Fundamentals of Computer Science

Macmillan Computer Science Series

Consulting Editor
Professor F. H. Sumner, University of Manchester

S.T. Allworth, *Introduction to Real-time Software Design*

Ian O. Angell, *A Practical Introduction to Computer Graphics*

G.M. Birtwistle, *Discrete Event Modelling on Simula*

T.B. Boffey, *Graph Theory in Operations Research*

Richard Bornat, *Understanding and Writing Compilers*

J.K. Buckle, *The ICL 2900 Series*

J.K. Buckle, *Software Configuration Management*

Robert Cole, *Computer Communications*

Derek Coleman, *A Structured Programming Approach to Data**

Andrew J.T. Colin, *Fundamentals of Computer Science*

Andrew J.T. Colin, *Programming and Problem-solving in Algol 68**

S.M. Deen, *Fundamentals of Data Base Systems**

J.B. Gosling, *Design of Arithmetic Units for Digital Computers*

David Hopkin and Barbara Moss, *Automata**

Roger Hutty, *Fortran for Students*

Roger Hutty, *Z80 Assembly Language Programming for Students*

H. Kopetz, *Software Reliability*

Graham Lee, *From Hardware to Software: an introduction to computers*

A.M. Lister, *Fundamentals of Operating Systems, second edition**

G.P. McKeown and V.J. Rayward-Smith, *Mathematics for Computing*

Brain Meek, *Fortran, PL/I and the Algols*

Derrick Morris and Roland N. Ibbett, *The MU5 Computer System*

John Race, *Case Studies in Systems Analysis*

B.S. Walker, *Understanding Microprocessors*

Peter J.L. Wallis, *Portable Programming*

I.R. Wilson and A.M. Addyman, *A Practical Introduction to Pascal*

* The titles marked with an asterisk were prepared during the Consulting Editorship of Professor J. S. Rohl, University of Western Australia.

Fundamentals of Computer Science

Andrew J. T. Colin

Professor of Computer Science,
University of Strathclyde

First edition 1980
Reprinted 1982, 1983

Published by
THE MACMILLAN PRESS LTD
London and Basingstoke
Companies and representatives
throughout the world

Typeset in 10/12 Press Roman by
STYLESET LIMITED
and printed and bound in Hong Kong

ISBN 0 333 30503 5

Contents

Preface

Computer science can be divided into two great streams of knowledge: one is programming, and the other deals with the principles, construction and applications of computer systems. This book is centred on the second stream; it is not primarily about programming, but assumes that the reader is following a parallel course on this key subject.

The range of knowledge needed to understand a computer system is large. It includes elementary physics, electronics, information theory, logic design, computer architecture, microcoding, machine code programming, compilers, interpreters, operating systems and a selection of typical applications. Most important of all is an over-all view which reveals how all these different areas can be made to work together in harmony to form an integrated system.

Traditional introductory computer science courses tend to consider a selection of these topics in isolation. Thus students may well be taught elementary logic design by one lecturer, assembly code programming by another and a high-level language by a third, but the links between these areas are never explored. The student's impression of the subject is of a few islands of clarity set in a sea of incomprehensible magic.

The aim of this book is to dispel the magic by providing a continuous and logically connected survey of the subject. For example, the section on logic design does not stop short at elementary combinatorial functions such as binary addition, but goes on to introduce multiplexers, sequential circuits, and buses. The chapter on over-all computer design does not therefore need to rely on abstractions which have no apparent connection with anything already covered in the course, but can use concepts which are familiar to the student.

This continuity of treatment in a first-year course cannot be achieved except at a certain cost. First, the text moves fast, and does not often pause to examine details which are not essential to the main theme. Second, the book traces but a single path across the subject. The aim is to show just one way in which a computer system could be implemented. The route chosen is largely arbitrary, and alternative routes that exist at every stage are simply ignored.

Every teacher of computer science will be able to name numerous topics which are given the briefest treatment, or not even mentioned. Nevertheless, the student who reads and understands the book will know at least one way to implement a working computer system. His knowledge will not have any conceptual gaps, and he will have a unified framework on which to hang new concepts that he may learn in the future.

A computer system is one of the most complex artefacts in existence. The only way to understand it is by a holistic approach. This word, first used by Koestler, describes any hierarchic system in which every component part is itself a system constructed from more elementary components. In computer science, the principle of holism appears at every stage, both in software and hardware, and this book puts it to considerable use. Sometimes, as in describing hardware, the approach is from 'bottom-up'. Some functional unit (say a full adder or a multiplexer) is fully described in terms of its elementary components, then it is notionally sealed in a box with the appropriate number of terminals, and used as an 'elementary' component in a more complex structure such as a parallel adder or arithmetic unit.

In software, the design method is more often 'top-down'. The book recommends the use of flow charts in which the portions which are not clearly understood at any stage are drawn as 'clouds'. Later, these clouds are expanded and elaborated, perhaps through several levels, until the entire algorithm can be expressed in elementary terms.

The use of structure to describe complex systems is perhaps one of the most important mental tools at our disposal. It is hoped that the integrated approach used in this book will help its readers to become totally familiar with the method, and be able to apply it in their everyday study and work.

At the end of the book there are ten 'assignments', each based on the ground covered by one or two chapters. Sample solutions are provided.

The three assignments on machine coding assume the use of a simple simulator for the SNARK abstract machine. Appendix B includes the listing of a suitable BASIC program for an 8K Commodore PET 2001*. The program does not make use of graphics or any other of the special features of this machine, and can easily be adapted to run on other systems.

My thanks are due to many people who have made the publication of this book possible: to students and colleagues at the University of Strathclyde, who have read the manuscript, made comments and found errors; to Frank Sumner and Simon Lavington, who gave me constant encouragement and detailed, constructive criticism; to Miss Agnes Wisley who typed the book (parts of it many times over); and above all to my wife and family, who left me undisturbed at times when they had every legitimate claim on my time and attention.

Glasgow
January, 1980

ANDREW COLIN

* A cassette tape of this program can be bought from Commodore Ltd, 360 Euston Road, London, NW1

Abbreviations

ACC	Accumulator
ARPA	Advanced Research Project Agency
ASCII	American Standard Code for Information Interchange
BASIC	Beginners' All-purpose Symbolic Information Code
BNF	Backus–Naur Form
CIR	Current Instruction Register
COBOL	Common Business-oriented Language
DEC	Digital Equipment Corporation
EBCDIC	Extended Binary Coded Decimal Interchange Code
EMI	Electrical and Musical Industries Ltd
GPO	General Post Office
IBM	International Business Machines Ltd
ICL	International Computers Ltd
JCL	Job Description Language
MAR	Memory Address Register
PET	Personal Electronic Transactor

1 Information

A computer is a machine designed to store and handle *information*. The book therefore begins with a chapter on some of the properties of this strange substance.

1.1 THE FOUR INFORMATION REVOLUTIONS

Today, a large and growing number of people spend their lives collecting, distributing or producing information. The 'information professions' include writers, broadcasters, teachers and lecturers, postmen, telephone engineers, signalmen, code experts, and many others.

Newspapers sometimes say that civilisation is in the midst of an 'information revolution', which is to have a major effect on all our lives. This is true; but it would be more accurate to refer to current events as 'the Fourth Information Revolution', because there have been at least three others before.

The first and perhaps the most profound revolution was the development of *speech*. When our ancestors learned to talk, they obtained the means of expressing ideas and concepts far more subtle than they could have managed with grunts and gestures alone. Everything they had learned could be passed on to their children, so that the stock of human knowledge increased generation by generation. Speech is at the root of human intellectual achievements, and serves to distinguish us from the rest of the animal kingdom.

The second information revolution was the development of *writing*. Written documents are far more accurate and durable than human memory, and they can easily be copied and sent from place to place. Writing allows information to be stored reliably over very long periods, and permits it to be exchanged between people who have never met one another. It is difficult even to imagine a civilisation which does not rely on writing to keep its organisation intact.

The third information revolution was brought about by the invention of *printing* in the late Middle Ages. Up to that time, it had been difficult to spread information widely. Books existed, but every copy had to be written out by hand, so books were rightly regarded as precious and scarce. Most people could not read and write, and the only book they ever saw was the Bible chained to the lectern in the parish church.

Printing changed this picture completely. Books, magazines and newspapers are mass produced, and many countries have a high literacy rate. Printed material is used to inform, entertain, influence and control people everywhere.

Each of these three information revolutions eventually brought about major differences in everyday life, although the effects took hundreds, or even thousands of years to work through. The current revolution is due to the introduction of the computer. These machines have only existed for 30 years, but they have already made whole industries obsolete, and brought about radical changes in others. Everybody is affected.

The role of the computer can best be explained by contrasting it with the techniques of talking, writing and printing. These last three are all essentially methods of sharing ideas between human minds. The intention is that the listener or reader should end up with the same concepts and mental images as the talker or writer, and if this cannot be achieved the failure is seen as a defect in communication. The processes of speech, writing or printing are not supposed to alter the information they carry in any way.

On the other hand, the computer is an *information processing* machine. The computer can certainly receive information from its environment, often through a keyboard, much like a printing press; but instead of simply passing the information on, the computer can store it, condense it, translate it into a different layout, use it to make logical deductions, check it for consistency with other items of information, or use it directly to make important decisions. The computer mechanises many routine thought processes, in much the same way as the steam engine replaced human muscles in the nineteenth century.

Up to 1975 computers were expensive, but the recent development of cheap computers called 'microprocessors' will ensure that the changes to our daily lives will continue at an accelerating pace.

1.2 SOME PROPERTIES OF INFORMATION

Information is fundamentally different from any material substance. It is essentially abstract, and has no weight and no size; it cannot exist by itself but needs a physical 'vehicle' or medium such as a net of human brain cells, sound waves in the air, patterns of ink on paper or holes in punched cards. Nevertheless, it is often valuable, and can be traded or forged. Information is particularly easy to steal because it can be copied without destroying the original. Some information is so important and confidential that great precautions are taken to ensure its security.

Like most material objects, information is subject to corruption and decay. A set of information such as a list of names and addresses may begin by being totally correct, but as time passes some people move, some change their names by marriage and some die. The *quality* of the list becomes gradually worse until after a few years the list is unusable.

To derive some of the properties of information, we must investigate it in an artificial context, much as a physicist might study the laws of gravitation by dropping objects from great heights. To begin, we shall make some definitions. Like all definitions they will be abstractions, broad enough to include a good proportion of all practical cases.

Consider a simple information system with three parts: a *source*, a *medium* and a *destination*. They are arranged as shown in figure 1.1.

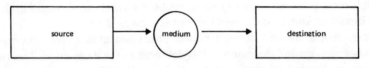

Figure 1.1

In this system, we assume that the source intends to send some information to the destination. The source begins by selecting a *message* from a limited group of possible messages, and transmits it to the medium using a set of rules or *code*. After a time interval the medium passes the message on to the destination, which uses the same code to interpret its meaning.

This somewhat bald description covers a large number of practical situations. Some of them, by way of illustration, are given in table 1.1.

Several points are worth noting. First, we asserted that the number of possible messages available to the source is limited — that is, that there are just so many messages and no more. It is difficult to square this with our freedom of speech, our evident ability to say anything we like. In actual fact everything we say or write consists of *sequences* of symbols — spoken words or written letters.

If we regard each symbol as a message in its own right, then the number is indeed finite. The English language has about 30 000 words, and its alphabet has

Table 1.1

Source	Medium	Destination	Code
Person speaking	Air	Person listening	Any human language
Person writing	Paper and ink	Person reading	The alphabet; rules of spelling; etc.
Diver signalling	Rope	Attendant on surface	'1 pull — let out more air-line' '2 pulls — I am OK' '3 pulls — bring me up!'
Satellite transmitting weather data	Radio waves	Monitor computer	Television picture conventions

26 letters. If you invent new words or letters, you will not be understood, and no information will pass to its intended destination.

Second, each message has to be coded as part of the process. A code is a convention that is known in advance to both source and destination. In some conditions the code is specially chosen to be compact, or secret, or suitable for transmission along a rope; but in ordinary speech the coding process is so automatic that we do not realise its existence until we meet someone who does not speak our language. The important properties of a code are two: first, each possible message should have its own unique representation, and second, the code should be known and agreed before the message is sent.

Next, there is always a time gap between the moment that the medium receives a message and the moment it is delivered to the destination. This time depends on the physical characteristics of the medium. Some typical times are shown in table 1.2.

Some information systems are made as fast as possible, but others actually take advantage of the time delay to store the information being transmitted.

When a message is passed from the medium to a destination, it is not necessarily destroyed. This makes it possible for a given message to reach many destinations, possibly at different times.

This abstract model of an information system covers most systems of communication. There is, however, one area in which it can only offer a caricature — in discourse between people. The model provides no way of taking into account the shades of meaning we can convey to one another by facial gestures or tone of voice, and it is quite incapable of representing the process by which a child learns a language in the first place. Fortunately, this chapter will be considering only mechanical systems, where the model is adequate.

In the model there is an information flow from source to destination. It will be useful to measure the rate at which the information flows (just as one can measure the flow of water in a river), but first we must establish a suitable unit of measurement.

Table 1.2

Place	Time
Inside a computer	10^{-8} seconds (approx.)
Radio signal (300 km)	10^{-3} seconds
Radio signal to Mars	20 minutes (approx.)
Telegram	2 hours
Letter	2 days
Scientific paper	1 year
Rosetta Stone	4000 years

To measure information, we use the idea of *probability*. We argue that if a message is unexpected, then it carries a great deal more information than if it is the one you have been waiting for all along. To give a concrete example, suppose you have bought a lottery ticket where the chance of winning is 1 in 10 000. You arrange for a friend to look up the winning number, and telephone you with the result. Stripped of inessential details the two possible messages are 'win' and 'lose'. Being a realist, you expected to lose all along, so the message 'lose' tells you hardly anything. On the other hand 'win' is an important piece of news, and may affect your actions for a considerable time.

The mathematical idea of probability can be applied to any *event* which has a fixed number of possible outcomes, but where the actual outcome on any occasion is unpredictable. The notions of probability were first developed in connection with gambling, where the 'event' is a hand of cards, a throw of dice, or a spin of a roulette wheel. Now the theory has a much wider application; some typical 'events' are listed in table 1.3.

Table 1.3

Event	Possible Outcomes
Tossing a coin	Heads/Tails/Balanced on edge
Throwing a dart at the bull on a dartboard	Hitting the inner bull/ Hitting the outer bull/ Hitting another part of the board/ Missing the board entirely
Going on a plane journey	Arriving at destination/ Flight cancelled before departure/ Flight diverted to a different place/ Plane crashes

If we collect figures about large numbers of different events, we can count the number of times each outcome actually occurs. The ratio of this number to the total number of events is called the *probability* of the outcome.

Let us give an example. Suppose that 1 million advertised plane flights had the following outcomes

Arrived at destination	950 000
Cancelled	45 000
Diverted	4 983
Crashed	17

If these flights were representative of air travel as a whole, the probabilities of the various outcomes would be

Arrival	950 000/1 000 000	= 0.95
Cancellation	45 000/1 000 000	= 0.045
Diversion	4 983/1 000 000	= 0.004983
Crashing	17/1 000 000	= 0.000017

The probabilities, when added together, total 1. This means that every event must have *an* outcome.

Sometimes we have good logical reasons for predicting the probabilities of the various outcomes of an event without making lengthy observations. For example, we feel that in throwing a die, any one of the six faces is equally likely to come uppermost; so we give each face a probability of 1/6. If we then check by throwing a die a large number of times and recording the results, we will usually find that the measured probability is quite close to the predicted value. A large discrepancy would suggest that the die is loaded.

Now consider a source of messages in an information system. We have already decided that the choice of possible messages is limited. We can regard each message as an *event*, and the actual selection as an *outcome*. If we observe the source for a period of time, we can measure the probability of each message. To give an example, if the messages are the letters of an English text, the probabilities are as follows.

space: 0.137	I : 0.082	R : 0.055
A : 0.069	J : 0.001	S : 0.055
B : 0.010	K : 0.006	T : 0.063
C : 0.031	L : 0.035	U : 0.025
D : 0.039	M : 0.020	V : 0.002
E : 0.119	N : 0.070	W : 0.016
F : 0.012	O : 0.051	X : 0.001
G : 0.033	P : 0.016	Y : 0.008
H : 0.033	Q : 0.006	Z : 0.001

(We include 'space' because it is the most common symbol.)

It now remains only to relate the probability p of any message to its information content I. Claude Shannon, the originator of information theory, showed that a suitable function is

$$I = \log (1/p) \qquad (1)$$

or its equivalent

$$I = -\log (p) \qquad (2)$$

This function has the right properties; when p is small the message is unexpected and its information content is correspondingly large. On the other hand, if a message is totally predictable, $p = 1$ and $I = 0$, meaning that it carries *no* information.

It is still necessary to decide the base of the logarithms in equations 1 and 2. You will be familiar with 'common' logs which use base 10, and also 'natural' logs to the base e. It is possible to have logs to the base of any positive number except 1.

It is convenient to define *one* unit of information as the amount needed to signal one of the outcomes 'yes' or 'no' to an event where both outcomes are equally likely ($p = 0.5$). We choose this unit because it is the least amount which can be transmitted independently from source to destination; it is called one *bit*.

It turns out that if we use logs to the base 2 in equations 1 and 2, the calculation will automatically produce the right answer in bits. A practical way of doing this is to take logs to the base 10 and multiply by $\log_2 10$ or 3.322.

We can now work out the amount of information in each of a number of alternative messages. Consider the answer to an enquiry about a plane flight. For example

Event : Plane Flight

Outcome	Probability p	1/p	log_{10} (1/p)	log_2 (1/p) = I
Arrived safely	0.95	1.053	0.0223	0.074 bits
Cancelled	0.045	22.22	1.347	4.474 bits
Diverted	0.004983	200.68	2.303	7.649 bits
Crashed	0.000017	58823.5	4.769	15.844 bits

An important general property of an information source is the *average* amount of information per message. Consider a source with two possible messages, with probabilities p_1 and p_2. Suppose the source transmits some large numbers of messages, say n. This will include np_1 of the first and np_2 of the second. Using our formula, the *total* amount of information will be

$$np_1 \log_2(1/p_1) + np_2 \log_2(1/p_2) \tag{3}$$

The average (dividing the total by the number of messages) is

$$\frac{np_1 \log_2(1/p_1) + np_2 \log_2(1/p_2)}{n} \tag{4}$$

n cancels out, leaving

$$p_1 \log_2(1/p_1) + p_2 \log_2(1/p_2) \tag{5}$$

This quantity is called the *entropy* of the source, and is measured in bits. The formula extends easily to any number of possible messages.

Example 1.1
An information source signals the result of a football match. Based on past experience, the possible results and their probabilities are as follows

Win	0.39
Lose	0.47
Draw	0.10
Match cancelled	0.04

Calculate the entropy of the information source.

Lay out your calculations as shown below. You will find a calculator with a 'log' key useful. It is best to work in logs to base 10 and to save the multiplication by 3.322 to the end.

Message	p	$log_{10}(1/p)$	$p \times log_{10}(1/p)$
Win	0.39	0.4089	0.1595
Lose	0.47	0.3279	0.1541
Draw	0.10	1.000	0.1000
Cancelled	0.04	1.3979	0.0559
			0.4695

Source entropy in bits = 3.322 x 0.4695 = 1.560 bits

1.3 CODING

In computers (and indeed in most other modern systems of information transmission and storage) information is represented as a sequence of binary digits or 'bits'. Each is a sign which can have *two* possible values called '1' and '0'. These bits can have all kinds of representations — some are shown in table 1.4.

Information engineers have the job of designing codes which represent messages in terms of binary digits. These codes have to satisfy diverse requirements. For example, in a digital watch or calculator the code for each decimal digit has to light up a suitable combination of segments; one possible arrangement is partly shown in figure 1.2 (the reader should fill in the missing lines).

A common requirement is for the code to be short. If a source has only two messages ('yes' and 'no') then a coding scheme is obvious: we use '1' for 'yes' and '0' for 'no'. (We could equally well use '0' for 'yes' and '1' for 'no' if the destination were warned in advance.)

Table 1.4

Medium	'1'	'0'
Paper tape	Hole	No hole
Telegraph line	High voltage	Low voltage
Telephone line	High-pitched tone	Low-pitched tone
Magnetic tape	Area magnetised in one direction	Area magnetised in the other direction
Electronic circuit	High current	Low current
Light-emitting diode	Light	Darkness

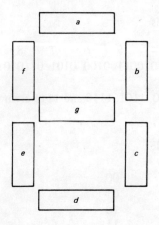

Codes	a	b	c	d	e	f	g
Digit	Representation						
'0'	1	1	1	1	1	1	0
'1'	0	1	1	0	0	0	0
'2'	1	1	0	1	1	0	1
'3'							
'4'							
'5'							
'6'							
'7'							
'8'							
'9'	1	1	1	1	0	1	1

Figure 1.2

If there are more than two possible messages, we must use a *sequence* of bits for each one. With n bits per message, the number of possible messages is 2^n. Thus when $n = 3$, there can be eight messages represented by 000, 001, 010, 011, 100, 101, 110 and 111. For any number of possible messages, we can always choose a value of n which gives enough combinations. The combinations can be assigned to the messages in an arbitrary way which constitutes a code. Some combinations may not be used.

Example 1.2

In a certain game, two dice are thrown and the numbers on the uppermost faces added together to find a score. Devise a code for transmitting this score.

First we note that there are 11 possible outcomes, from 2 to 12. Now $2^3 = 8$ and $2^4 = 16$, so 4 bits will be needed for each message.

A possible assignment is

Score	2	3	4	5	6	7	8	9	10	11	12
Code	0000	0001	0010	0011	0100	0101	0110	0111	1000	1001	1010

The five codes 1011, 1100, 1101, 1110 and 1111 are not used.

Example 1.3

Assume the following code

Win	00
Lose	01
Draw	10
Match cancelled	11

Construct a summary of the season's play of a football team from the following record

000001101001010101001110000001011001000010101101100100

We divide these bits into pairs, and look up the meaning of each pair, thus

00 00 01 10 10 01 01 01 01 00 11 ...
W W L D D L L L L W C ...

The summary is

Win	*Lose*	*Draw*	*Cancelled*
8	10	7	2

In these examples, all the messages in each group are the same length, so this is clearly the average length of the message. A fundamental theorem of information theory states that for any ergodic source (one where the probabilities do not change with time) the average message length must always be equal to or greater than the entropy. This is the case in our two examples

Source	Entropy	Message Length
Dice score	3.274	4
Football results	1.560	2

2 Information Inside Computers

The primary purpose of any computer is to handle and store information. This chapter discusses the way in which two of the most important types — characters and numbers — are represented within a computer.

A major component of any computer is its information store. A machine may use several different storage mechanisms, including purely electronic circuits and magnetic components, but all of them have one aspect in common: every element of store has precisely two possible states, called '1' and '0'. This allows each element to hold one 'bit' of information.

In most computers the individual storage elements are arranged in groups called 'words'. All the bits in any word are processed at the same time. Large machines tend to have longer words than small machines, but in most types of computer the word size is fixed. Table 2.1 shows the word length in several widely used machines.

Table 2.1

Machine	Word Size (bits)
INTEL 8080 (microprocessor)	8
Commodore PET (microcomputer)	8
PDP-11 (minicomputer)	16
IBM 370/145 (computer)	32
ICL 2980 (large computer)	64

In principle, the various items of information in a computer can be represented by any arbitrary code. In practice, certain constraints are imposed by the structure of the store and the need to make information handling as simple as possible. For example, information items should not spill over word boundaries unnecessarily.

2.1 REPRESENTATION OF CHARACTERS

Characters are the individual symbols — letters, spaces, digits and punctuation signs – which go to make up a text. Most computers receive information in the form of a stream of characters flowing from a keyboard like the one on a type-writer. The keyboard can be connected directly to the computer, or it can be linked through a telephone line, or it can be used to punch holes in cards which are collected and fed to the computer later; these are all variants on the same basic theme.

A normal keyboard can produce about 90 different characters, including the special ones like 'end-of-line'. If each character is regarded as a message, then it can be represented by a fixed-length binary code. Since $2^6 = 64$ and $2^7 = 128$, 7 bits are sufficient, and there will be a few spare combinations.

A designer who lived on a desert island could assign codes to characters quite arbitrarily, but in normal circumstances there is great pressure to conform to one or other of the existing standards so that, for example, a new computer can take over existing workloads or be connected to other machines.

Two well-known character codes are the ASCII (American Standard Code for Information Interchange) and EBCDIC (Extended Binary Coded Decimal Interchange Code). In broad terms IBM machines use EBCDIC while all the others use ASCII.

The ASCII code has *8* bits rather than 7. The extra binary digit is called a *parity bit*; it has no independent meaning but is derived from the other 7 bits in such a way as to make the total number of 1s *even*. It acts as a powerful check against errors, for if one bit of a character should be accidentally changed (perhaps when being transmitted over a noisy telephone line) the number of 1s will no longer be even and the mistake can be detected.

You may have noticed that in all the machines mentioned in table 2.1 the word size is either 8 bits, or a multiple of 8 bits. This arrangement is almost universal, and allows 8-bit characters to be stored efficiently without waste or overlapping word boundaries. The larger machines 'pack' several characters into one word.

2.2 REPRESENTATION OF NUMBERS

Inside a computer numbers are as important as characters. The nature of the store makes the use of decimal numbers somewhat clumsy, and it turns out that the binary system offers a much more efficient internal way of representing numbers. This does not mean that computers have to be *fed* with binary numbers – as we shall see they can easily convert sequences of decimal digits into their binary equivalents.

2.2.1 The Binary System

The binary system is a positional notation, similar to the normal decimal system we use in everyday life, except that it is based on radix *two* instead of radix *ten*.

Consider a decimal number like '1979'. This is a shorthand way of writing

$$1.10^3 + 9.10^2 + 7.10^1 + 9.10^0$$

(You will remember that $n^1 = n$, and $n^0 = 1$ for any value of n.)

Ten is called the *radix* of the decimal system because every decimal number is a polynomial in 10, as you can see by writing

$$1979 = x^3 + 9x^2 + 7x + 9 \quad \text{where } x = 10$$

By contrast, a binary number like 10110 can be expanded in powers of two, thus

$$1.2^4 + 0.2^3 + 1.2^2 + 1.2^1 + 0.2^0 = \text{twenty-two}$$

It is a polynomial in 2.

A major advantage of the binary system over the decimal is that is requires only two symbols: '0' and '1'. There is no need for '2' because two is written '10'.

2.2.2 Conversion between Binary and Decimal Systems

To understand the binary system fully, you should be able to convert numbers between the normal decimal and the binary notations.

A decimal number can be converted to binary by a series of divisions by 2. The exact rule is as follows.

(1) Prepare a space for the result.
(2) Divide the decimal number by 2. Write the remainder (which must be 0 or 1) in the 'result' space, to the *left* of any digits you have already written.
(3) If the quotient of the division is 0, stop. The result space now contains the answer in binary.
(4) Otherwise, take the quotient as the new decimal number and go back to step 2.

Example 2.1
Convert 47 to binary notation.

$$2 \overline{\smash{)}47} \div \quad \text{23 r 1}$$

$$\boxed{101111}$$

$$2 \overline{\smash{)}23} \div \quad \text{11 r 1}$$

result

$$2 \overline{\smash{)}11} \div \quad \text{5 r 1}$$

$$\begin{array}{r} 2 \text{ r } 1 \\ 2 \overline{\smash{\big)}\, 5 \ \div} \end{array}$$

$$\begin{array}{r} 1 \text{ r } 0 \\ 2 \overline{\smash{\big)}\, 2 \ \div} \end{array}$$

$$\begin{array}{r} 0 \text{ r } 1 \\ 2 \overline{\smash{\big)}\, 1 \ \div} \end{array}$$

Therefore 47 (decimal) = 101111 (binary).

To convert in the other direction, it is convenient to use a table of the powers of 2

2^{10}	2^9	2^8	2^7	2^6	2^5	2^4	2^3	2^2	2^1	2^0
1024	512	256	128	64	32	16	8	4	2	1

The decimal value of a binary number can be found by adding up the powers of 2 which correspond to the 1s in the number.

Example 2.2
What is the decimal equivalent of the binary number 10101101?

$$10101101 = 2^7 + 2^5 + 2^3 + 2^2 + 2^0$$

$$= 128 + 32 + 8 + 4 + 1$$

$$= 173 \text{ (decimal)}$$

2.2.3 Binary Addition, Subtraction and Multiplication

Binary addition is similar to decimal addition except that a 'carry' is produced whenever the result of adding digits is *two* or more. A typical binary addition would run as follows.

1111	0 and 0 is 0;
10110	1 and 1 is 0 carry 1;
01110 +	1 and 1 and 1 is 1 carry 1;
100100	1 and 0 and 1 is 0 carry 1;
	1 and 1 and 0 is 0 carry 1;
	1 and 0 and 0 is 1 carry 0.

(The carries are shown in their usual place above the addition sum.)

Binary subtraction can be done in a similar way, using 'borrows'. However, it is awkward for people to carry out in this form, and is in fact hardly ever necessary, even for computer scientists.

Binary multiplication is normally done by the traditional 'long multiplication' method, but it is very much easier since the only multipliers are 0 and 1, and no tables are needed. For example

```
       1110
       1001 ×
     ──────
       1110
      00000
     000000
   1110000 +
   ────────
   1111110
```

(The equivalent in decimal terms is 14 × 9 = 126.)

2.2.4 Numbers in Computers

The binary system is a good one for computers because of its simplicity and use of only two symbols. Nevertheless, its adaptation to this new environment brings certain problems.

First, our normal positional notation allows numbers to be of any size, and to have any number of digits, but in a computer each item of information must fit into a word of fixed length.

Second, it is necessary to use some method of representing negative numbers.

Third, computers in many applications need a way of handling fractions.

Unsigned Whole Numbers
We shall begin by discussing only unsigned whole numbers. Consider a machine with 8-bit words. Each word can take 2^8 = 256 possible values. They can be used as straightforward binary codes for the numbers 0 to 255, so that, for example

```
      00000000 = 0
      01010101 = 85
and   11111111 = 255
```

This system can handle correctly any numbers between 0 and 255. If the computer does an addition where the correct result is more than 255, the computer's answer will be wrong because the result overflows the number of digits available for it. For example, '144' and '177' can both be represented as 8-bit binary numbers, but their sum, '321', needs 9 bits in binary. In the computer's result, the ninth, most significant bit is not represented.

The position is similar to a car with 99 995 miles on its mileometer: if it is driven another 12 miles it will go 'round the clock' and register 00 007 miles only. Unlike the car, the computer can detect that an overflow has occurred, but special action is needed to correct the result.

In many applications of computers the only numbers used are small ones, so the limitation in range can be ignored. If larger numbers are unavoidable, then the range can be extended by using more than one word for each number. For example, a number stored in *four* 8-bit words could range between 0 and $(2^{32} - 1)$ or 4 294 967 295. Of course, calculations with four-word numbers are much more laborious than for those which occupy only one word, because the machine must handle each word in turn and arrange for carries between them; an overflow from one word gives a 'carry' of 1 into the next word on the left.

Example 2.3
Two 8-bit words contain the (unsigned) binary numbers 10110100 and 01110101. What is the result of adding them, and is it correct?

First we add, remembering that the result must be 8 digits long

```
  10110100
  01110101 +
(1)00101001
```

The carry generated at the left is lost. This suggests that the 8-bit result is *wrong*. This is confirmed by converting the numbers to their decimal equivalent, as follows

```
  180
  117 +
  ---
   41
```

Signed Numbers
In most areas of computer use, it is convenient to have access to negative numbers as well as positive ones.

Our own experience with signed numbers may suggest that handling them in a computer must be complicated. The normal 'school' rule for adding two signed numbers goes like this

If the two numbers have the same sign, *add* them and attach the common sign.
If the two numbers have different signs, then *subtract* the smaller from the larger and attach the sign of the larger.

This rule is based on the 'sign-magnitude' notation, where each number is written as a sign (+ or −) and an absolute value.

In computers, signed numbers are usually represented by a completely different and far simpler method.

Consider a computer with only 4 bits per word. The largest number available would be $(2^4 - 1)$ or 15. If we start with 0 and repeatedly add 1, then after 16 additions the number will return to 0. This can be shown as a 'circle diagram' (figure 2.1). Every step clockwise corresponds to an addition, and every step anti-clockwise represents a subtraction.

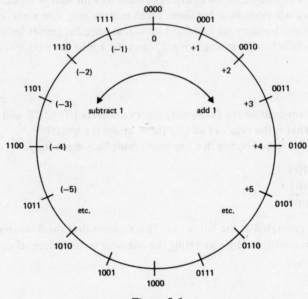

Figure 2.1

One way of defining a negative number $-n$ is to say that it is that number which produces zero when $+n$ is added to it. On this definition the code 1111 in our circle diagram takes the value '−1', because when 1 is added to it, the result is zero. Similarly, 1110 stands for −2, 1101 for −3, and so on. These (new) values have been marked in on the diagram.

This method of representing negative numbers, which is called the 'two's complement notation' leads to far simpler arithmetic than the sign-magnitude notation. So long as the numbers are small enough, one simply goes through the mechanism of adding or subtracting without regard to the signs or sizes of the quantities, and the result is automatically correct. For example

(a)   (7) + (−5) :   0111

                        1011 +

              (1) 0010

The 'carry' in this case drops off the end, leaving the correct (4-bit) result +2.

(b) 3 + (−6) :   0011
                    1010 +
                    ‾‾‾‾
                    1101

Again, the 4-bit result is −3, which is correct.

Genuine overflow can occur in signed addition and subtraction. It can be detected, but the test is more complicated than in unsigned arithmetic. Again, special action is needed to correct a calculation which has overflowed.

As it stands, the system is ambiguous. Each point on the circle can be reached from 0 either by going forwards, or by going backwards. Should '1000', for example, be taken to mean '+8' or '−8'?

This dilemma can be resolved by a neat convention. The circle is *cut*, as nearly as possible opposite zero, so as to give as many negative numbers as non-negative ones. The exact position is chosen so that all negative numbers begin with a 1, as shown in figure 2.2.

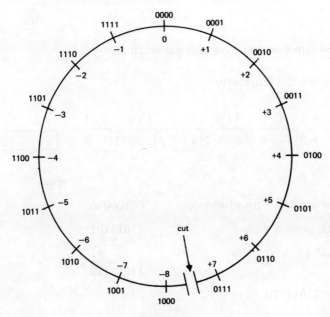

Figure 2.2

The two's complement system can be extended to binary numbers of any size. The largest positive number in an n-bit word always has the form 01111111 ... and the value $+(2^{n-1} - 1)$, while the largest negative number looks like 10000000... and equals $-(2^{n-1})$.

Example 2.4

Write down the form and the value of the largest positive and negative numbers that can be expressed in the two's complement notation, using words of (a) 10 and (b) 16 binary digits.

(a)   10 digits

Largest positive : 0111111111 = $+(2^9 - 1)$ = +511
Largest negative : 1000000000 = $-(2^9)$ = −512

(b)   16 digits

Largest positive : 0111111111111111 = $+(2^{15} - 1)$ = +32767
Largest negative : 1000000000000000 = $-(2^{15})$ = −32768

The conversion of positive decimal numbers into two's complement notation can be done with the process already described for unsigned binary numbers. For negative numbers, it is best to convert the absolute value, and then take the binary complement, by inverting every digit and adding 1.

Example 2.5

Convert −34 into 8-bit, two's complement notation.

Step 1: Convert +34 into binary

$$\overset{\text{17 r 0}}{2\overline{\smash{)}34}} \div \overset{\text{8 r 1}}{2\overline{\smash{)}17}} \div \overset{\text{4 r 0}}{2\overline{\smash{)}8}} \div \overset{\text{2 r 0}}{2\overline{\smash{)}4}} \div \overset{\text{1 r 0}}{2\overline{\smash{)}2}} \div \overset{\text{0 r 1}}{2\overline{\smash{)}1}} \div \qquad \boxed{100010}$$

result

Step 2: Pad out to 8 digits with zeros   00100010

Step 3: Change every digit   11011101

Stem 4: Add 1   +1
                                                    ──────────
                                                     11011110

Thus −34 ≡ 11011110.

Conversion from two's complement notation into decimal is made easy by a trick: if the first digit of the number is 1, *subtract* the appropriate power of 2 instead of adding it.

Example 2.6

Convert the following two's complement numbers into decimal: (a) 00101101,

(b) 10110100.

$$00101101 = 2^5 + 2^3 + 2^2 + 2^0 \quad = \quad 32$$
$$8$$
$$4$$
$$1 +$$
$$\overline{45}$$

$$10110100 = -2^7 + 2^5 + 2^4 + 2^2 = -128$$
$$32$$
$$16$$
$$4$$
$$\overline{-76}$$

note sign

Fractions and Large Numbers

In certain areas of computer use, such as science, mathematics and engineering, the limitations imposed by a fixed word size are often embarrassing. The two's complement notation described in the previous section is quite unsuitable either for fractions or for large numbers which lie beyond the permitted range.

The standard way of handling both fractions and large numbers is called the 'floating-point' notation. Every value is represented by a pair of quantities called the 'mantissa' and the 'exponent'. The mantissa is a signed integer which lies within a given range. The exponent is a scale factor (or more accurately the log of a scale factor) which indicates by how much the mantissa should be multiplied to give a true value.

Although mantissa and exponent are both stored in binary, the system is very like the 'scientific notation' used on hand calculators. There, for example, it is understood that

$$1387 \text{ E } 24 = 1387 \times 10^{24} = 1387000000000000000000000000$$

or

$$339 \text{ E} - 9 = 339 \times 10^{-9} = 0.000000339$$

In practice, typical sizes for the mantissa and exponent are 40 bits and 8 bits respectively. This gives a wide range but means that on small machines each floating-point number needs several words of store.

The processes of arithmetic on floating-point numbers are complicated and will not be discussed here.

2.3 EXTERNAL REPRESENTATIONS OF BINARY NUMBERS

Binary numbers are efficient and convenient inside computers, but they are awkward and tedious for human manipulation. When computer scientists handle binary numbers, they usually do so in one of two shorthand notations, called the 'octal' and 'hexadecimal' respresentations.It is emphasised that these forms have no existence or meaning in a computer, but are used *solely* for human convenience.

An octal number is one written in radix 8. Since $8 = 2^3$, each octal digit corresponds to a group of 3 binary digits according to the code

Binary	000	001	010	011	100	101	110	111
Octal	0	1	2	3	4	5	6	7

To convert an octal number to binary, replace each octal digit by its binary code.

To form the octal representation of a binary number, first mark off the digits in groups of 3, starting from the right. Then replace each group by its octal equivalent.

Example 2.7

(a)   What is the *binary* equivalent of the octal number 3172?

Replace octal digits by their codes, giving: 011001111010.

(b)   What is the *octal* equivalent of the binary number 01101110?

First, mark off the digits in groups of 3: 01, 101, 110. Next replace each group by an octal digit, assuming initial zeros, giving: 156.

Example 2.8

The octal form of an 8-bit two's complement binary number is 314. What is its decimal value?

First, convert 314 (octal) to binary (8 bits): 11001100. (Discard leading zero to keep length to 8 bits.) Next, convert to decimal

$$11001100 = -2^7 + 2^6 + 2^3 + 2^2$$
$$= -128 + 64 + 8 + 4 = -52$$

The hexadecimal notation ('hex' for short) uses radix 16 or 2^4. The notation handles binary digits in groups of 4, and needs 16 different symbols, allocated as follows.

Binary	0000	0001	0010	0011	0100	0101	0110	0111
Hex	0	1	2	3	4	5	6	7

Binary	1000	1001	1010	1011	1100	1101	1110	1111
Hex	8	9	A	B	C	D	E	F

Otherwise, the hex notation is similar to the octal. For example, 1100 0000 1101 1110 in binary appears as 'CODE' in hex.

When there is any risk of ambiguity between radices, subscripts are used, thus

$$1100100_2 = 144_8 = 100_{10} = 64_{16}$$

3 *The Basic Structure of a Computer*

3.1 AN OVER-ALL VIEW

A computer consists of a *processor*, a *store*, and several *peripheral units*. The processor is in over-all control of the system, and is responsible for data storage, logic and arithmetic. The store records numbers and other information in immediate use by the processor. The peripheral units connect the whole system to the outside world. Each unit is either a *sensor*, feeding information into the processor, or an *actuator*, conveying the decisions of the processor back to its environment. Some units can be switched from one function to the other.

The pattern shown in figure 3.1 is repeated in computers of every size. In a small personal computer, for example, the peripheral units would comprise a keyboard, a display screen and perhaps a cassette recorder. In a larger system the peripherals might include magnetic tape decks, exchangeable disc drives, line printers, card readers, terminals, and links to other computers.

This chapter is mainly concerned with the processor — the discussion of peripheral units will be left until later.

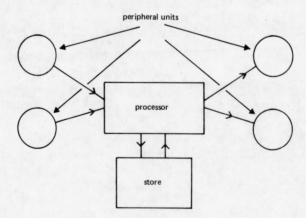

Figure 3.1

3.2 LOGIC NETWORKS

The processor of a computer is a network of elements called *logic gates*, connected by paths which carry signals from one gate to another. These signals are invariably binary, that is, each signal indicates exactly one of two possibilities, which we call 1 and 0.

Every gate has one or more *inputs* and one *output*. The inputs to any gate are usually the outputs of other gates, or signals from peripheral devices; similarly the output of a gate can serve as the input for other gates, or it can be sent to an actuator for transmission to the external world.

At any moment the output signal of a gate is a *function of* (that is, it depends on) the input signals at that moment. There are several types of gate, which differ in the precise way that the output is derived from the input. Three basic families of gate are

(1) The 'AND' gate. This has two or more inputs and one output. The output is only 1 if all the inputs are 1s; otherwise it is 0.
(2) The 'OR' gate. This again has two or more inputs and one output, but the output takes the value 1 if *any* of the inputs is 1.
(3) The 'NOT' gate or 'Inverter'. This gate has one input and one output which is always the opposite of the input: 0 in gives 1 out, and 1 in gives 0 out.

The symbols for these three gates are shown in figure 3.2.

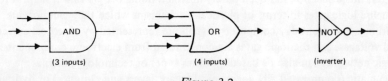

Figure 3.2

These three gates — or indeed the inverter and either of the other two — are in principle sufficient to construct a logic network of any kind, such as a complete computer. In practice, computer engineers often find it convenient to use gates with different specifications. One type — the so-called NAND gate — can be used for all purposes, and it is the only one we shall describe here.

The *n*-input NAND gate is a logic element with *n* inputs and one output. The output signal is always 1 *unless* all the inputs are 1s, in which case it is 0.

The general symbol for a NAND-gate is shown in figure 3.3.

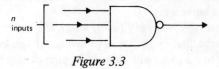

Figure 3.3

The name NAND is a contraction of 'NOT—AND', given because it is possible to duplicate the action of a NAND gate with an AND gate and an inverter as shown in figure 3.4.

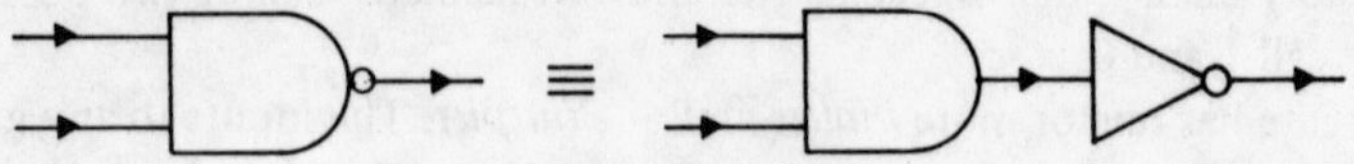

Figure 3.4

Manufacturers of logic elements offer families of gates with one, two, three, four or more inputs. The NAND gate with one input has precisely the same action as an inverter, and is usually represented by the symbol shown in figure 3.5.

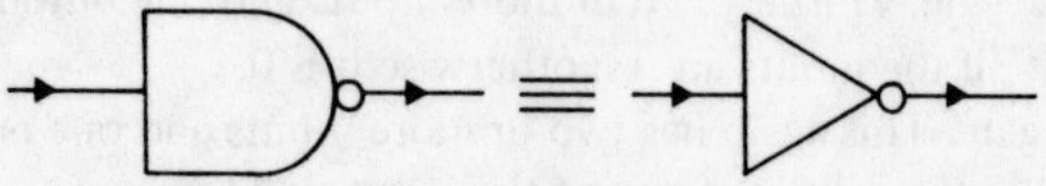

Figure 3.5

3.3 THE HYDRAULIC ANALOGY

So far, this discussion has been purely abstract. Some people find it helpful to visualise logic gates in terms of physical mechanisms which they can imagine working. In present-day computers, signals are represented by electrical currents and voltages, and the logic gates are constructed from electronic components. Logic networks can also be based on other types of technology, such as pneumatic (compressed air), mechanical (gears, levers and clutches) or hydraulic (water). Hydraulic logic is particularly easy to visualise for anyone who has ever turned on a tap or used a garden hose.

In a hydraulic logic network, signals are carried by currents of water in pipes. We can take the presence of a current to signify 1, and its absence to mean 0. (Remember that the pipes are always full of water, whether it is flowing or not.)

Figure 3.6 shows how this code could be used to send a message along a pipe. You have placed a bet on a horse in the 3 o'clock race, but you are obliged to be at a place several miles away when the race is run. Fortunately there is a hosepipe joining the race track to the place where you are waiting, and you arrange with a friend to signal the result of the race by turning on the tap for a few seconds if you horse wins.

Because the hose pipe is already full of water, the water will start flowing at your end almost immediately the tap is turned on. If you know that a race takes about 10 minutes to run, you will observe the pipe closely between, say, 3.10 and

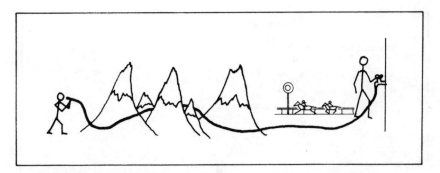

Figure 3.6

3.15. If any water runs out during this period you will know that you have won; but if none comes you can assume that you have lost.

This fable illustrates several important aspects of the transmission of signals in logic networks.

(1) The information transmitted at any time consists of *1* binary digit. We have not specified how large the current of water is to be, so a small current has the same meaning as a large one: a dribble brings the same news as a squirt in the eye. This means that it is easy for the transmission to stay accurate in spite of leaks, blockages, and so on — all that matters is that *some* water should get through.

(2) The speed at which the information is transmitted is very high. In our example it is roughly equal to the speed of sound in water (about 1.6×10^3 m/s) but in electrical circuits it is nearer the speed of light $(2.9 \times 10^8$ m/s). In neither case does it depend on any physical object, such as a drop of water, moving from the source to the destination. In our example the particles of water in the pipe may only move a few metres.

(3) To understand the message, the receiver must know *when* to look. If you didn't know what time the race was, then the absence of a current could mean either 'You have lost' or 'The race has not yet been run'.

Next, we discuss a way in which logic gates based on hydraulics could actually be constructed. Figure 3.7 shows two cross-sections through a special valve. In figure 3.7a, a current of water flows through the input pipe, down the left-hand chamber, and out to waste. In flowing, it pushes a pivoted flap down against its spring.

When the left side of the flap moves down, the right side moves up, and blocks the right-hand chamber. Consequently, no current flows from the water supply through to the output.

Figure 3.7b shows what happens when the input current stops. The spring pulls the flap back up. This unblocks the right-hand chamber, and a current of water is free to flow through the output.

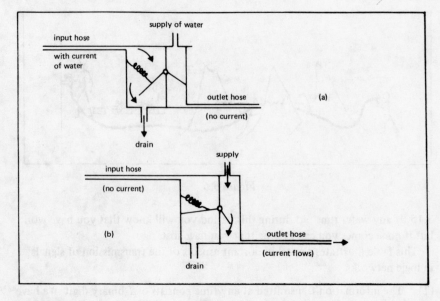

Figure 3.7

A moment's thought will show that this is the action of a one-input NAND gate or inverter — the output is 1 *unless* all (that is, the only) input is 1.

A NAND gate with more than one input can be constructed by connecting the outputs of several special valves, as shown in figure 3.8. In this diagram, if *all* valves have input currents there will be no output current. Otherwise at least one of them will produce an output current. This again satisfies the requirements of a NAND gate.

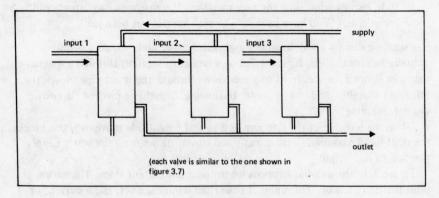

Figure 3.8

3.4 ELECTRONIC CIRCUITRY

A computer built of hydraulic valves would be a working proposition, but it would be bulky, expensive and extremely slow. Each valve might take one-fifth of a second to respond to a change in its input, and at this speed the machine would take days to complete the simplest calculation.

Electronic components are currently favoured for computers because they are fast, reliable and cheap. An electronic NAND gate will react to changes of input within a few nanoseconds (10^{-9} s) so that it can get through 100 million operations a second. Gates can be etched on to the surface of silicon wafers by a process which is basically similar to printing. When complete, the wafers are broken into chips, which are then encapsulated and mounted for use as *integrated circuits* in electronic equipment.

The number of gates on a chip varies widely. Four categories are recognised

Small-scale integration: 1 to 9 gates per chip (SSI)
Medium-scale integration: 10 to 99 gates per chip (MSI)
Large-scale integration: 100 to 10000 gates per chip (LSI)
Very-large-scale integration: over 10 000 gates per chip (VLSI)

At one end of the spectrum, there are chips with groups of unconnected gates, costing a few pence. One family of such chips is the '7400 Series', which includes

Part number	7404	6 inverter gates
Part number	7400	4 two-input NAND gates
Part number	7410	3 three-input NAND gates
Part number	7420	2 four-input NAND gates
Part number	7430	1 eight-input NAND gate

Other families include elements with various speeds and electronic characteristics.

Moving towards the more complex, there are chips which add, subtract and multiply binary numbers, and chips for calculators, watches and TV games. Among more recent developments are *store chips*, each of which can store many thousands of bits of information, and *microprocessors*, which are complete processors needing only some peripheral devices to do useful work. All these chips are mass-produced at low individual cost. On the more complex chips, the price *per gate* is a minute fraction of a penny.

3.5 TRUTH TABLES

Truth tables are an important way of describing logic networks. Consider any network with several — say n — inputs and one output. The corresponding truth table will have one column for each input, and one for the output. It will have

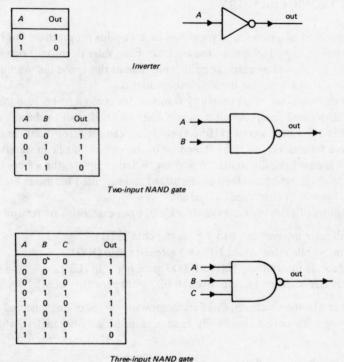

Figure 3.9

one row for every possible *combination* of inputs: 2^n rows in all. The output
cell in each row simply specifies the output for that combination of inputs.

Figure 3.9 shows truth tables for an inverter, a two-input NAND gate and a
three-input NAND gate.

It is worth noting that 'all combinations' of *n* inputs can be listed simply by
writing down the binary numbers 0 to $(2^n - 1)$.

3.6 CONVERSION BETWEEN TRUTH TABLES AND LOGIC NETWORKS

This section describes how any truth table can be represented in terms of a
network of gates.

When a gate distinguishes one possible combination of inputs by treating it
differently from other combinations, we say that the gate *responds* to that
input. Thus a NAND gate will respond by producing a 0 only when all the inputs
are 1s.

Logic networks often need to respond to other combinations. For example, a network might be specified with the following truth table.

A	B	Out
0	0	1
0	1	1
1	0	0
1	1	1

A gate can be *adapted* to respond to the combination $A = 1, B = 0$ by placing an inverter in the B-input signal line, as shown in figure 3.10.

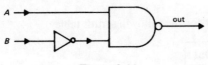

Figure 3.10

The inverter ensures that when $B = 0$, the NAND gate actually receives a 1. Thus it only receives, and responds to, the combination of inputs $(1, 1)$ when $A = 1$ and $B = 0$, as required by the truth table.

Again, the special response is sometimes required to be a 1, rather than a 0. This can be arranged by feeding the output of the NAND gate into another inverter.

Example 3.1
What is the truth table of the network in figure 3.11?

Figure 3.11

Stage 1: The NAND gate has two inputs, so the truth table will have three columns and four rows. We can draw a 'skeleton' table

A	B	Out
0	0	
0	1	
1	0	
1	1	

Stage 2: Both inputs are inverted, so the gate will respond when $A = B = 0$. The 'distinguished' row in the table is therefore the first (apart from the title).

Stage 3: The output is inverted, the distinguished combination therefore produces a 1, and all the others 0s. The final truth table is

A	B	Out
0	0	1
0	1	0
1	0	0
1	1	0

Example 3.2
Draw a logic network for the following truth table

A	B	C	Out
0	0	0	0
0	0	1	1
0	1	0	0
0	1	1	0
1	0	0	0
1	0	1	0
1	1	0	0
1	1	1	0

The table has three input columns, and will need a three-input NAND gate.
    There is only one distinguished row, and it generates a 1. An inverter will be needed at the output.
    The distinguished row has $A = 0$, $B = 0$ and $C = 1$, so that inverters are needed in the A and B signal lines.
    The final result is shown in figure 3.12.

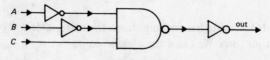

Figure 3.12

In many cases there is a need to distinguish more than one row of a truth table: in other words, several of the input combinations must be treated as equivalent.
    Suppose that the distinguished rows have 1s in the output column. The

corresponding network can be designed in two stages, as follows.

(1) Draw a suitable gating system for each distinguished row, *omitting* the inverter on the output of the NAND gate.

(2) Connect the outputs of all these NAND gates to the inputs of yet another NAND gate. The output of this gate is the required function.

Example 3.3

When 2 binary digits *A* and *B* are added, the *sum* digit is given by the following truth table

A	B	Sum
0	0	0
0	1	1
1	0	1
1	1	0

Design a logic network to implement this truth table.

Stage 1: The distinguished rows are (0, 1) and (1, 0). We draw two gating systems, one below the other (see figure 3.13).

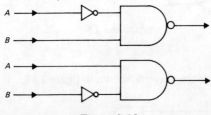

Figure 3.13

Stage 2: Connect both outputs to the inputs of another NAND gate (figure 3.14).

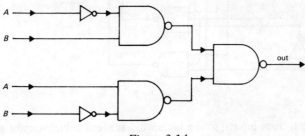

Figure 3.14

Stage 3: Tidy up by connecting together all the *A*-inputs, all the *B*-inputs, and so on. Lines that cross are not deemed to be connected to one another! (see figure 3.15).

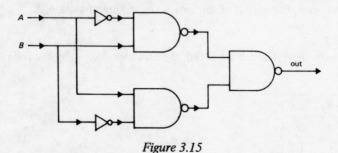

Figure 3.15

Logic networks can often be improved by eliminating inverters. One inverter can easily drive several inputs (figure 3.16).

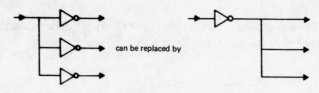

Figure 3.16

Example 3.4
Derive the truth table for the network shown in figure 3.17.

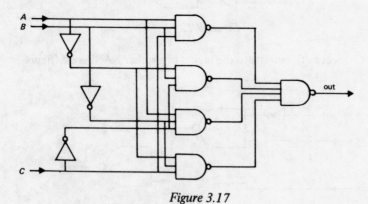

Figure 3.17

The network has three inputs, so the table will have four columns and eight rows.

Careful inspection shows that the combination distinguished by each gate (working downwards) is

$A = 1, \ B = 1, \ C = 1$
$A = 0, \ B = 1, \ C = 0$
$A = 1, \ B = 0, \ C = 0$
$A = 0, \ B = 0, \ C = 1$

The truth table can be written down

A	B	C	Out	
0	0	0	0	
0	0	1	1	(Distinguished by 4th gate)
0	1	0	1	(Distinguished by 2nd gate)
0	1	1	0	
1	0	0	1	(Distinguished by 3rd gate)
1	0	1	0	
1	1	0	0	
1	1	1	1	(Distinguished by 1st gate)

The logic network derived by this method will always be correct, but it may not be the most economical. It is often possible to design another network which does the job with fewer gates, or even to buy a single chip which has the necessary function. This is illustrated in the next example.

Example 3.5
How many chips are needed for the network in example 3.4, assuming that chips in the 7400 Series are to be used?

First solution: A preliminary 'gate count' shows the following

3 inverters
4 three-input NAND gates
1 four-input NAND gate

Using the data on p. 29, this could be satisfied by

1 7404 chip (leaving 3 spare inverters)
2 7410 chips (leaving 2 spare three-input gates)
1 7420 chip (leaving 1 spare four-input gate)

Total: 4 chips

Second solution: A NAND gate with n inputs can always be used as a gate with fewer inputs, just by connecting some of the input lines together (figure 3.18).
This allows us to use one of the four-input gates on the 7420 chip as a three-input gate, and reduces the chip count by 1.

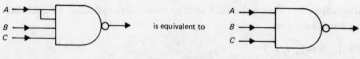

Figure 3.18

Third solution: The manufacturer's catalogue indicates that the 7489 MSI chip (also part of the 7400 series) has precisely the right truth table, and is the only chip needed.

The over-all cost of a machine is strongly related to the number of chips it contains, and hardly at all to the complexity of the individual chips. The third solution is therefore the best.

3.7 PROPAGATION TIME

Earlier it was mentioned that in an electronic gate, any change of input was reflected in the output within a few nanoseconds. Although this period of time is small, it cannot be neglected — it is called the 'gate propagation delay'. A common assumption is that it is the same for all gates, and it is referred to by the symbol δ.

If a signal has to pass through several gates on its way through a logic network, the delays in the individual gates add together. Consider a network like the one in example 3.4. The longest path through the network has three gates: an inverter, a three-input NAND gate and a four-input NAND gate. The over-all propagation time is therefore 3δ.

4 The Implementation of Binary Arithmetic

This chapter shows how some of the simple arithmetic operations described in chapter 2 can be mechanised with logic gates, giving the first real example of the holistic approach to understanding computers. At one level in the discussion, a mechanism can be described in terms of its component parts. We discover *what* it does and *how* it does it. Later, we enclose the mechanism in a box, and make it into a component which may be used as part of a 'higher', more complex device. We still need to know *what* it does, but *how* is no longer relevant. Even though a device may be extremely complicated in absolute terms (that is, it may involve thousands of gates) it can always be easily understood in terms of the functions of its component parts.

4.1 SERIAL AND PARALLEL TRANSMISSION OF WORDS

Chapter 2 explained how various quantities — characters and numbers — are represented by groups of binary digits called *words*. There are two main methods of moving a word between any two places inside a computer system. In the *serial* mode, the signals representing the binary digits are all sent down the same line, one after the other. In the *parallel* mode the signals are all transmitted at the same time, along a bundle of lines called a 'highway'. There are, of course, as many lines in the highway as there are bits in the word.

Serial transmission is slower than parallel, but it uses less equipment. The earliest computers, which were built when logic gates were still very expensive, relied mainly on the serial mode, but most present-day machines use the parallel mode, except for certain specific purposes such as sending information down public telephone lines.

Highways vary from 8 bits in microcomputers to 64 or more in large machines. In diagrams it is not sensible to show every line individually — instead the whole highway is drawn as a broad arrow (see figure 4.1).

4.2 ADDITION OF NUMBERS

When two binary numbers are added, each step of addition yields a *sum* digit

Figure 4.1

(which is part of the answer) and a *carry* digit, which is passed on to the next step. This implies that every step of addition except the first has to handle 3 input digits: one from each of the numbers being added, and a carry from the previous step. The truth tables for the addition are shown below. X and Y represent the digits of the numbers being added.

X	Y	Carry in	Out (sum)		X	Y	Carry in	Out (carry)
0	0	0	0		0	0	0	0
0	0	1	1		0	0	1	0
0	1	0	1		0	1	0	0
0	1	1	0		0	1	1	1
1	0	0	1		1	0	0	0
1	0	1	0		1	0	1	1
1	1	0	0		1	1	0	1
1	1	1	1		1	1	1	1

Sum digit	*Carry digit*

The logic networks for these truth tables can easily be designed by the methods presented in chapter 3. However, the carry network can be simplified and speeded up by noticing that it represents 'any two out of three'. This halves the number of gates and reduces the propagation delay to 2δ.

One possible form of the sum and carry circuits is shown in figure 4.2. In practice, the two networks are always formed on the same integrated circuit and used together. The entire component is called a 'full adder', and is represented in technical drawings by a box with a σ-sign. (This is the Greek letter 'sigma', which mathematicians used to indicate summation.)

When two numbers are added, a full adder is needed for every step of the addition. The adders are arranged in a chain, and each one sends the carry it produces to the input of the next adder to its left. The exceptions are at the ends: the first, or least significant stage has its carry input fixed at zero (at least for now) and the carry which emerges from the most significant stage is thrown away or used to detect overflow.

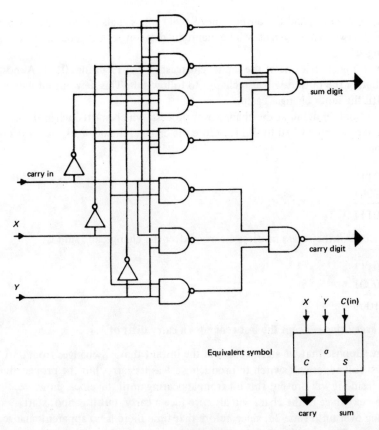

Figure 4.2

Figure 4.3 shows an adder for two 4-bit numbers, with digits X_3, X_2, X_1, X_0 and Y_3, Y_2, Y_1, Y_0 respectively. The 4-digit sum is called S_3, S_2, S_1, S_0.

It is worth considering the operation of this circuit. Suppose that the X and Y lines are connected to switches or push-buttons, and that (for the sake of argument) X brings 0110 and Y brings 0001. The circuit will continuously add

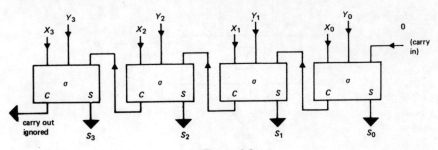

Figure 4.3

these two numbers, and the output lines S will carry signals which represent the sum of the two. These signals will be maintained as long as the input lines remain unchanged.

Now suppose that one of the inputs changes: perhaps X brings 0111. Almost immediately the output will also change to follow suit. This new output will last until the input changes again.

Let us look in detail at the change-over process, which started when the input changed from 0110 to 0111. Before the change, the network was doing the addition

$$\begin{array}{r} 0110 \\ 0001\ + \\ \hline 0111 \end{array}$$

where none of the stages involves a carry. After the change, the sum is

$$\begin{array}{r} 0111 \\ 0001\ + \\ \hline 1000 \end{array}$$

where *every* stage except the last generates a carry digit of 1.

Now suppose that we start a clock at the instant that X_0 changes from 0 to 1. The first full adder will switch to producing a 1 as its carry, but the propagation delays inside it will prevent this bit from appearing until the clock shows 2δ.

The next stage in the chain will also produce a carry, but it cannot start changing over until time 2δ, since before that time there is no apparent change in its input. The new value of the carry does not emerge from the second stage until time 4δ.

The same argument can be extended all the way along the chain. In our example, the most significant digit S_3 takes up to nine gate propagation delays to reach its correct value after new inputs have been applied. It does not always

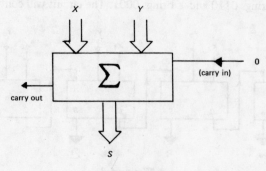

Figure 4.4

take as long as this — it depends on the numbers being added both before and after the change — but a computer designer must allow for the worst case.

The effect is called the 'carry propagation delay', and is roughly $2n$ gate delays when the numbers being added are n bits long. In large computers, where the word length may be 30 or 40 bits, this is significant even if the individual gate delay is very small, and special circuits are used to speed up the process of addition by predicting carries in advance.

A chain of full adders is called a 'parallel adder', and is often shown as in figure 4.4. Parallel adders with many stages are manufactured as single integrated circuits.

4.3 SUBTRACTION OF NUMBERS

With two's complement notation, a simple way to complement a number (that is, to find its negative) is to change every bit and then add 1. The mathematics behind this process was described and illustrated in chapter 2; it leads to a convenient method of subtraction. Let us rewrite $X - Y$ as $X + (-Y)$. We can now change each bit of Y by using an inverter, and add the result to X with a full adder. The extra 1 can be supplied as an initial carry to the least significant stage. This is illustrated in figure 4.5, which includes a conventional notation for showing a row of inverters as a single component.

4.4 THE MULTIPLEXER

In a television studio the producer sits in front of a bank of monitor screens, each one showing the picture seen by a different camera. His job is to select and transmit just one of the pictures available. In a similar way, a computer has certain places where there are a number of alternative signals, of which exactly one must be selected for onward transmission. The selection mechanism is called a *multiplexer*.

Figure 4.6a shows a simple multiplexer. There are two signal inputs A and B, a control input X and an output. When $X = 0$ the selected input is A, and the output takes the same value as A, quite independently of anything that may happen to B. When $X = 1$, B is selected and A is ignored.

Truth tables are not especially helpful in designing multiplexers. It is easier to go directly to the logic diagram, which is shown in figure 4.6b. When $X = 0$, gate p is 'disabled' because its output is 1 no matter what the value of B may be; q, on the other hand is 'enabled' because its output is the inverse of A. The output of the entire network is therefore the same as input A.

When $X = 1$, q is disabled and the only data path through the network starts at B. B is therefore selected.

Multiplexers are built with four, eight or sixteen inputs. The number of

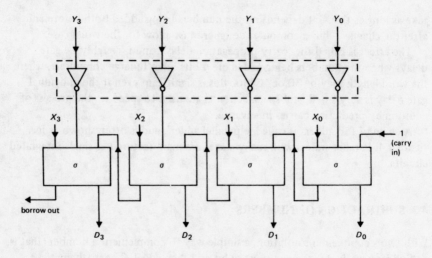

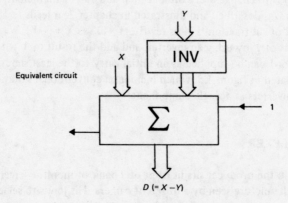

Figure 4.5

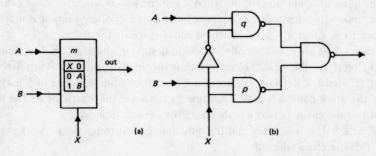

Figure 4.6

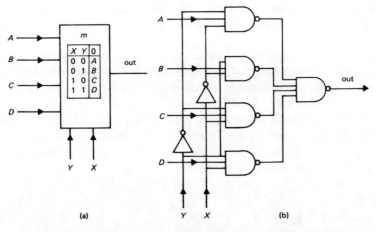

Figure 4.7

control lines is always enough to select exactly one of the inputs: two controls for four inputs, three for eight, and so on. A multiplexer has a gate for every input, but only one of them is enabled at a time. Figure 4.7 shows the symbol for a four-input multiplexer and its corresponding network.

Frequently the information to be selected occupies a complete highway rather than a single line. Individual multiplexers can be assembled in banks to make a 'parallel multiplexer', such as the one shown in figure 4.8. Note that the control signals are *not* highways but individual lines.

4.5 SHIFTING BINARY NUMBERS

In the decimal system, any number can be divided by ten simply by shuffling each digit one place to the right. If a whole number result is needed the least

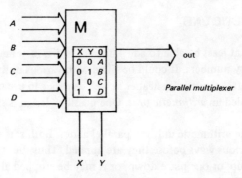

Figure 4.8

significant digit on the right is discarded. Similarly, a number shifted one place left is multiplied by ten, so long as there is no loss of a significant digit from the left.

In the binary system, a number shifted to the right is halved, and one shifted left is doubled — always provided that bits are not lost from the ends. These shifts are often useful, particularly as elementary steps in the much more complex processes of general multiplication and division.

In a parallel machine, a shift network can be constructed without any gates whatever. All that is necessary is to 'stagger' the lines of the highway and to insert a zero at the appropriate end. Figure 4.9 shows networks for shifting left and right, and the corresponding symbols.

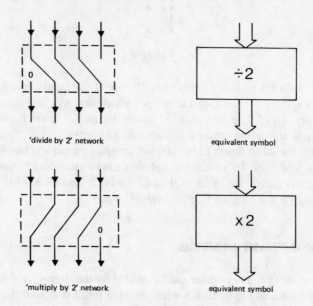

Figure 4.9

4.6 AN ARITHMETIC UNIT

A computer must at least be able to add, subtract, shift, increment and complement binary numbers. It could be filled with various units devoted to these different tasks, but it is cheaper as well as easier to use one general-purpose device called an *arithmetic unit*. One possible design is shown in figure 4.10.

The heart of the arithmetic unit is a parallel adder. Both sets of inputs may be transformed in various ways before they are applied. Thus the *A*-input may be shifted one place up, or one place down, or it may be stopped altogether (replaced by 0s). Similarly the *B*-input can be inverted if necessary.

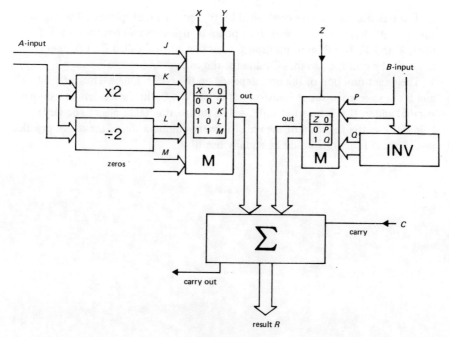

Figure 4.10

X	Y	Z	C	Effective function
0	0	0	0	$R = A + B$
0	0	0	1	$R = A + B + 1$
0	0	1	0	$R = A - B - 1$
0	0	1	1	$R = A - B$
0	1	0	0	$R = 2A + B$
0	1	0	1	$R = 2A + B + 1$
0	1	1	0	$R = 2A - B - 1$
0	1	1	1	$R = 2A - B$
1	0	0	0	$R = \tfrac{1}{2}A + B$
1	0	0	1	$R = \tfrac{1}{2}A + B + 1$
1	0	1	0	$R = \tfrac{1}{2}A - B - 1$
1	0	1	1	$R = \tfrac{1}{2}A - B$
1	1	0	0	$R = B$
1	1	0	1	$R = B + 1$
1	1	1	0	$R = -B - 1$
1	1	1	1	$R = -B$

The transformations are controlled by two parallel multiplexers. The one for the A-inputs has to select one of four possible highways and has two control lines, X and Y. The B-input multiplexer has one control called Z. A further input to the unit is C, an initial value for the carry.

The exact function of the unit depends on the control lines. Thus when A and B are selected without transformation and $C = 0$, the device acts as a simple parallel adder. If B is inverted and $C = 1$, a subtraction takes place. The table below shows the function of the unit for every combination of inputs. In practice not all these functions would be equally useful.

5 Sequential Networks

5.1 STORAGE ELEMENTS

An essential part of any computer is its information store. In processors, stores are usually implemented with flip–flops, which are networks each consisting of several NAND gates, and capable of storing one binary digit.

5.1.1 The Bistable Circuit

Consider the network shown in figure 5.1. Suppose (for the sake of argument) that the output of inverter a is high. Following the signal round the loop, we find

	Output from a high
Therefore	Input to b high
Therefore	Output from b low
Therefore	Input to a low
Therefore	Output from a high

This result is in keeping with the original assumption, and shows that the state of the network is stable: the outputs at P and Q will remain at their present values indefinitely.

Now take the opposite assumption: that the output of a is low. Since the network is completely symmetrical, this assumption will also be justified by working round the loop. The conclusion is that the network has *two* stable

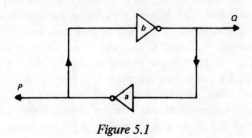

Figure 5.1

states, either of which can be maintained indefinitely. The names given to the states are as follows.

Output		Name
at P	*at Q*	
1	0	0
0	1	1

5.1.2 The R–S Flip–Flop

In practice, a bistable circuit made of two inverters is useless because there are no input lines and therefore no way of changing its state. This fault disappears if each inverter is given an extra input, making it into a two-input NAND gate. This is shown in figure 5.2, where the *same* network is drawn in two different ways — one to bring out the essential similarity to figure 5.1, and the other showing its more conventional form.

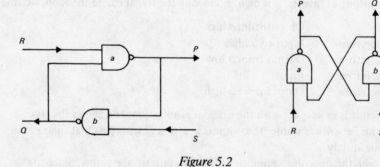

Figure 5.2

Suppose that the network is in state 0 ($P = 1$, $Q = 0$) and that both R and S are *high*. The network is stable in this state. Now let the signal on S go *low*. This drives the output of gate b high, which in turn sends the output of a low. The flip–flop has switched state. When S goes high again, the flip–flop does not switch back — it 'remembers' that S was momentarily low.

When a signal changes from high to low, and then back again after a short time to 'high', this is called a 'negative pulse'. We say that the flip–flop is switched from 0 to 1 by a negative pulse on S. If the device is already in state 1, then further negative pulses on S will have no effect.

The circuit is again symmetrical, and a similar analysis shows that a negative pulse on R will switch the device into the 0 state if it is not already there. A table describing the action of the device is as follows.

Input	Starting State	Result
Negative pulse on *S*	0	Switches to state 1
Negative pulse on *S*	1	Remains in state 1
Negative pulse on *R*	0	Remains in state 0
Negative pulse on *R*	1	Switches to state 0

A basic assumption about this circuit is that the outputs at *P* and *Q* must always be different. The inputs at *S* and *R* are never allowed to go *low* at the same time because this would send both *P* and *Q* high, so violating the rule.

The circuit is called an *R–S* flip–flop (the letters stand for 'reset' and 'set'), or sometimes a toggle. It is indeed somewhat like a light switch mounted on a wall. If it is off, a downward blow (at least in the United Kingdom) will turn it on, but further blows downwards will have no effect. When the switch is on the first upward blow will turn it off, but any further blows upwards will be ignored. Blows in both directions delivered at the same time would lead to undefined results, and are not permitted.

Figure 5.3 is a 'timing diagram' for an *R–S* flip–flop changing state in response to a negative pulse. The horizontal axis represents time, and the vertical axis represents the various labelled inputs and outputs.

Initially, the flip–flop is in the 0 state, with *P* = 1 and *Q* = 0. At a certain moment the *S*-input changes from 1 to 0. After one unit of gate propagation delay *Q* changes to 1, and after another unit *P* changes to 0. *S* can now be allowed to go back to 1 without affecting the new state of the flip–flop. Note that the outputs of the flip–flop are not valid until two units of propagation delay after the change in the input signal.

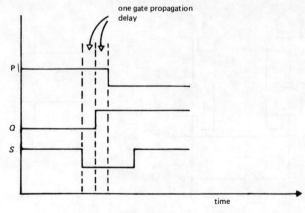

Figure 5.3

5.1.3 The Clocked 'D' Flip–Flop

A computer contains many flip–flops, each connected to each other and to various logic networks such as adders and multiplexers. An $R-S$ flip–flop can change state as soon as one of its inputs changes to 0. The logic networks all have their own propagation times, so that in a machine built of $R-S$ flip–flops each one will, in general, change state at a different time. Although it is not impossible to design a machine which runs correctly under these circumstances, it is difficult and expensive. Most smaller computers use a modified form of circuit which ensures that all flip–flops change at the same moment — like players in a well-disciplined orchestra. A machine built with this property is called *synchronous*.

In a synchronous computer, there is a special component called a 'clock' which produces a sequence of pulses and transmits them to all the flip–flops in the system. The clock is like the conductor of the orchestra, except that it beats time rather more quickly — usually between 1 and 10 million pulses per second.

The flip–flops in a synchronous machine have two inputs: a 'data' input and a 'clock' input. When the clock input is low, the data input is ignored, but when it goes high, the data is 'clocked' into the device, replacing the previous information there.

Figure 5.4 shows the network of a D flip–flop. Gates a and b form an ordinary $R-S$ flip–flop, and gates x and y use the data signal, the present state of the flip–flop and the clock pulse (which is *positive*) to steer a negative pulse to a or b, as necessary, if a change is required.

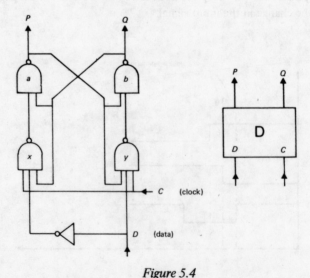

Figure 5.4

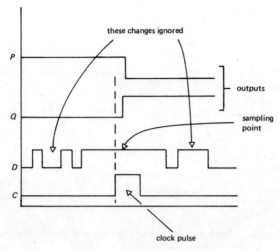

Figure 5.5

In practice, the clock pulse is kept short so that the data input can have no chance to change while it is being sampled. A timing diagram for a D flip–flop is shown in figure 5.5.

Logical networks which involve flip–flops are called *sequential* because they pass through sequences of states. By contrast, networks which can be described by truth tables, and where (ignoring propagation time) the outputs depend only on the current inputs, are called *combinatorial*.

5.2 REGISTERS

In machines which use parallel transmission of data (that is, the majority) most of the D flip–flops are arranged in groups called *registers*. A register can store a complete word, 1 bit being kept in each flip–flop.

Figure 5.6 shows a 3-bit register and its equivalent symbol. The input and output lines are all connected to other parts of the network such as a parallel adder or a multiplexer.

The input highway is distributed to the D-inputs of the individual flip–flops. When a clock pulse is received, the information on this highway is taken into the register, replacing the previous contents. Note that the clock signal is a single line, not a highway.

Figure 5.7 shows two possible ways of connecting registers and combinatorial networks. In both cases, the registers are assumed to contain numbers. In figure 5.7a, the network is a 'divide by 2', so that the number returned to the input of the register is half its present contents. One clock pulse will effectively halve the

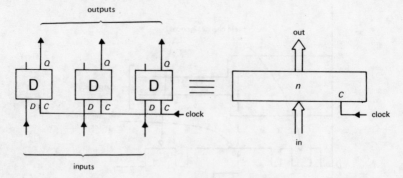

Figure 5.6

contents of the register, and a sequence of t pulses will divide the original contents by 2^t.

In figure 5.7b, two registers, A and B, are connected to the inputs of a parallel adder. The output, which is the sum of the numbers in the registers, is connected back to the input of A. A single clock pulse will therefore add the contents of B to A. A register used to receive the result of an arithmetic operation is often called an 'accumulator'.

Figure 5.8 illustrates the relationship between the clock rate (expressed as the interval between successive clock pulses) and the circuit propagation time. In general, the inputs to a combinatorial circuit like the adder in figure 5.6b change at the beginning of each clock pulse. Thereafter, the outputs of the circuit may not reach their correct values until the maximum propagation delay through the network: this may be several dozen gate delays. If the next clock pulse comes after the maximum delay, the system will always work correctly, but if it comes before, there is a danger that the outputs are used before they have reached their correct values. Thus the propagation delay is a major factor in determining the speed of a central processor.

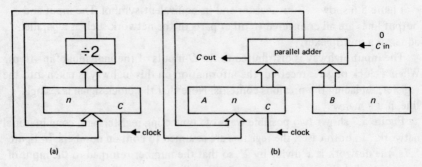

Figure 5.7

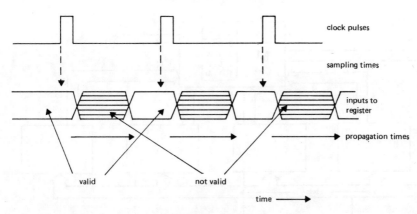

clock pulses

sampling times

inputs to register

propagation times

valid

not valid

time ⟶

Figure 5.8

5.3 BUS STRUCTURES

A typical central processor contains about a dozen registers, and it is necessary to move information among them without restriction.

One approach is to provide a separate highway between every pair of registers, and to equip each register with a multiplexer to select the appropriate signal. However, this approach leads to a very large number of signal lines, and is only used in expensive computers designed for great speed. A more economic method is to use a *bus*, which is a single highway linking all the registers and other components of the system.

Each clock pulse defines a 'bus cycle'. For any one cycle, one device (which may be a register or a combinatorial network) is selected, and its output is transmitted over the entire bus.

The destination of the information is always a register. The actual register concerned during any one bus cycle is given a clock pulse. This transfers the information from the bus into the register, replacing its previous contents.

For any bus cycle, the source of the information is called the 'bus master', and the destination is referred to as the 'bus slave'. It is clear that at any instant there can only be one bus master, but there may be any number of bus slaves — the information is sent to all of them.

The bus is like a long pipe with openings. For any cycle, the bus master is permitted to shout a message into his opening, and the bus slaves are instructed to listen.

In principle, the bus could be driven by a large parallel multiplexer, as shown in figure 5.9. Here the bus master for any cycle would be selected by the control lines X and Y. However, this system would also lead to a great deal of cabling (since highways from all the registers would have to be returned to a central point) and this is undesirable. A better system consists of attaching the various

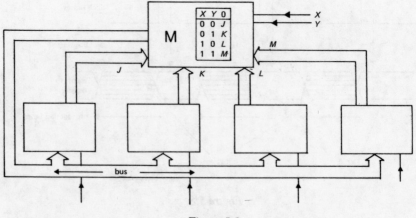

Figure 5.9

highways directly to the bus itself. Since only one bus master is permitted, the connection must be made through a special isolating switch which can disconnect any highway which is not the master for that cycle. Such a switch can be controlled by a conventional signal, and for technical reasons, is called a 'tri-state buffer'.

A simple bus-organised system is shown in figure 5.10. The tri-state buffers are shown as circles.

Suppose that information is to be transferred from register X to register Y. Register X is made the bus master, and its tri-state buffer is switched *on* by the control signal S_x. All other tri-state buffers are off.

Register Y is the bus slave. At the end of the bus cycle, a pulse is applied to its clock input (but *not* to the inputs of the other registers). This completes the transfer.

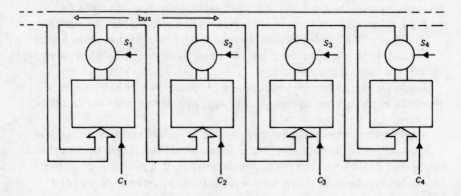

Figure 5.10

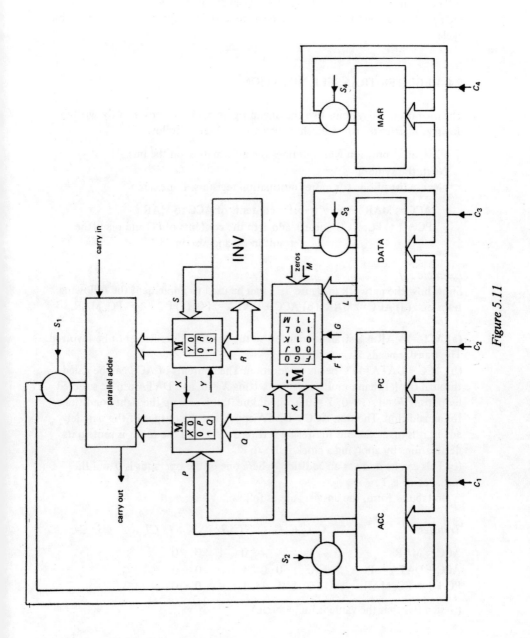

Figure 5.11

A more complex system with a bus structure is shown in figure 5.11. Leaving aside certain details such as the choice of names for the registers, it is clear that the network can be made to do one of many different operations in any one bus cycle.

5.4 REGISTER TRANSFER NOTATION

The operations of systems like the one in figure 5.11 are conveniently written down as *register transfers*. Each bus cycle is written as follows.

First, an expression which defines the information on the bus
Next, the symbol =⟩
Next, a list of one (or more) destination registers. For example

ACC =⟩ MAR means 'transfer contents of ACC to MAR'
PC + 1 =⟩ PC, ACC means 'add 1 to the contents of PC and place the
result in PC and also in ACC'

Example 5.1
Show how the network in figure 5.11 can be used to implement the following transfers: (a) ACC =⟩ MAR; (b) ACC + DATA =⟩ PC; (c) PC + 1 =⟩ PC, MAR.

(a) ACC =⟩ MAR is a straight transfer, so the parallel adder need not be involved. The transfer needs $S_2 = 1$, C_4 pulsed.
(b) ACC + DATA =⟩ PC needs an addition. The contents of ACC can be gated through the left-hand multiplexer by setting $X = 0$, and DATA can be selected by putting $F = 1$, $G = 0$, $Y = 0$. C should be 0; this sets up the right conditions for an addition. The sum ACC + DATA appears at the output of the parallel adder; it is made the bus master by setting $S_1 = 1$, and the result is sent to its destinations by applying a clock pulse to PC.
(c) This can be done as an addition, where one of the operands is 0 and the initial carry is 1.

In tabular form, the answers are as follows.

Transfer	X	Y	F	G	C	S1	S2	S3	S4	C1	C2	C3	C4
ACC ⇒ MAR	–	–	–	–	–	0	1	0	0				⎍
ACC + DATA ⇒ PC	0	0	1	0	0	1	0	0	0	⎍			
PC + 1 ⇒ PC, MAR	1	0	1	1	1	1	0	0	0	⎍			⎍

(– signifies that the value is immaterial.)

6 Immediate Access Stores

6.1 RANDOM ACCESS MEMORY

Most of the storage in a processor is provided in the form of *random access memory* or RAM. The memory is an array of registers or 'cells' each capable of holding one word. The number of cells varies between 64 in small microprocessor systems to several millions in large computers. The term 'random access' implies that the information in all the cells in accessible equally quickly.

In the array, each cell has its own unique identification which is called an 'address'. The addresses are numerical, and generally start at 0, going up in steps of 1 as far as necessary.

When the computer is running, each register transfer can involve at most one of the cells in the memory (that is, it would be impossible for the bus master and the bus slave both to be memory cells). The cell actually used is determined by an *address selection mechanism*, which is in turn controlled by the contents of the *memory address register*, a special register used only for this purpose – its name is often abbreviated to MAR.

Figure 6.1 shows how a random access memory could be attached to a bus

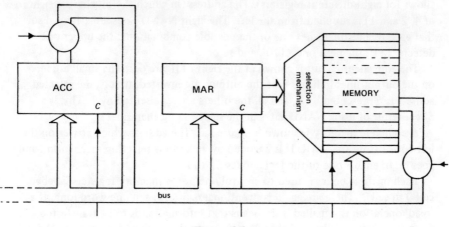

Figure 6.1

system. Whenever the memory is to be used, the address of the cell required must first be sent to the MAR. When this address is loaded, the corresponding cell in the memory is selected automatically, and the memory behaves as if this cell were a conventional register, and the others did not exist at all. In principle, the cell remains selected indefinitely until the MAR is supplied with a new address, but in practice it is unusual for the same cell to be used even twice running, so each memory reference normally takes *two* register transfers — one to load the MAR and one to transfer information to or from the selected cell.

Example 6.1

Referring to figure 6.1, list the register transfers needed (a) to load the contents of cell 57 to the accumulator; (b) to copy the contents of cell 3 to cells 4 and 5.

Using a symbolic notation, we can put

(a) 57 =)MAR   (load address 57 to MAR; this selects cell 57)
     MEM =) ACC (copy contents of *selected* cell to ACC)
(b) 3 =) MAR   (copy contents of cell 3 to ACC; a direct
     MEM =) ACC   transfer between cells 3 and 4 is impossible)
     4   =) MAR (copy contents of ACC to cell 4)
     ACC =) MEM
     5   =) MAR (copy contents of ACC to cell 5)
     ACC =) MEM

Internally, the MAR is a conventional register composed of D flip—flops. It has no tri-state buffer on its output because it is never called on to be the bus master; its output highway is always connected to the memory address selection mechanism.

Figure 6.2 shows an address selection mechanism for a 3-bit address (which allows for eight different registers). The address (in which the bits have weights of 4, 2 and 1) is supplied from the left. The eight NAND gates are arranged so that each one distinguishes one of the possible combinations: the upper one detects '111', the next one, '110', and so on.

The equivalent circuit is shown at the right of figure 6.2. The small circles on the output lines indicate that the outputs are inverted, that is, the selected address is represented by 0, and all the others are represented by 1. This is a direct result of using NAND gates in the selection mechanism.

A complete memory is shown in figure 6.3. The address which arrives on the left comes from the MAR. It is decoded by an address selection mechanism, and goes on to enable *one* of the logic boxes L_0 to L_7.

Each of these boxes is used to control one of the memory registers labelled cell 0 to cell 7. These are again conventional registers each one word long. If a 'read' operation is signalled, this means that information is to be transferred *from* the selected cell *to* another destination in the system. Accordingly, the

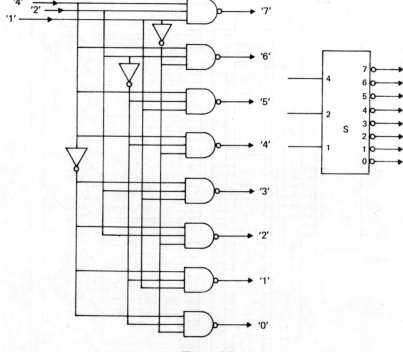

Figure 6.2

selected logic box opens the tri-state buffer of its cell, and allows the contents
on to the bus. The selected cell is therefore bus master for the current bus cycle.

When a 'write' operation is invoked, information must be taken from the bus
and loaded into the selected cell, replacing its previous contents. The selected
logic box directs the write signal into the clock input of the selected register,
thus making it a bus slave for the current cycle.

The logic boxes are all identical. Each one is a simple combinational circuit
with three inputs and two outputs, and the design of its truth table and
corresponding network are entirely straightforward.

In practice, memories are hard to make because of the sheer number of
components needed. A basic *D* flip–flop needs five gates. In a memory, when
the selection mechanisms and tri-state buffers have been taken into account, a
more realistic measure is six to eight gates per bit stored. A store consisting of
1024 words of 8 bits each (a very modest requirement) would need about 50 000
gates. The difficulty of manufacturing and testing a single chip with 50 000
components can well be imagined, because a single defective gate destroys the
usefulness of the entire chip.

At any time, there is a practical limit to the number of components which
can be etched on to a single chip, with a reasonable chance that all of them

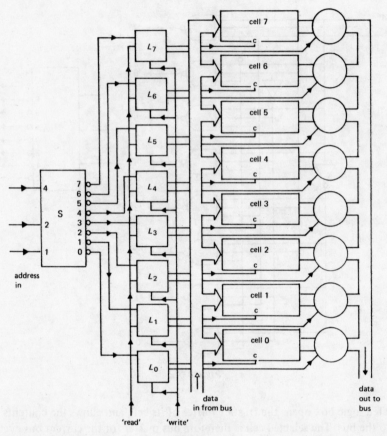

Figure 6.3

should work. At the time these words are written, chips with 64K (2^{16}) bits
are commercially available. The recent tendency has been for the chip capacity
to quadruple every two years, and the cost per bit to halve; this trend may well
continue. In the meantime, most computer systems will need far more storage
than can be accommodated on a single chip, so the question arises of how to sub-
divide the store while keeping the number of connections to each chip as low as
possible. (Connections are made manually and are one of the most expensive
parts of chip production.) One immediate conclusion is that each chip must
have its own address selection mechanism, otherwise it would have an 'enable'
line for each of thousands of cells.

Internally, the storage can either be bit-oriented (with each bit having its
own address), or word-oriented (with the flip—flops arranged in groups of 4 or
8). Thus a 16K 'chip' can either provide a single bit at each of 16K different
addresses, or 2048 8-bit registers. A complete memory can be assembled from
either type of chip, and there is little to choose between them, except that

using word-oriented chips would need an additional selection mechanism to identify the chip which corresponded to any address. To give a practical example, the 8K of 8-bit store in the PET microcomputer is made of 16 memory chips, each one of 1K x 4 bits.

The type of random access memory we have described is called 'static semiconductor memory'. Certain other types are also available. *Core store*, which is obsolescent but still used in many existing computers, relies on a tiny ring of magnetic material to record each bit. For many years core store was the only type of random access memory, and many people and books still refer to 'core' when they mean 'memory'. *Dynamic semiconductor memory* is broadly similar to the static type. It is somewhat cheaper, but more complicated to use.

6.2 READ-ONLY MEMORY

Most types of random-access memory are *volatile*. This means that whenever the power to a computer is switched off, the information in such a memory is lost.

For many applications it is important to store information permanently, so that it is always available to the processor and can be used as soon as the computer is switched on.

This facility can be provided by *read-only memory* or ROM. In most ways, a ROM chip is similar to a random access component, but the storage elements are not flip–flops but fixed networks which always contain the same information. The data can be put in either when the chip is manufactured, or by a process called 'field programming', in which the appropriate bit is set into each storage network by passing a heavy current of electricity for long enough to vapourise a thin metallic link. This is equivalent to storing a binary number on a domestic switchboard by blowing selected fuses, except that in the ROM chip the fuses cannot be repaired.

Another way of providing protection against loss of information is to use non-volatile RAM. There are two main types: core store, and static semiconductor memory with an emergency battery to maintain the power. This latter method is not really permanent but will usually retain the information until the main power supply is restored.

6.3 TIMING

All the types of memory we have considered fall into the general category of 'random access' because the contents of *any* cell can be accessed in just two bus cycles. There exist many other types of memory, but they all rely on physical motion or its electrical analogue, and generally require the system to wait for as long as several minutes before it can gain access to any item of information. These other types will be discussed later.

7 Introduction to SNARK

A computer system for any specific task (perhaps running an airline booking scheme or looking after the welfare of a patient in the intensive care unit of a hospital) is designed as a holarchy, and consists of several 'layers'. At the bottom, there are the individual NAND gates and their connections, which are used to form networks capable of arithmetic and information storage. This layer is called the 'hardware' of the system. Left to itself, the hardware can do no useful work, any more than a non-programmable hand calculator can solve any problem entirely on its own. The hardware of a computer needs to be driven by a sequence of instructions, each one of which represents a simple step in the execution of the present task. The collection of instructions for a complete job is called a *program*. Programs generally are referred to as *software*, and form the next layer, above the hardware, in the system hierarchy.

Unlike hardware, programs are *abstract*. They are not constructed but written, and they exist only to be executed by hardware, much as a piece of music exists only to be performed on an instrument. The analogy goes a little further, for a musical score can be thought of as a set of instructions, or program, to be executed by the player.

The final, uppermost layer in the system hierarchy is the over-all system design. Here, however, we shall focus our attention on programming, leaving the systems aspect to be considered later. We begin by discussing *machine coding*, the style of programming most closely related to the hardware of the computer itself.

7.1 THE SNARK COMPUTER

Barring only the most superficial level, it is impossible to learn anything about programs without actually writing them. Most existing computers are not suitable for the study of machine code programming, for one of two reasons.

Some computer systems allow programs to be written only in a so-called 'high-level language' such as BASIC or PASCAL. Such a language is convenient for solving practical problems precisely because it disguises the actual properties of the underlying hardware with an impenetrable layer of software. To give a practical example, many expert BASIC programmers know nothing about the binary system, even though the hardware of the computer uses this notation to express all the numbers in their programs.

Other systems admit machine code programs, but the testing of these programs is laborious and complicated for reasons which have nothing to do with the fundamental principles involved.

A way out of this difficulty is to use an 'abstract' machine — an imaginary computer called the SNARK. This forms a useful teaching vehicle because it illustrates many basic principles without introducing unnecessary complexity, and because it can be simulated on an existing computer. This allows programs written for SNARK to be executed in such a way that their detailed operation is immediately apparent. The execution is done by a special program called a 'simulator', which makes the existing computer behave exactly as if it were a SNARK. Practical details of the program are included in appendix A. The SNARK, of course, is only one out of many possible designs.

7.2 THE BASIC STRUCTURE OF THE SNARK

As we have explained in previous chapters, central processing units are made up of registers, arithmetic units and stores. The SNARK is no exception. It contains

An arithmetic unit capable of adding and subtracting 16-bit numbers.
Two 16-bit registers called 'accumulator *A*' and 'accumulator *B*' ('ACC *A*' and 'ACC *B*' for short).
A 9-bit register called the 'program counter' (abbreviated to 'PC').
An addressable memory, containing up to 512 cells of 16 bits each. The addresses start at 0, and this enables the PC to 'point' to any cell uniquely.

The SNARK also includes other registers (such as a memory address register), but because they are effectively concealed from the programmer, we shall not describe them here.

A diagram of SNARK appears in figure 7.1.

7.3 INSTRUCTIONS

The SNARK can obey some 16 different instructions, most of which are designed to manipulate the contents of the registers and the store. In general the instructions have numerous variants. Here are some examples

'Load ACC *A* with the number 17'
'Add 1 to the contents of ACC *A*'
'Subtract 6 from the contents of ACC *A*'
'Stop'

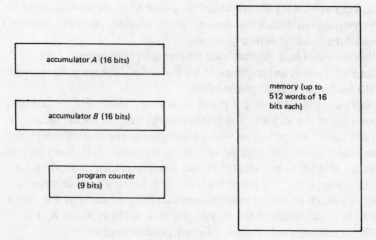

Figure 7.1

When the machine executes the first of these instructions, it places the binary pattern 0000000000010001 (decimal 17) in accumulator *A*, destroying the original contents of ACC *A* as it does so. If it then goes on to obey the other instructions in sequence, it eventually stops with 12 (binary equivalent 0000000000001100) in ACC *A*. It will have executed a trivial but complete program to evaluate (17 + 1 − 6).

In this example, 'load', 'add', 'subtract' and 'stop' are all instructions in the SNARK's repertory. Each of these instructions except the last can specify either of the two accumulators, and can use any value between 0 and 511.

When writing programs it is convenient to use a compact formal notation for the various instructions. Every instruction starts with a *mnemonic* or code which indicates the operation: thus 'LDA' means 'load the accumulator'. In most cases the mnemonic is followed by an *A* or a *B* to show which accumulator is intended. Next comes the number to be used, written in decimal and preceded by the # sign.

Programs are often made more comprehensible by comments addressed to the human reader. The formal notation has room for this material: it is put to the right of the instruction itself, and separated from it by a ↑ sign.

Here are some examples of instructions with comments

LDA	A	#17	↑	LOAD 17 TO ACC A
LDA	B	#400	↑	LOAD 400 TO ACC B
ADD	A	#1	↑	ADD 1 TO ACC A
SUB	B	#103	↑	TAKE 103 FROM B
END			↑	STOP

So far, we have said little to suggest that the SNARK is different in any important way from a hand calculator. The essential distinction is that SNARK is a *stored program* machine. The instructions are not supplied and executed one at a time; instead they are all supplied in advance, placed in the memory, and then extracted and executed automatically. This allows the machine to run at its own speed without constant human attention.

When it is fed in, each instruction of a program is coded as a 16-bit binary pattern and stored in one of the cells of memory. Later, when the machine is obeying the program, it fetches the coded instructions from the memory and executes them one after the other. At any stage, the PC register contains the *address* of the cell which contains the next instruction. Normally, the instructions are taken from cells with consecutive addresses, so that during every instruction 1 is automatically added to PC to ensure an orderly progression through the program.

When you write a program for the SNARK, you must decide which registers to use for holding the instructions. The *address* of each instruction is written, as a decimal number, at the *left* of the line. Suppose, for example, that you pick cell 0 for the first instruction in your program. Then the complete program might be

```
0   LDA   A   #17        ↑ CALCULATE (17 + 1 − 6)
1   ADD   A   #1
2   SUB   A   #6
3   END                  ↑ STOP
```

When you enter this program into the SNARK simulator, and type RUN (as described in appendix A), the simulator will display exactly what happens at each step, and will eventually halt with the contents of ACC *A* shown as '12'.

It is important to note that the numerals on the left are *addresses*, not *statement numbers* as in BASIC or FORTRAN. You must use consecutive numbers because the SNARK obeys instructions taken from cells which are next to one another.

Every line in a program is coded and placed in the SNARK store as soon as it is typed, replacing the previous contents. This means that you can type the lines in any order, and that you can correct a line by retyping it, but you cannot insert extra commands between existing ones — there is simply no room for them.

Example 7.1
Write a SNARK program to calculate (400 +173 − 416 + 51) using accumulator *B*.

We choose 0 as a starting cell.

```
0   LDA   B   #400
1   ADD   B   #173
2   SUB   B   #416
3   ADD   B   #51
4   END
```

7.4 ADDRESS MODES

All the instructions in the previous section (except END) specified their
operands explicitly, in the form #17, #400. Such instructions are said to be in
the *immediate mode*. A program written only with this kind of instruction
would be extremely limited since it could only ever do one calculation.

Another possibility is to use the *direct mode*. Here the operand is assumed to
be present in the store, and is specified by giving the address of its cell. Direct
mode instructions are distinguished by *not* having the # sign in front of the
address. Thus

        LDA   A   57

means 'Load accumulator *A* with the contents of cell 57'.

When necessary, the initial value in any cell can be specified by writing it as
an addressed, signed number, thus

        57   +999   ↑ START WITH 999 IN CELL 57

However, the important point is that programs which use the direct mode
would work with *any* numbers.

Example 7.2
Write a program which adds the numbers in cells 100, 101 and 102, leaving the
result in accumulator *B*.

0	LDA	B	100	↑ LOAD CONTENTS OF CELL 100
1	ADD	B	101	↑ ADD CONTENTS OF CELL 101
2	ADD	B	102	↑ ADD CONTENTS OF CELL 102
3	END			↑ STOP
100	+ 4			↑ NUMBERS TO BE ADDED
101	+ 7			
102	+11			

The operands used by instructions in the direct mode are 16-bit numbers in
two's complement notation. A number may be kept in any cell except one
already occupied by another number *or an instruction!*

A useful instruction is one which copies the contents of the specified
accumulator into a designated store cell. Its mnemonic is 'STA', which stands
for 'store accumulator'. This instruction cannot be used in the immediate mode:
it would make no sense to store the accumulator into a *number*.

Example 7.3

A number *a* is stored in cell 50. Write a program which places $(a + 1)$ in cell 51, and $(100 - a)$ in cell 52.

0	LDA	A	50	↑ CALCULATE $(A + 1)$
1	ADD	A	#1	↑ NOTE IMMEDIATE MODE
2	STA	A	51	↑ STORE IN 51
3	LDA	A	#100	↑ CALCULATE $100 - A$
4	SUB	A	50	
5	STA	A	52	↑ STORE IN 52
6	END			
50	+31			↑ POSSIBLE VALUE FOR A

7.5 INPUT AND OUTPUT

In practical use (as opposed to the artificially simple 'learning' situation implied by this book) a program is written by one person, and then used later by others. The users must be able to supply the program with their own particular 'data', so that it does exactly the task they need at that moment. The program must be much more flexible than those we have considered in this chapter.

Programs normally have 'specifications', which describe what they do. The specification of a very simple program might be

'This program accepts three numbers from the user, and displays their sum'

The SNARK has a special instruction which can accept numbers from the user after the execution of the program has begun. Its mnemonic is INA, and its effect is to ask the user for a number by displaying a question-mark. When the number has been typed on the keyboard (and ended by RETURN) the SNARK loads its value into the selected accumulator and passes on to the next instruction. INA can specify either accumulator, but does not need an operand.

The SNARK is unusual in that it displays everything that it does. Most computers give no outward sign of their internal calculations, and must be explicitly programmed to display the results of their work.

The SNARK simulator has a mode in which display is not automatic, and it is therefore equipped with a special display instruction. This command is called OUT. When executed, it prints the contents of the selected accumulator as a signed decimal number, on a line by itself. Like INA, OUT must specify an accumulator but needs no operand.

Example 7.4

Write a program which reads three numbers supplied by the user, and displays their sum. Sketch the display produced by a typical run of the program, assuming that the SNARK monitor is switched off.

0	INA	A	↑ INPUT FIRST NUMBER
1	STA	A 50	↑ STORE IN 50
2	INA	A	↑ INPUT SECOND NUMBER
3	ADD	A 50	↑ ADD FIRST
4	STA	A 50	↑ STORE RESULT IN 50
5	INA	A	↑ INPUT THIRD
6	ADD	A 50	↑ ADD FIRST AND SECOND
7	OUT	A	↑ DISPLAY RESULT
8	END		↑ STOP

```
? 17  ⎫
? 19  ⎬  over-all display; numbers typed by the user are
? 327 ⎭  underlined
+ 363
```

8 Jump Instructions on SNARK

The SNARK, as we explained in chapter 7, is a *stored program* computer. One major advantage of this arrangement is that the computer can choose to repeat certain sequences of instructions many times over, or else to skip them entirely, depending on the circumstances of the problem. This ability of the computer to choose which instruction to do next distinguishes it from a simple calculator, which has to be guided from step to step by its human user.

Normally the computer obeys a sequence of orders which it takes from consecutive cells in the store. It is built so that when it has completed the order it took from cell n, it *automatically* goes on to obey the order from cell $(n + 1)$. The 'current address' is kept track of in the *program counter* register, which is increased by 1 for every instruction. There are, however, certain orders which make the machine break this regular sequence. One of them is the unconditional jump instruction. Its mnemonic is JMP, and its operand — which is normally written in the direct mode — indicates the address of the next instruction to be obeyed. When the jump instruction is executed, the normal sequencing mechanism is suspended, and the new address is loaded into the program counter, replacing the previous contents. Consider this program

```
0   LDA   B   #3
1   ADD   B   #7
2   JMP   1              ↑ NOTE: NO ACCUMULATOR (A OR B)
                         ↑ NEEDED
```

If this program is started at register 0, it begins by loading 3 into accumulator *B*, and adding 7 (giving 10). Then it obeys the jump instruction, which sends it back to register 1. The machine again adds 7, jumps again, and so on, indefinitely until someone intervenes from outside. The program generates a display like

```
0   LDA B #3    A = 0    B = 3
1   ADD B #7    A = 0    B = 10
2   JMP  1      A = 0    B = 10
1   ADD B #7    A = 0    B = 17
2   JMP  1      A = 0    B = 17
1   ADD B #7    A = 0    B = 24
.   .
.   .
.   .
```

Jump instructions can transfer control forwards as well as back.

8.1 CONDITIONAL JUMPS

A jump which always transfers control to a given register is a somewhat rigid device. If the new address is before the present one (as 5 is 'before' 10) the jump will lead to a loop which runs on for ever (or until the system is stopped externally). If the new address comes beyond the present one, some of the instructions are skipped, never to be obeyed.

A more flexible method of control is provided by the conditional jump instructions, which only transfer control if some explicit condition is true.

The SNARK has four conditional jumps, all of which apply to the contents of either accumulator.

BZE : Jump if contents of selected accumulator equal zero
BNZ : Jump if contents of selected accumulator not equal to zero
BMI : Jump if contents of selected accumulator less than zero
BPL : Jump if contents of selected accumulator greater than or equal to zero

Consider the following program

```
 0   INA   A          ↑ INPUT A NUMBER
 1   STA A 100        ↑ STORE IT IN CELL 100
 2   INA   A          ↑ READ
 3   STA A 101        ↑ STORE IT IN CELL 101
 4   SUB A 100        ↑ CALCULATE (SECOND-FIRST)
 5   BMI A 9          ↑ JUMP IF RESULT < 0
 6   LDA A 100        ↑ GET FIRST
 7   OUT   A          ↑ DISPLAY IT
 8   END              ↑ STOP
 9   LDA A 101        ↑ GET SECOND
10   OUT   A          ↑ DISPLAY IT
11   END              ↑ STOP
```

The program starts by reading two numbers from the keyboard and storing them in cells 100 and 101. It then compares them by subtracting one from the other. If the first is larger than the second — that is, the result of the subtraction in cell 4 is negative — the program jumps to cell 9, skipping the instructions in cells 6, 7 and 8. Otherwise the program does not jump but continues in sequence. In either case, the result is that the program chooses the *smaller* of the two numbers and displays its value.

Example 8.1
Write a program which reads a number x from the keyboard and displays its absolute value: x if x is positive, but $(-x)$ if x is negative.

```
0   INA    A          ↑ READ NUMBER TO ACCUMULATOR
1   BPL  A 5          ↑ JUMP IF NUMBER POSITIVE
2   STA  A 100        ↑ OTHERWISE NEGATE IT
3   LDA  A #0
4   SUB  A 100
5   OUT  A            ↑ OUTPUT RESULT
6   END              ↑ STOP
```

(It is worth noting that there is a single instruction, NEG, which negates the contents of the selected accumulator. A shorter solution is therefore

```
0   INA  A
1   BPL  A 3
2   NEG  A
3   OUT  A
4   END                          )
```

8.2 FLOW CHARTS

Programs with jumps are easier to design and understand if they are represented by flow charts. A flow chart is a network of special shapes — boxes, diamonds and clouds — connected by arrowed lines. Each shape indicates some action which the machine must take, and the lines show the sequence in which the actions are to occur. In particular, when a line connects shape *a* to shape *b*, thus

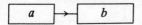

the meaning is that when the machine has completed the action in shape *a*, it must begin that in shape *b*.

The two *basic* shapes are the box and the diamond. The box is used to record some simple and invariable action which can be directly translated into a SNARK

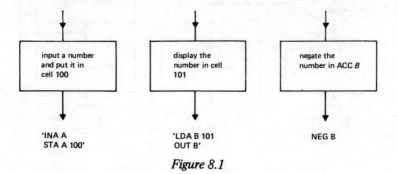

Figure 8.1

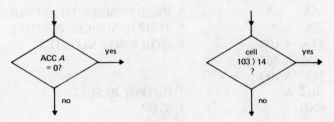

Figure 8.2

instruction, or a small sequence of instructions which do not include a jump of any kind. Examples of such boxes are shown in figure 8.1.

The diamond contains a question, of the sort which must have one of the two replies *yes* and *no*. It has one entry line and two exit lines, one for each of the possible answers. It is often convenient to place the entry line at the top, the 'no' exit line at the bottom, and the 'yes' line at one of the sides. Some examples appear in figure 8.2

Complete flow charts are constructed from these basic boxes and small circles to show the starting and finishing points. The flow charts for the programs on pp. 70 and 71 are shown in figures 8.3a and b.

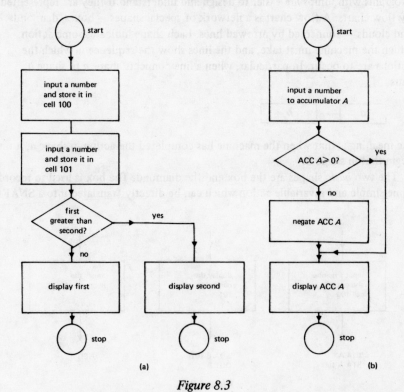

Figure 8.3

The *cloud* is not a basic shape. It is used to contain actions which are not yet fully defined, or which we don't — yet — know how to carry out. The implication is that every cloud is eventually expanded into a network of the basic shapes (and possibly simpler clouds).

8.3 CONTROLLED LOOPS

All practical computer programs include one or more 'controlled' loops, in which a group of instructions is repeated many times over (but *not* indefinitely). These loops can be divided into two categories: the first where the number of repetitions is known in advance, and the second where the termination of the loop depends on some condition calculated in the loop itself.

When the number is known in advance, the standard technique is to use an accumulator for a 'counter', which shows how many times the loop is still to be obeyed. Every time the loop is executed the count is reduced by one. Initially, the accumulator is loaded with the required number of repetitions. When the counter reaches zero, the loop must have been executed the right number of times, so the repetitions can stop. Figure 8.4 shows the corresponding flow chart.

Example 8.2
Calculate and display the 13-times table, up to 12 x 13.

Since the SNARK has no direct multiplication instruction, we solve this problem by repeated addition. We use accumulator *B* to hold the sequence 0–13–26–39 . . . and accumulator *A* to count down from 12 to 0. The action, each time round the loop, will consist of adding 13 to ACC *A*, displaying the result, and taking 1 from *B*. The flow chart appears in figure 8.5.

The corresponding program is written in three stages. First the instructions are written down, with all addresses left blank. Next, the address of each order is added at the left. Finally, the operands of the jumps can be filled in. In its various stages, the program might look something like this

LDA	B	#0		0	LDA	B	#0		0	LDA	B	#0
LDA	A	#12		1	LDA	A	#12		1	LDA	A	#12
ADD	B	#13		2	ADD	B	#13		2	ADD	B	#13
OUT	B			3	OUT	B			3	OUT	B	
SUB	A	#1		4	SUB	A	#1		4	SUB	A	#1
BNZ				5	BNZ				5	BNZ	2	
END				6	END				6	END		
	(1)					(2)					(3)	

(In practice there is no need to copy out the program three times.)

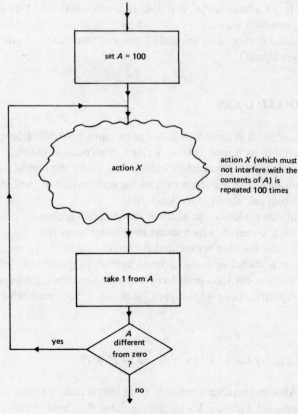

Figure 8.4

In the second category of loop, the test at the end is made on the result calculated by the action itself. A good example is given by Euclid's algorithm for finding the highest common factor (HCF) of two numbers. The algorithm consists of the following steps.

(1)   If the two numbers are equal, stop. Their common value is the HCF.
(2)   Otherwise subtract the smaller from the larger, and return to step 1.

. Consider the following example.

The starting values are   8   20
They are not equal, so take the smaller (8)
    from the larger (20), giving   8   12
They are not equal, so take the smaller (8)
    from the larger, (12), giving   8   4
They are not equal, so take the smaller (4)
    from the larger, (8), giving   4   4
They *are* equal, so the HCF of 8 and 20 is 4

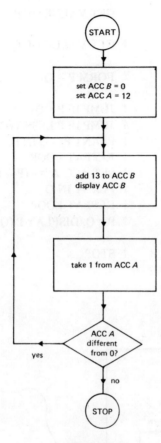

Figure 8.5

This algorithm can be translated into a flow chart, which is shown in figure 8.6. Initially we suppose that the two numbers are stored in cells p and q. We shall leave the actual addresses of p and q to be decided later, when we know how many cells are occupied by the program itself.

To make the algorithm into a computer program we add an input section, where the values of p and q are read from the keyboard and stored, and an output section, where the result is displayed. The complete flow chart is drawn in figure 8.7.

The final program is shown below. p and q have been assigned to cells 50 and 51. The values are compared by the subtraction in cell 5, and the rest of the code uses the fact that after the subtraction accumulator A contains $(p - q)$.

```
 0   INA   A            ↑ GET VALUE OF P
 1   STA   A   50
 2   INA   A            ↑ GET VALUE OF Q
 3   STA   A   51
 4   LDA   A   50       ↑ FORM P – Q
 5   SUB   A   51
 6   BZE   A   13       ↑ JUMP IF P = Q
 7   BMI   A   10       ↑ JUMP IF P LESS THAN Q
 8   STA   A   50       ↑ PLANT P – Q IN P
 9   JMP   4            ↑ REPEAT LOOP
10   NEG   A            ↑ SET ACC A = –(P – Q) = Q – P
11   STA   A   51       ↑ PLANT IN Q
12   JMP   4            ↑ REPEAT LOOP
13   LDA   A   50       ↑ P = Q. DISPLAY P (Q WOULD DO)
14   OUT   A
15   END                ↑ STOP
```

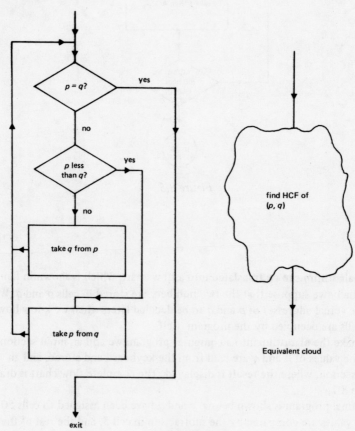

Figure 8.6

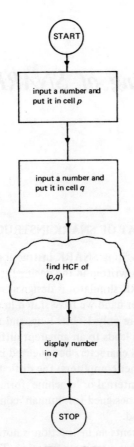

Figure 8.7

9 Array Handling of SNARK

9.1 THE INTERNAL FORMAT OF SNARK INSTRUCTIONS

The most convenient way of writing SNARK instructions is to use mnemonics such as ADD or STA, numbers written in the decimal scale, and other symbols such as A, B and #. The SNARK simulator is designed so that it accepts instructions in this form. On the other hand we have stated in several places that the cells in the SNARK memory are only 16 bits long, and that each instruction occupies exactly one cell. This leads to an apparent difficulty: how can an instruction written with 7 or 8 characters be squeezed into a 16-bit word?

In the SNARK (as in all other computers) the difficulty is overcome by storing the instructions in an internal or 'machine' format. The internal layout is extremely compact and is not designed for 'human' consumption; nevertheless its details should be understood.

A 16-bit word which represents an instruction is notionally divided into several 'fields', each of which has a separate function. The layout of SNARK instructions is shown below.

←		16 bits	→
FUNCTION	ACC	Mode	Address
4 bits	1 bit	2 bits	9 bits

Each field contains a coded representation of part of an instruction. The *function* field holds the code for a mnemonic, thus

Mnemonic	LDA	STA	ADD	SUB	AND	ORA	JMP	BZE
Code	0000	0001	0010	0011	0100	0101	0110	0111

Mnemonic	BNZ	BMI	BPL	LRS	NEG	INA	OUT	END
Code	1000	1001	1010	1011	1100	1101	1110	1111

The *ACC* field contains 0 if the instruction refers to accumulator *A*, and 1 if it refers to accumulator *B*.

The *mode* field holds a 2-bit pattern as follows

Immediate mode   : 00
Direct mode   : 01
Index mode (by *A*) : 10
Index mode (by *B*) : 11

(The two 'index' modes are explained later on in this chapter.)

The *address* field holds the binary equivalent of the written decimal address part. This is an integer in the range 0 to 511.

To illustrate this layout, consider the instruction

ADD   B   99

The function is ADD, which is represented by 0010

The accumulator is *B*, which is coded as   1
The mode is direct, and is recorded as   01
The address is 99, which in 9-bit binary   001100011

The complete internal representation of this instruction is therefore

0010   1   01   001100011
Function   ACC   mode   address

In a 16-bit word this appears as '0010101001100011'.

Example 9.1
What written instruction is represented by the following binary form?

1000001000001111

When this word is spit into its fields, it gives

Function = 1000   or BNZ
ACC   = 0   or *A*
Mode   = 01   or 'direct'
Address   = 000001111 or '15'

The entire instruction therefore represents 'BNZ A 15'.

A vital point to note is that both instructions and numbers are stored as 16-bit words, and there is no internal distinction between them. A word is taken as an instruction whenever it is pointed to by the program counter. This allows us to solve problems like the following.

Example 9.2

What will the following program do?

```
0    LDA    A    #7
1    +12291
2    OUT A
3    END
```

The key to the problem is that the word written as '+12291' is used as an instruction; the machine reaches it after obeying the 'LDA A #7' in cell 0. Some tedious arithmetic shows that the binary equivalent of +12291 is

0011000000000011

and this, in turn, can be converted to 'SUB A #3' The program is therefore precisely equivalent to

```
LDA     A    #7
SUB     A    #3
OUT     A
END
```

and its result is 4.

To end this section we note that where a field is not used, its contents are ignored. This would apply, for example, to the address and modifier fields of an OUT instruction.

In normal conditions the translation between the written and machine forms of instructions is done automatically by a program in the computer itself.

9.2 INDEX MODIFICATION

An important concept in programming is the table of values. There are many important problems which cannot be solved by manipulating individual quantities (as we have done hitherto) but need 'families' or 'arrays' of values in finding the answer. Some obvious examples are

The calculation of a total invoice or bill for a selection of items, where the price of each item is shown on a price list.
Solving simultaneous equations.
Searching related travel timetables to determine 'through' connections.
Setting up a page of type for printing.

At the machine code level, the table handling facility is provided by a special addressing mechanism called *index modification*.

In general, the *mode* of an instruction defines the way in which the written address part is used to provide the operand. Thus, as we already know, the address part in the immediate mode *is* the operand. In the direct mode, the address part gives the cell which *contains* the operand.

The SNARK has two further modes called the *index* modes. Each of them involves the contents of one of the accumulators in finding the operand. The two modes are identical except that one signifies modification by ACC A, and the other by ACC B.

When an index modified instruction is executed, the SNARK adds up the written address part and the contents of the modifying accumulator, and uses the result as the *address* of the operand.

To show index modification, an A or B is placed after the address part, as in these examples

> LDA   A   37B   or   STA   B   0A

To illustrate the action of the index mode, consider the sequence

> LDA   A   #17
> LDA   B   5A

The first instruction loads ACC A with the number 17. The second instruction then refers to the contents of cell 22 (because it is index modified by A) and the contents of A (17) are *added* to the written address part (5) immediately before the instruction is executed.

It is worth noting that the process of modification does *not* alter the contents of the modifying accumulator. In most cases, (but not necessarily) the modifying accumulator is not the same as the one used for the result of the operation. Thus an instruction which adds to ACC A might be index modified by ACC B, or vice versa.

9.3 TABLE LOOK-UP

An important use of index modification lies in extracting values from tables. This is shown in the example below.

Example 9.3
Write a program which inputs a number n (in the range 0 to 7) from the keyboard and displays factorial n. [Factorial n, often written $n!$, is defined as $n(n-1)(n-2) \ldots \times 3 \times 2 \times 1$. For example $6! = 6 \times 5 \times 4 \times 3 \times 2 \times 1 = 720$. 0! is defined as 1.]

The standard way to calculate $n!$ is by repeated multiplication; but in practice it is faster to look up the answers in a table. We do so with the help of index modification

```
0    INA    A              ↑ INPUT N
1    LDA    B    4A        ↑ FETCH N! FROM TABLE
2    OUT    B              ↑ DISPLAY N!
3    END
4    +1                    ↑ TABLE OF FACTORIALS : 0!
5    +1                    ↑ 1!
6    +2                    ↑ 2!
7    +6                    ↑ 3!
8    +24
9    +120
10   +720
11   +5040                 ↑ 7!
```

It is worth tracing through this program with an example. Suppose the input number is 5.

INA   A   will load 5 into ACC A

LDA   B   4A   is index modified, so the address is calculated by adding 4 (the written address part) and 5 (the contents of A). The result is 9, so the number loaded to ACC B is the contents of cell 9, or 120. This is the value of 5!

OUT   B   the value of B, 120, is displayed

Needless to say, this happy result did not come about by accident. It happened because the program contains a table in which the nth entry is $n!$, and because the written address in the index modified instruction is that of the beginning of the table.

9.4 ACCESS TO ENTIRE TABLES

When an index modified instruction is included in a loop, it can be used to refer to all the elements in a table, one after the other. Here, for example, is a program which *clears* (that is, sets to zero) the fifty cells with addresses 20 to 69

```
0    LDA    A    #0
1    LDA    B    #50
2    STA    A    19B
3    SUB    B    #1
4    BNZ    B    2
5    END
```

In this example, ACC B is used to count down from 50 to 0, in precisely the way discussed in chapter 8. ACC A contains zero all the time. The actual storage is done by the instruction in cell 2

STA   A   19B

which is index modified. The first time through the loop ACC B = 50, so the actual address used is $(50 + 19)$ or 69. The second time, B = 49, so the cell cleared is $(49 + 19)$ or 68. The program continues this way, working backwards from cell 69, until the last time round the loop ACC B = 1, and the cell cleared is $(1 + 19)$ or 20.

This example can be expanded into a general rule: To work through an array of p elements, starting at cell q

(1)   organise a count to start at p, and work towards zero;
(2)   to refer to the individual elements, use index modification and a written address part of $(q - 1)$.

Example 9.4
Write a program to add up and display the numbers in cells 50 to 60 (inclusive).

Here p = 11, and q = 50. We can put

```
0   LDA   A   #0        ↑ CLEAR A
1   LDA   B   #11       ↑ ORGANISE 11 CYCLES
2   ADD   A   49B       ↑ ADD A NUMBER FROM THE LIST
3   SUB   B   #1        ↑ JUMP BACK IF
4   BNZ   2             ↑ LOOPING NOT ENDED
5   OUT   A             ↑ DISPLAY RESULT
6   END                 ↑ STOP
```

9.5 TABLE SEARCHING

A common operation is to search a table of numbers to test whether any of them complies to some specified condition. This is normally done by testing each number in turn, and jumping out of the loop as soon as a number is found which satisfied the condition. Here, for example, is a fragment of program which examines the numbers in locations 80 to 99, and tests whether any of them has the value '3'. If so, the program displays '3', otherwise it displays '0'.

```
0    LDA   B   #20       ↑ SET UP COUNT FOR 20 CYCLES
1    LDA   A   79B       ↑ GET A NUMBER FROM TABLE
2    SUB   A   #3        ↑ COMPARE WITH 3
3    BZE   A   8         ↑ JUMP IF SAME
4    SUB   B   #1        ↑ ELSE COUNT AND
5    BNZ   B   1         ↑ JUMP BACK
6    OUT   B             ↑ '3' NOT FOUND. DISPLAY 0
7    END                 .
8    LDA   A   #3        ↑ 3 FOUND.
9    OUT   A             ↑ DISPLAY 3
10   END
```

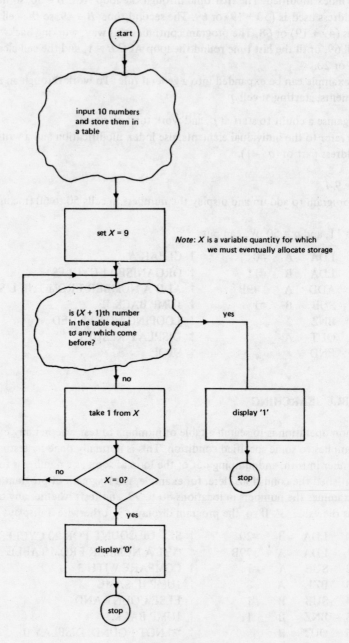

Figure 9.1

Example 9.5

Write a program which inputs ten numbers from the keyboard, and displays a '1' if any two of them are the *same*; if the numbers are all different, the program is to display '0'.

This program is complex enough to warrant a careful design procedure using flow charts.

Our general strategy will be as follows.

First, input all the ten numbers and place them in a table.

Next, choose one number in the table and compare it with all the rest. If an exact match is found, the program can display a '1' and stop; otherwise the chosen number can be discarded (for it must be different from all the others) and the process repeated with another number chosen from the table. This is continued until all the numbers have been compared with one another and found *different*: then the machine can display a 0.

The program can be most easily organised if the table is scanned from high addresses to low addresses. On the first pass, we shall compare the *tenth* number with the preceding nine; on the second, the *ninth* with the preceding eight, and so on. Nine passes are needed in all, and on the last pass the second number is compared with the first. A series of flow charts for the program is in figures 9.1, 9.2 and 9.30.

Next, we allocate space for the various quantities. First, we consider the inner loop. One accumulator is needed for Y, and the other to compare numbers. We shall use A and B. The other quantities are the table numbers, the counter X, and the current selected number Z. We cannot use accumulators for these numbers, so we (arbitrarily) assign storage as follows

Table of numbers	:	50–59
X		60
Z		61

The complete program can now be written

0	LDA	A	#10	↑ READ IN NUMBERS
1	INA	B		
2	STA	B	49A	
3	SUB	A	#1	
4	BNZ	A	1	
5	LDA	A	#9	↑ SET X = 9
6	STA	A	60	
7	LDA	A	60	↑ SET Y = X
8	LDA	B	50A	↑ GET VALUE OF Z
9	STA	B	61	↑ AND STORE IT
10	LDA	B	49A	↑ GET A NUMBER

11	SUB	B	61	↑ COMPARE WITH Z
12	BZE	B	20	↑ JUMP IF EQUAL
13	SUB	A	#1	↑ ELSE GO ROUND INNER LOOP
14	BNZ	A	10	
15	LDA	A	60	↑ DECREMENT X
16	SUB	A	#1	
17	BNZ	A	6	↑ GO ROUND OUTER LOOP
18	OUT	A		↑ DISPLAY 0
19	END			
20	LDA	A	#1	↑ DISPLAY 1
21	OUT	A		
22	END			↑ STOP

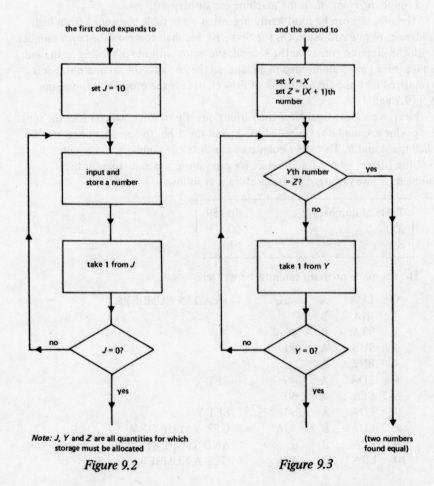

the first cloud expands to

set J = 10

input and
store a number

take 1 from J

J = 0?

no

yes

and the second to

set Y = X
set Z = (X + 1)th
number

Yth number
= Z?

yes

no

take 1 from Y

Y = 0?

no

yes

Note: J, Y and Z are all quantities for which
storage must be allocated

(two numbers
found equal)

Figure 9.2   *Figure 9.3*

10 Computers – the Grand Design

A computer system is a blend of hardware and software. In this book these two streams have so far been kept separate, but now they can be combined and used to explain how a computer is actually built. There are several methods of constructing computers but only one of the simplest will be explained.

This chapter forms a focal point of the book, and it may be as well to list the topics you should understand before reading it. You may find it useful to revise chapters 2 to 6 for the hardware, and chapters 7 to 9 for the software. The necessary concepts are

Hardware	Software
Binary arithmetic	Machine instructions and their internal
Parallel representation	representation
Gates and multiplexers	Sequences
Arithmetic units	Conditional commands
Registers and stores	Loops
Bus-oriented systems	Index modification
Register transfer notation	

10.1 SEQUENCES OF OPERATIONS

Many important operations in a computer – and in particular, the execution of a machine instruction – cannot be done in a single register transfer, but need sequences of transfers which takes several clock pulses to be completed. We begin by considering how these sequences can be organised.

Suppose a machine has a register called A, and that we need a mechanism for multiplying this number by 10 (decimal ten).

Let the machine have another register, B. One way of organising the multiplication is to move the contents of A to B, and then to add B back to A

nine times. In RT (register transfer) notation we put

$$
\left.
\begin{array}{l}
A \Rightarrow B \\
A + B \Rightarrow A \\
A + B \Rightarrow A \\
\quad . \\
\quad . \\
\quad . \\
A + B \Rightarrow A
\end{array}
\right\} \quad \text{nine times}
$$

This sequence would take 10 clock pulses in all.

A faster method uses doubling as well as addition

$A \Rightarrow B$	Copy A to B	
$A * 2 \Rightarrow A$	Double A	
$A * 2 \Rightarrow A$	Double it again	(making 4 times original)
$A + B \Rightarrow A$	Add B to A	(making 5 times original)
$A * 2 \Rightarrow A$	Double A	(making 10 times original)

Figure 10.1 shows a bus-organised arithmetic unit which provides these transfers (doubling A is done by adding it to itself). In terms of control gates the five transfers could be written

Transfer	F	S_1	S_2	C_1	C_2
$A \Rightarrow B$	–	0	1		⊓
$A * 2 \Rightarrow A$	0	1	0	⊓	
$A * 2 \Rightarrow A$	0	1	0	⊓	
$A + B \Rightarrow A$	1	1	0	⊓	
$A * 2 \Rightarrow A$	0	1	0	⊓	

10.1.1 Microcoding

As explained in chapter 5, every synchronous computer has a clock which delivers a sequence of clock pulses. When the machine is set to carry out a predetermined sequence of transfers (such as the ones needed to multiply a number by 10) matters must be organised so that each successive pulse makes the machine do the next transfer in the list. Two things must be ensured for each transfer. First, the appropriate control signals and clock pulses must be applied to the arithmetic unit. Second, the machine must in some way keep track of its place in the sequence so that when the current transfer is completed the next one is selected correctly.

In a microcoded machine, all the details of every transfer are coded as groups of binary digits and stored as a control word or *microinstruction* in a read-only memory. This memory is used only for storing microinstructions, and is often

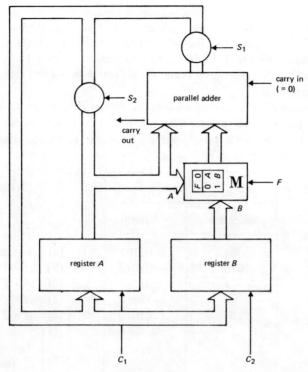

Figure 10.1

called a 'control memory'. In each cycle the machine fetches a microinstruction from the control memory and executes the transfer which it describes.

In any machine, all the microinstructions have the same layout. The microinstruction is arranged in two parts: the 'transfer' field which is used to define the current register transfer, and the 'sequence' field, which ensures the correct succession of microinstructions. In the simplest case, the sequence field 'points to', or contains the address of, the next microinstruction in the read-only memory.

Suppose that the multiplication by 10 described above is to be controlled by microcode with the microinstruction stored in an eight-word ROM. Then the microinstruction format would be

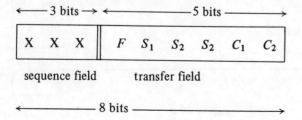

The sequence field is 3 bits long because this is enough to indicate any word in the eight-word ROM. Likewise, the transfer field has 5 digits because five signals (F, S_1, S_2, C_1 and C_2) are sufficient to describe any transfer in the arithmetic unit shown in figure 10.1. The presence of a clock pulse in C_1 or C_2 can be coded as a '1'; and a 'don't care' signal (as in F in the first transfer) can be represented by 0.

Let us suppose that the control words for the five transfers are to be stored in words 0 to 4 (as we shall see later they need not be in consecutive words; this arrangement simply makes the microprogram easier to read). The contents of these words would be

| Address | Contents | | (Transfer) |
	Successor	Transfer	
000	001	00101	(a) $A \Rightarrow B$; goto b
001	010	01010	(b) $A * 2 \Rightarrow A$; goto c
010	011	01010	(c) $A * 2 \Rightarrow A$; goto d
011	100	11010	(c) $A + B \Rightarrow A$; goto d
100	101	01010	(e) $A * 2 \Rightarrow A$; goto f
101	.	.	(f)
110	.	.	further transfers
111	.	.	(underlined)

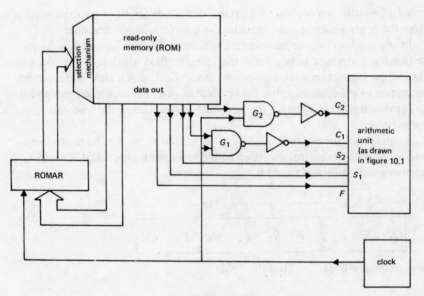

Figure 10.2

Locations 5, 6 and 7 of the ROM may hold detials of other transfers (possibly those which use the result of the multiplication) but we have no need to discuss them here. We originally specified an eight-word ROM only because these components always have sizes which are exact powers of 2; 'five-word ROMs' don't exist.

Figure 10.2 shows a possible arrangement. The address used in the ROM is controlled by a register, labelled ROMAR, similar in function to the MAR described in chapter 6. One important difference is that the register is only 3 bits wide, and is supplied with new contents directly from the ROM itself.

The action of the machine is best described by considering its timing, and the contents of the ROM given in the table above. Suppose that a certain clock pulse has just placed 000 into the ROMAR. After some propagation time the pattern in location 0 (which is 001 00101) appears at the output of the ROM. The lines which carry bits 4, 3 and 2 are connected directly to the arithmetic unit as F, S_1 and S_2. They set up the condition for the transfer $A \Rightarrow B$. Bits 1 and 0 are sent to gates G_1 and G_2, and bit-lines 7 to 5 are applied to the inputs of the ROMAR.

Eventually, after enough time has passed for all the signals to be propagated through the network, the next clock pulse occurs. It has two effects: first it is *gated* to C_2, because bit 0 is 1, but not to C_1, because bit 1 is 0. This makes the arithmetic unit *execute* the transfer which is already set up, by clocking the value of A into register B. At the same time, the clock pulse moves the information on lines 7 to 5 into ROMAR, replacing the previous contents. The new value in ROMAR is 001. The ROMAR, selection mechanism and ROM have a finite propagation time, which means that the transfer can be completed before the controlling signals actually change.

During the next cycle, the ROM produces the word in location 001. This microinstruction sets up the transfer '$A * 2 \Rightarrow A$', and defines 010 as the address of the next microinstruction. The clock pulse which follows again effects this transfer and changes the ROMAR to its next value of 010.

The system continues in this way, and over the five cycles the multiplication is completed. Finally, the system fetches the microinstruction in word 5, which we have not defined here, because it is presumably the first of the next sequence of transfers.

At this point you may feel that the description of microcoding is suspiciously like that of machine code. There are indeed some obvious likenesses: each cycle of the machine is defined by a word which is read from a store, and which contains the description of an operation and an address. As we continue to study microcode, further similarities will emerge. You should therefore be vigilant agianst confusing the two concepts, because they are fundamentally different. In particular, a machine instruction is an abstract concept used by a programmer to carry out a calculation, whereas a microinstruction is used by an engineer to control a register transfer. Instructions and microinstructions do *not* have the same format, and the ROM and its address register are *not* the same as the main computer memory. The operations which can be specified by microinstructions are limited to those which can be executed in a single machine cycle, while functions indicated by machine instructions all take several cycles.

A further point of confusion is that you have seen the contents of ROMAR start at 0 and reach 5 in steps of 1, somewhat like a program counter. In our microcoded system each microcoded instruction defines its successor quite explicitly and there is *no* automatic mechanism for incrementing ROMAR by 1 as in machine code. The microinstructions in our sequence could equally well have been jumbled up in any order and scattered throughout the ROM, without making any difference to the working of the system.

To summarise, microinstructions are not a different *kind* of machine instruction, but provide a mechanism by which machine instructions can be implemented.

Example 10.1

Write down the ROM contents for the 'times 10' sequence so that the microcode starts at word 7 and runs backwards. The last microinstruction is to be in word 3, and is to jump to word 2 on completion.

We note that no change need be made to the mechanism. The ROM contents would be

Address	Contents		(Transfer)	
	Sequence	Transfer		
000	.	.		
001	.	.		
010	.	.	(f)	
011	010	01010	(e)	$A * 2 \Rightarrow A$; goto f
100	011	11010	(d)	$A + B \Rightarrow A$; goto e
101	100	01010	(c)	$A * 2 \Rightarrow A$; goto d
110	101	01010	(b)	$A * 2 \Rightarrow A$; goto c
111	110	00101	(a)	$A \Rightarrow B$; goto b

10.2 VARIABLE SEQUENCES

In most practical applications of microcoding the sequence of register transfers is not fixed but depends in some way on the quantities being used. A simple example is afforded by a shifting mechanism. Consider a machine with two registers, X and Y, both 16 bits long. It is required to shift the contents of X to the right by y places, where y is the initial contents of Y. For example, suppose that the initial values in X and Y are '1101001001011111' and '0000000000000101' respectively. The final contents of X must then be '0000011010010010' (which is the original contents shifted five places right) and the eventual result in Y is immaterial.

Figure 10.3 shows part of an arithmetic unit which can do the necessary transfers. It has one new and vital aspect: it not only has control lines S_1, S_2, C_1 and C_2 going in, but an information line coming out. The signal on this line is the NOR function of all the flip–flops in Y, and takes the value *true* if only the contents of Y are *zero*.

The $\div 2$ unit in figure 10.3 can only shift one place at a time, so that in general, a shift of y places needs several transfers. This can be done by a microprogram, which includes a shift operation on X, a subtraction of 1 from Y, and a conditional microjump. Only two microinstructions are needed

(a) $Y - 1 \Rightarrow Y$; goto b
(b) $X \div 2 \Rightarrow X$; if $Y \# 0$ then goto a else goto c
(c)   . . .

Figure 10.4 shows a mechanism which can support this microprogram. We assume – more realistically than in the previous example – that the microinstructions are stored in a 64-word ROM along with various other sequences of microcode, so that 6 bits are needed to specify the address of a successor.

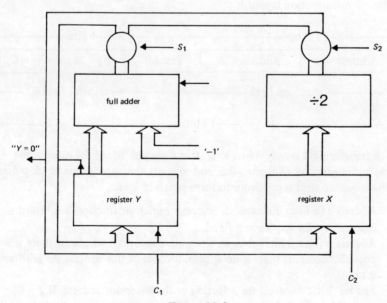

Figure 10.3

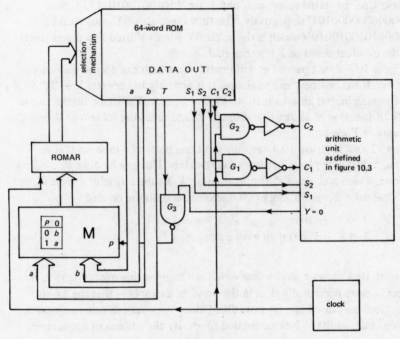

Figure 10.4

The microinstruction layout is

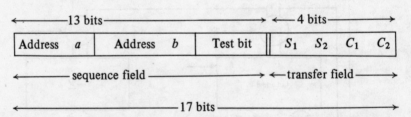

The transfer field is only 4 bits long; this is enough to set the gates in the simple arithmetic unit of figure 10.3, and to apply the appropriate clock pulses. The sequence field is divided into three separate areas.

(1)   Address a (6 bits) indicates the successor microinstruction in all normal cases, when the sequence is fixed.

(2)   Address b (also 6 bits) gives an alternative successor whenever there is a possible choice. If there is no choice, the bits of this address are arbitrarily set to 0.

(3)   The test bit T controls the selection of the successor address. If $T = 0$, then address a is taken as successor. If $T = 1$, the successor depends on the

line '$Y = 0$' which comes from the arithmetic unit. If the line is *true*, then *address b* is the successor; otherwise address *a*. This is summarised below.

Test bit T	$Y = 0$	Successor
0	false	address *a*
0	true	address *a*
1	false	address *a*
1	true	address *b*

The design shows how the input to ROMAR is selected by a multiplexer controlled by T and $Y = 0$.

We can now write down the microinstructions for the shift. We assume — quite arbitrarily — that the microinstructions will occupy words 3 and 4 of the ROM, and when the shift is completed control is to pass to the microinstruction in word 63.

ROM Address	Contents							(Transfer)
	Address *a*	Address *b*	T	S_1	S_2	C_1	C_2	$Y - 1 \Rightarrow Y$; goto 4
								$X \div 2 \Rightarrow X$; if $Y = 0$
000011	000100	000000	0	1	0	1	0	then goto
000100	000011	111111	1	0	1	0	1	else goto 3

This microprogram can be traced (just like a program). The trace will show that as long as $Y \# 0$, the microinstruction in word 4 selects 3 as its successor; but when $Y = 0$, control passes to word 63.

You may be puzzled by the order of the microinstructions. Why is it

$$Y - 1 \Rightarrow Y$$
$$X \div 2 \Rightarrow X$$

and not the more natural-seeming

$$X \div 2 \Rightarrow X$$
$$Y - 1 \Rightarrow Y?$$

The reason is that each microinstruction contains a transfer *and* possibly a conditional jump. The condition for the jump must be present when the microinstruction is started. It would not be possible to take 1 from Y and test the result for 0, all in the same microinstruction.

Example 10.2
Figure 10.5 shows an arithmetic unit with three registers X, Y and Z, and

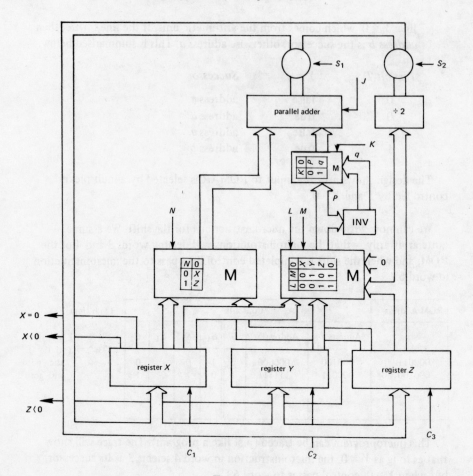

Figure 10.5

various combinatorial elements. There are ten control lines, and three information lines coming out: '$X = 0$', '$X < 0$', and '$Z < 0$'. The last two merely indicate the states of the left-most flip–flops in their respective registers.

Assuming a 64-word ROM, show how the control structure in figure 10.4 can be modified to drive this arithmetic unit, and design a suitable microcode layout.

The transfer field of the microinstruction can be widened to 10 bits, and the various control lines can be allocated in any order. Likewise the general structure of the sequence field with its two addresses can be kept. The only difficulty is that there are now not one but *three* different signals which may affect the sequencing.

This aspect may be easily handled by replacing the test bit with a 2-bit test

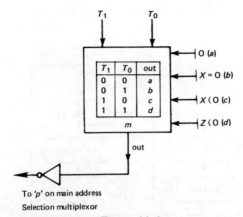

Figure 10.6

field. The bits, which are called T_1 and T_0, can be given the following significance

T_1	T_0	Meaning
0	0	Use address a as successor (always)
0	1	If $X = 0$ use address b; otherwise use address a
1	0	If $X < 0$ use address b; otherwise use address a
1	1	If $Z < 0$ use address b; otherwise use address a

This arrangement can be implemented in hardware by replacing the gate G_3 in figure 10.4 by a multiplexer (note: *not* a parallel multiplexer) as shown in figure 10.6.

The microcode layout can now be defined. It is 24 bits long.

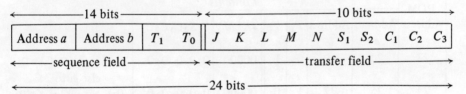

Example 10.3
Use the system described in example 10.2 to code a general-purpose shift operation. Initially, Z holds an arbitrary binary pattern, and X holds a number – say x – which may be positive, negative or zero.

The overall effect of the operation is to shift Z x places *left*, in other words, to multiply it by 2^x. It is possible, however, for x to be less than zero, in which case Z must be shifted $(-x)$ places *right*. The microcode you write must in word 23, and on completion it must transfer control to word 60.

We begin by devising a suitable algorithm. It is often useful to draw a microflow chart, as in figure 10.7. Each block corresponds to a single microinstruction, and

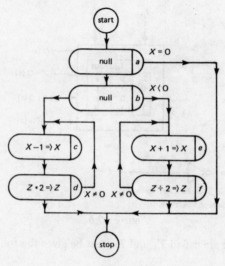

Figure 10.7

may contain a transfer *and* a test, but the test must be based on conditions which exist *before* the transfer takes place. Some blocks are concerned only with sequencing and do not specify any transfers at all.

All that remains is to translate this algorithm into microcode. To make the result more readable, we attach labels *a, b, c, ...*, to each of the blocks in the flow chart and use corresponding labels in the code. We also use decimal numbers for addresses, remembering that each number stands for an equivalent binary value 8 digits long.

ROM Address	Contents						
	Address a	Address b	T_1	T_0	$JKLMN$	$S_1 S_2 C_1 C_2 C_3$	
23	24	60	0	1	00000	0 0 0 0 0	(a) goto 60 if $X=0$; else goto 24
24	25	27	1	0	00000	0 0 0 0 0	(b) goto 27 if $X<0$; else goto 25
25	26	00	0	0	01110	1 0 1 0 0	(c) $X-1 \Rightarrow X$; goto 26
26	25	60	0	1	00101	1 0 0 0 1	(d) $Z*2 \Rightarrow Z$; if $X=0$ goto 60 else goto 25
27	28	00	0	0	10110	1 0 1 0 0	(e) $X+1 \Rightarrow X$; goto 28
28	27	60	0	1	00000	0 1 0 0 1	(f) $Z \div 2 \Rightarrow Z$; if $X=0$ goto 60 else goto 27

10.3 DESIGN OF THE SNARK

The final section of this chapter shows how a machine with the characteristics of the SNARK could be constructed from hardware components.

The basic design method is to begin at an abstract level, and then to refine and elaborate, stage by stage, until we reach a description which can be implemented directly in hardware components such as parallel adders and multiplexers. Read each section carefully, and make sure you understand it before moving on to the next stage.

10.3.1 The Abstract Machine and its Order Code

The starting point of our design process is the abstract SNARK computer, which was discussed in chapters 7, 8 and 9. Since this machine is our point of departure, it is as well to re-state its various properties here. From the *programmer's* point of view, SNARK has a 512-word 16-bit memory, two 16-bit accumulators, a 9-bit program counter and devices for reading and displaying numbers. A diagram of this abstract structure is shown in figure 10.8. A slight change has been made from the presentation in chapter 7, because now the output from the machine (that is, the numbers displayed by the OUT instruction) is handled by a special register. We assume that any number sent to this register is automatically displayed on a screen in its decimal form. Similarly, any number typed on the keyboard as input makes its way to the input register, from which it can be transferred to other parts of the machine. We shall not be too concerned with the details of the mechanisms which look after the display, the keyboard and the conversion between decimal and binary, because this would make the

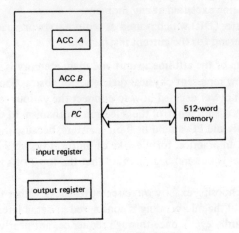

Programmer's view of the SNARK

Figure 10.8

chapter too long and overburdened with detail, but we note that the various operations of input and output take a considerable amount of time. In particular, no input operation is complete until the user of the program has actually typed a number, and this may take seconds, minutes or even hours.

The SNARK is driven by instructions expressed in a specific *order code*. (Remember that we have temporarily moved back to the programmer's level and are considering instructions, not microinstructions!) Each SNARK instruction has an internal 16-bit representation with four fields: function (4 bits), accumulator (1 bit), mode (2 bits) and address (9 bits). Although the SNARK simulator makes the conversion automatically, the internal representation is different from the written form. The rules of conversion were fully described in chapter 9.

10.3.2 Internal Registers

We can now begin the actual design process, which consists of 'mapping' the abstract parts and functions of the SNARK on to physical components. We start by defining the registers which the machine needs in its arithmetic unit.

It is clear that each of the abstract registers in SNARK needs a corresponding physical register. This leads us to five registers called A, B, PC, IN and OUT. We say that register A *models* accumulator A, and so on. The system also needs three registers which are 'secret' in the sense that they are hidden from the programmer and do not model any part of the abstract machine

(1)   the memory address register (MAR) which holds the address of the location currently being accessed in the memory;
(2)   the current instruction register (CIR) which holds the 16-bit SNARK instruction being executed at any moment;
(3)   the data register (DR) which is used as temporary workspace and normally holds the operand for the current instruction.

A partial diagram of the arithmetic unit and main memory is shown in figure 10.9. The boxes now represent physical registers, not abstractions as in 10.8. Note that we have not yet decided how to connect the various registers together, except that MAR is used to control the selection mechanism of the memory.

In principle MAR and PC should be 9-bit registers, because the store is only $512\,(2^9)$ bits long. In practice, for the sake of uniformity, we shall specify 16-bit registers throughout and bear in mind that the top 7 bits in PC and MAR remain unused.

The reason for choosing exactly *three* secret registers, rather than two or five, will not emerge until the microcoding is considered in detail later on. The actual design process is hardly ever a once-through sequence, but nearly always contains false starts, and loops where some particular part of the system is refined several times. We can say that three secret registers are necessary only because we have

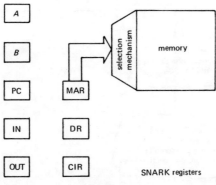

Figure 10.9

already tried using different configurations and found there are either not enough registers or too many.

10.3.3 Microcoding the SNARK

When the internal registers have been defined, the next stage is to express the functions of the SNARK in terms of register transfers. This process is strictly not programming, but it is somewhat similar, and we can borrow various programming techniques, such as the use of flow charts and clouds.

The execution of a *single* SNARK instruction is shown in the microflow chart in figure 10.10. Initially (at the top of the flow chart) the address of the next instruction to be obeyed is in PC.

The first cloudet has the job of fetching the next instruction from the store and putting it in CIR where it can be executed. The program counter is also advanced by 1 at this time (even though this operation is wasted if the instruction to be obeyed is a jump).

The cloudlet can be decomposed into *three* register transfers

(1) PC =⟩ MAR   Copy PC to MAR. This selects the right location to fetch the instruction
(2) MEM =⟩ CIR   Copy the contents of the selected memory cell to CIR
(3) PC + 1 =⟩ PC   Add 1 to PC

Figure 10.11 shows the corresponding microflow chart, where the boxes are labelled *a, b, c* for further reference.

The second cloudlet prepares the current instruction for execution by doing as much work as possible before the function code is taken into account.

The SNARK instructions can be divided into three types

(1) those which need an *operand* or quantity to be used in some operation:
     LDA, ADD, SUB, AND, ORA;

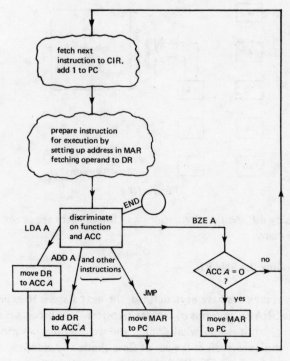

Figure 10.10

(2)   those which need an *address*: STA and the various jumps;

(3)   those which need neither: LRS, NEG, INA, OUT, END.

The aim of the cloudlet depends on the type of instruction. For type 1 the operand is placed into the data register. For type 2, the required address is left in the memory address register. For type 3 no action is necessary.

It turns out that if we tolerate an occasional redundant or unnecessary transfer, all three types of instruction can be prepared by a single sequence which takes into account the mode of the instruction being executed, but is independent of its function.

The necessary transfers are

For immediate mode

CIR *and* 777_8 => DR   (This selects the address field of the current instruction and moves it to the data register. The selection is made by *and*'ing the current instruction with a mask which is, in binary, 0000000111111111)

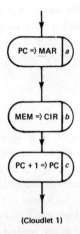

(Cloudlet 1)

Figure 10.11

For direct mode

    CIR *and* 777_8 =⟩ MAR   (Moves address part to MAR)
    MEM =⟩ DR   (Fetches operand)

For index modified mode (modification by ACC *A*)

    CIR *and* 777_8 =⟩ DR   (Move address part to DR)
    DR + A =⟩ MAR   (Add contents of *A* and put result in DR)
    MEM =⟩ DR   (Fetch operand)

For index modified mode (modification by ACC *B*)

    CIR *and* 777_8 =⟩ DR   (Move address part to DR)
    DR + B =⟩ MAR   (Add contents of *B* and put result in DR)
    MEM =⟩ DR   (Fetch operand)

(Note that all the MEM =⟩ DR transfers are actually wasted when the instruction being executed is a STA or a jump. This price is worth paying for the simplification achieved.)

We can now translate the cloudlet into a detailed microflow chart. The precise action of the cloudlet depends on the mode of the instruction, and we can use two control signals to 'steer' the control accordingly

M0 is taken from the right-hand bit of the mode field in CIR,
M1 is taken from the left-hand bit of the mode field.

Note that if the instruction is in immediate mode, M1 = M0 = 0; if in direct mode M1 = 0, M0 = 1, and so on.

One practical difficulty is that, as far as we know, any microinstruction can have at most *two* possible successors, whereas the cloudlet has to select one of *four* possible courses of action. One way of organising the flow of control is to have the system find its way through a 'tree' of microinstructions with null transfers until the appropriate sequence is reached. This is shown in figure 10.12.

The number of cycles needed for the cloudlet as a whole is

For immediate mode: 3
For direct mode   : 4
For an index mode   : 5

However, we can easily improve on these figures. Instead of wasting the initial microinstructions on null operations, we can use them to do transfers which may (or may not) be needed. This approach gives an advantage in some cases and costs nothing in the others, and leads to the arrangement shown in figure 10.13, where the boxes are again labelled for future use. This scheme needs an extra control signal 'M = 00', which is true only if the current instruction is in the immediate mode, but this signal is easily generated from M1 and M0.

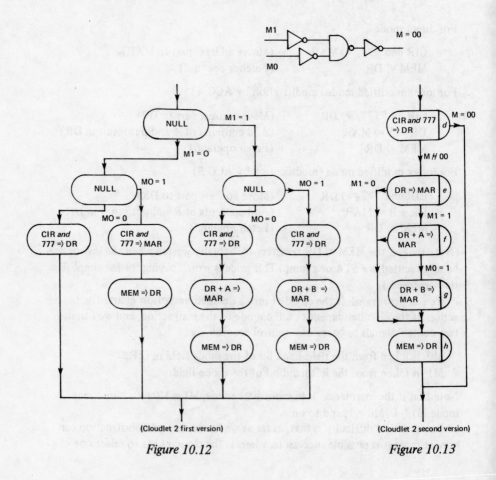

(Cloudlet 2 first version)   (Cloudlet 2 second version)

Figure 10.12   *Figure 10.13*

Example 10.4
Using figure 10.13, write down the transfers executed for an instruction in each
of the four modes, and identify any which may be redundant.

Immediate	CIR and 777 =⟩ DR	(Total = 1)

Direct	CIR and 777 =⟩ DR	
	DR =⟩ MAR	
	MEM =⟩ DR	(Total = 3)

Modified by A	CIR and 777 =⟩ DR	
	DR =⟩ MAR (Redundant)	
	DR + A =⟩ MAR	
	MEM =⟩ DR	[Total = 4
		(1 redundant)]

Modified by B	CIR and 777 =⟩ DR	
	DR =⟩ MAR ⎫ Redundant	
	DR + A =⟩ MAR ⎭	
	DR + B =⟩ MAR	
	MEM =⟩ DR	[Total = 5
		(2 redundant)]

The next box in the outline flow chart discriminates on the function and
selected accumulator, and chooses an appropriate sequence of transfers. For
example, if the instruction is 'ADD B', the machine must be directed to a transfer
which adds the operand to B.

There are 16 functions and a choice of 2 accumulators, giving 32 combinations
in all. It would be absurdly inefficient to have a string or tree of 32 'null'
operations to test for all the possibilities — we need a more efficient method
of discrimination.

In the earlier part of the chapter we have already met the idea that the
new contents of the ROMAR, which determines the next microinstruction,
should be selected by a parallel multiplexer. We now expand this notion, and
suppose that the ROMAR multiplexer has a third set of inputs, derived from the
function and accumulator fields of the current instruction register. When this set
is selected, the successor to the current microinstruction is neither address A nor
address B (for we assume that, as in earlier examples, there are two successor
addresses in the microcode), but depends only on the current contents of CIR.

It remains to settle some practical details. We decide to use 6-bit microcode
addresses because this gives 64 words of microcode, which is ample for the
SNARK. We construct the third set of inputs to the ROMAR multiplexer as
follows

Most significant bit : always 1
Next 4 bits   : the function code field of CIR
Least significant bit : the accumulator field of CIR

This generates a unique address for each combination of function and accumulator. For example

Instruction	Binary form	Corresponding address	Decimal value
LDA A	0000 0	100000	32
LDA B	0000 1	100001	33
BPL B	1010 1	110101	53
INA A	1101 0	111010	58

In practice, three-input multiplexers are not manufactured; the number of inputs is always an exact power of 2, and we must use a four input parallel multiplexer. However, this extra input can be used for an important function: that of starting (or re-starting) the whole system.

Every computer must have a 'start' or 'reset' button. When this button is pressed, the system must abandon anything it is currently doing and jump directly to a sequence of code (or microcode) which prepares to load and execute a new program.

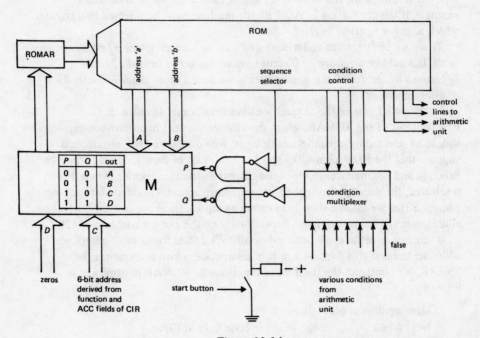

Figure 10.14

One possible sequencing arrangement is drawn in figure 10.14, where

(1)   The line from the *start* button takes the value 'false' (or 0) when the button is pressed. This forces the control lines *P* and *Q* to the main multiplexer to 1s, so that the address selected is *D*. This makes the system transfer control to the microinstruction in address 0, which we have arbitrarily selected as the beginning of the 'reset' sequence.

(2)   When the start button is not pressed, the sequencing is determined by the sequence selector bit in the microcode, and by the output from the condition multiplexer, according to the following table.

Sequence selector	Output from condition multiplexer	Successor
0	0	Address *A*
0	1	Address *B*
1	0	Address selected by fields of CIR function and accumulator
1	1	Not normally used

In the system as a whole the sequencing can at various times be controlled by many different condition signals (M1, M0 and M = 00 are three of them) and the condition multiplexer has the job of selecting the one appropriate for each microinstruction. When a microinstruction has only one successor, the multiplexer could in principle be bypassed by a direct signal to the input *Q*, but it is easier to leave it running and to make it select a 'dummy' condition signal which is always *false*.

The action of the condition multiplexer is controlled by a group of lines. One particular combination of lines makes it select the dummy condition, and this combination is always used when there is only one successor. It is also used when the successor is to depend on the contents of CIR, but in this case the sequence control bit is set to 1.

The details of the condition multiplexer will be defined later, when we have collected a list of all relevant conditions.

The final section of the outline flow chart is concerned with the execution of the various instructions. By this stage most of the work has already been done: the instruction has been fetched, the effective address has been worked out and left in MAR, and the operand (in one is needed) is ready in DR. The mode of the instruction has been taken fully into account and need no longer concern us.

It turns out that the sequences of register transfers needed for the various instructions are very short: usually one, and sometimes two, is all that is needed. A full list below gives all functions which refer to accumulator *A*. The list for *B* is similar.

LDA A   DR =⟩ A   (Move operand to A)

STA A   A =⟩ MEM   (Store contents of A. Address
                                     already in MAR)

ADD A   A + DR =⟩ A   (Add operand to A)

SUB A   A − DR =⟩ A   (Subtract operand from A)

AND A   A *and* DR =⟩ A (*And* A with DR)

ORA A   A *or* DR =⟩ A   (*Or* A with DR)

*JMP   MAR =⟩ PC   (Copy address to PC to make jump)

BZE A   If A = 0 then MAR =⟩ PC   (Copy address to PC only if
                                    condition is true)

BNZ A   If A ≠ 0 then MAR =⟩ PC

BMI A   If A < 0 then MAR =⟩ PC

BPL A   If A ⩾ 0 then MAR =⟩ PC

LRS A   A ÷ 2 =⟩ A   (Shift A one place right)

NEG A   (−A) =⟩ A   (Negate A)

INA A   (Wait until input
         register is ready)
         IN =⟩ A

OUT A   (Wait until output
         register is ready)
         A =⟩ OUT

*END   (Do nothing until
         RESET is pressed)

As we noted earlier, the input and output registers take some time to fulfil their functions. The input register has two possible states: 'busy', which implies that it is waiting for a number to be entered by the user, and 'ready', which indicates that the number has been typed and its value is available. The state is accessible as a condition signal, and permits the system to wait until the register is ready before using its contents.

The output register also has two states and emits a ready/busy control signal.

The END instruction merely makes the machine loop indefinitely until the RESET button is pressed.

We can now consider the detailed design of the arithmetic unit. First we collect all the different types of register transfer needed, by examining the design sketches already made, and allowing for operations on accumulator B as well as on A. The various transfers (in no particular order) are shown in the left-hand column of table 10.1.

Next, we make a 'skeleton' design. It is clear that the machine will need a parallel adder, with an associated inverter for the arithmetic functions, and an *and* box, an *or* box and a ' ÷ 2' box for the logic and shift operations. This leads to a configuration like that shown in figure 10.15, where the various boxes are

---

* JMP and END do not refer to an accumulator but are included in the list

Table 10.1

Transfer	Multiplexer Input Selected			C_{in}	Tri-state Switch Selected	Destination Register Clock
	M1	M2	M3			
PC =⟩ MAR	'0'	PC	X	0	S_4	C_7
MEM =⟩ CIR	'0'	MEM	X	0	S_4	C_3
PC + 1 =⟩ PC	'0'	PC	X	1	S_4	C_5
CIR *and* 777 =⟩ DR	'777'	CIR	–	–	S_3	C_6
DR =⟩ MAR	'0'	DR	X	0	S_4	C_7
DR + A =⟩ MAR	A	DR	X	0	S_4	C_7
DR + B =⟩ MAR	B	DR	X	0	S_4	C_7
MEM =⟩ DR	'0'	MEM	X	0	S_4	C_6
DR =⟩ A	'0'	DR	X	0	S_4	C_1
DR =⟩ B	'0'	DR	X	0	S_4	C_2
A =⟩ MEM	'0'	A	X	0	S_4	C_8
B =⟩ MEM	'0'	B	X	0	S_4	C_8
DR + A =⟩ A	A	DR	X	0	S_4	C_1
DR + B =⟩ B	B	DR	X	0	S_4	C_2
A – DR =⟩ A	A	DR	Y	1	S_4	C_1
B – DR =⟩ B	B	DR	Y	1	S_4	C_2
A *and* DR =⟩ A	A	DR	–	–	S_3	C_1
B *and* DR =⟩ B	B	DR	–	–	S_3	C_2
A *or* DR =⟩ A	A	DR	–	–	S_2	C_1
B *or* DR =⟩ B	B	DR	–	–	S_2	C_2
MAR =⟩ PC	'0'	MAR	X	0	S_4	C_5
A ÷ 2 =⟩ A	A	–	–	–	S_1	C_1
B ÷ 2 =⟩ B	B	–	–	–	S_1	C_2
(–A) =⟩ A	'0'	A	Y	1	S_4	C_1
(–B) =⟩ B	'0'	B	Y	1	S_4	C_2
IN =⟩ A	'0'	IN	X	0	S_4	C_1
IN =⟩ B	'0'	IN	X	0	S_4	C_2
A =⟩ OUT	'0'	A	X	0	S_4	C_4
B =⟩ OUT	'0'	B	X	0	S_4	C_4
NULL	–	–	–	–	none	none

Note: a dash (–) means that the input selected is immaterial

supplied by two parallel multiplexers, M1 and M2, which select the contents of specified registers or constants when they are needed. M3 selects the inverse of the output of M2 when it is needed for subtraction or negation.

It remains to allocate the connections to the multiplexers. The aim must be to use as few connections as possible, while allowing all necessary transfers to

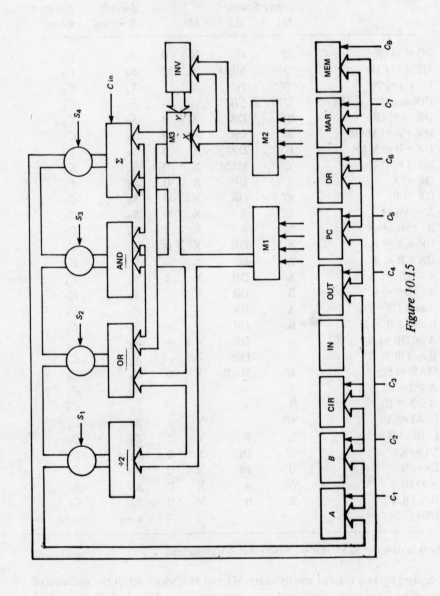

Figure 10.15

take place. One possible arrangement is tabulated below.

M1: 4 inputs

Control signals		Selected input
J	*K*	
0	0	ACC *A*
0	1	ACC *B*
1	0	Constant '0'
1	1	Constant '777_8'

M2: 8 inputs

Control signals			Selected input
L	*M*	*N*	
0	0	0	ACC *A*
0	0	1	ACC *B*
0	1	0	CIR
0	1	1	IN
1	0	0	PC
1	0	1	DR
1	1	0	MAR
1	1	1	MEM

M3: 2 inputs

Control signal	Selected input
T	
0	*X* (Output from M2)
1	*Y* (Output from parallel inverter)

The rest of table 10.1 can now be filled in. For each transfer we specify the inputs selected by the multiplexers, the carry digit to the parallel adder, the tri-state buffer to be activated, and the destination register clock. Later, this information can be converted into binary digits for the transfer field of each microinstruction. The table also confirms that all the transfers needed to implement the SNARK can be provided by the proposed configuration.

Next we define the format of the transfer field in the microcode word. It must be able to represent each of the transfers in table 10.1, and a simple arrangement is shown in figure 10.16. With this scheme some of the transfers

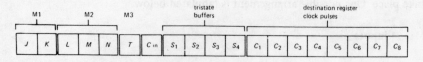

Figure 10.16

can be coded as follows

CIR and 777 ⇒ DR	'777'	CIR	–	–	S_3	C_6
	11	010	0	0	0010	00000100
B − DR ⇒ B	B	DR	Y	1	S_4	C_2
	01	101	1	1	0001	01000000
(−A) ⇒ A	'0'	A	Y	1	S_4	C_1
	10	000	1	1	0001	10000000

(Clearly more compressed coding schemes are possible but we shall not describe them here.)

The next stage consists of making a table of all the condition signals, and allocating a selection code to each one so that it can be picked out by the condition multiplexer. Table 10.2 gives a possible arrangement.

The final format of the sequence control field in the microcode word can now be determined. It is illustrated in figure 10.17 and has four subfields

Address a (6 bits)	Defines successor microinstruction
Address b (6 bits)	Defines alternative successor microinstruction
Sequence selector (1 bit)	Defines one of the control inputs to the sequence multiplexer
Condition multiplexer (4 bits) control field	Controls the condition multiplexer

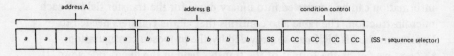

Figure 10.17

Table 10.2

Condition	Code	Code in Binary
False	0	0000
A = 0	1	0001
A # 0	2	0010
A < 0	3	0011
A ⩾ 0	4	0100
B = 0	5	0101
B # 0	6	0110
B < 0	7	0111
B ⩾ 0	8	1000
M0 (mode digit in CIR) = 1	9	1001
M1 (mode digit in CIR) = 1	10	1010
M = 00 (true if M0 = 0 and M1 = 0)	11	1011
IN ready	12	1100
OUT ready	13	1101

The design is now almost complete. Figure 10.18 shows the entire hardware arrangement of the SNARK, with a degree of detail sufficient for it to be used as a working drawing by the engineer who is to build the machine. The diagram shows how the arithmetic unit is linked to the sequence controller. The clock and clock gating circuits are omitted for clarity, and the connection between the CIR and the sequence multiplexer is not drawn in full because its path would be too tortuous in two dimensions.

The final design phase is the exact specification of the microcode. All the necessary register transfers and the sequencing rules have been designed already, so the production of microcode is essentially a mechanical process.

We use a design sheet divided into 64 lines (as shown in table 10.3): one for each word in the read-only memory. There are columns for the various parts of each microinstruction, and further columns for identification, and for noting the binary equivalent.

The positions of some of the microinstructions are predetermined. For example the transfer which carries out the 'LDA A' instruction must be in location 32 because the machine is built to jump to that location whenever it executes 'LDA A'. The same applies to all the transfers which correspond to the various SNARK machine instructions, so that words 32 to 63 are completely accounted for.

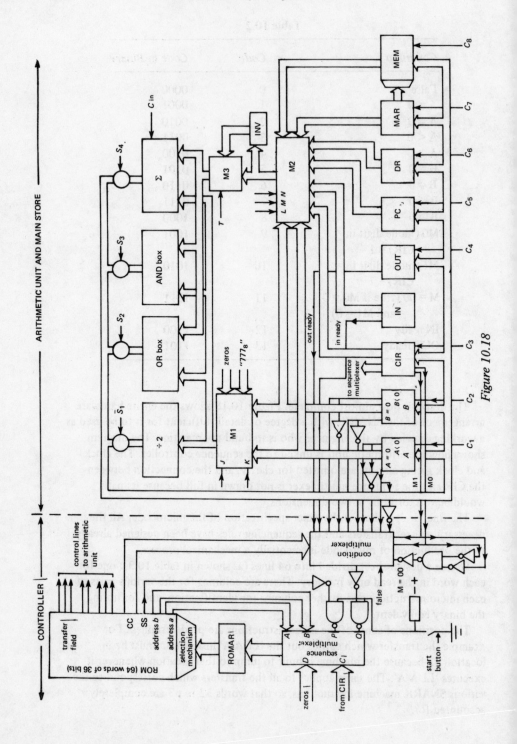

Figure 10.18

The starting sequence (which is entered whenever the 'start' button is pressed) begins at ROM address 0. A common way to make a machine start on a new program is to reserve a small area of the main store, construct it from read-only memory, and preload it with a very short program called a 'bootstrap' which can input and start the new program to be run. In the case of the SNARK we shall assume that the first instruction of the bootstrap is at location 511, so that the only job the initial microcode sequence needs to do is to load 511 (777_8) into PC, thereby making the machine jump to the beginning of the bootstrap. This needs two transfers, of which the first merely clears PC to zero.

The instruction decoding sequence is placed (arbitrarily) in words 2 to 10. The labels on the microinstructions are the same as those used in the microflow charts in figures 10.11 and 10.13.

When an instruction is in the immediate mode, the discrimination on the function takes place in microinstruction (i), which has a null transfer. For instructions in the other three modes the function is selected in microinstruction (h), saving a machine cycle.

When the function has been decoded, most of the SNARK instructions need only one transfer each. That transfer completes the execution of the current instruction, so that the successor can be defined as the first of the sequence which fetches and decodes the next instruction.

One exception to this simple rule is the family of conditional jumps. They may each need two machine cycles: one to test the condition, and one to copy MAR to PC if the condition is true. In table 10.3, the unconditional jump instruction is implemented in location 44 with the transfer MAR =) PC. Consider the conditional jump BZE A, in word 46. The condition selected is 'A = 0'. If this condition is false, the machine uses address *a*, and returns control to location 2 without making any transfers at all. Since PC has been incremented by 1 earlier in the instruction execution cycle, the effect is to make the SNARK obey the next instruction in line. If the condition is true, then address *b* is selected, and the system jumps to location 44 where the new address in MAR is transferred to PC before the next instruction is fetched.

Another group of exceptions consists of the sequences for INA and OUT. When executing one of these functions the machine has to wait until the input (or output) register is ready for another transfer. The sequence for each instruction must include a waiting loop, and this takes two microinstructions. The extra microinstructions are placed (arbitrarily) at words 11 to 14.

You may notice that the JMP and END functions are represented twice. In a SNARK JMP instruction the accumulator bit has no meaning, but it may be 0 or 1. The entries at words 44 and 45 allow the machine to handle both cases without error; the same applies to END.

In the present design words 15 to 31 are not used. It is often convenient to have some spaces in case the capabilities of the machine need to be extended — for example, by dealing more directly with input and output.

The logic design of the SNARK is now complete (apart from the input and

Table 10.3

Address Label	Address a	Address b	SS	Condition control	Transfer	Binary Equivalent									
						a	b	SS	CC	M1	M2	M3	Cin	S	C
0	1	0	0	False	PC and 0 => PC	000001	000000	0	0000	10	100	0	0	0010	00001000
1	2	0	0	False	PC or 777 => PC	000010	000000	0	0000	11	100	0	0	0100	00001000
2 a	3	0	0	False	PC => MAR	000011	000000	0	0000	10	100	0	0	0001	00000010
3 b	4	0	0	False	MEM => CIR	000100	000000	0	0000	10	111	0	0	0001	00100000
4 c	5	0	0	False	PC+1 => PC	000101	000000	0	0000	10	100	0	0	0001	00001000
5 d	6	10(i)	0	M = 00	CIR and 777 => DR	000110	001010	0	1011	11	010	0	0	0010	00000100
6 e	9(h)	7	0	M1	DR => MAR	001001	000111	0	1010	10	101	0	0	0001	00000010
7 f	9(h)	8	0	M0	DR + A => DR	001001	001000	0	1001	00	101	0	0	0001	00000100
8 g	9	0	0	False	DR + B => DR	001001	000000	0	0000	01	101	0	0	0001	00000100
9 h	–	0	1	False	MEM => DR	000000	000000	1	0000	10	111	0	0	0001	00000100
10 i	–	0	1	False	NULL	000000	000000	1	0000	00	011	0	0	0001	10000000
11	2	0	0	False	IN => A	000010	000000	0	0000	10	011	0	0	0001	01000000
12	2	0	0	False	IN => B	000010	000000	0	0000	10	011	0	0	0001	00010000
13	2	2	0	False	A => OUT	000010	000000	0	0000	10	000	0	0	0001	00010000
14	2	2	0	False	B => OUT	000010	000000	0	0000	10	001	0	0	0001	00010000
15															
16			Registers 15 to 31 not allocated												
.															
.															
30															
31															
32 LDAA	2	0	0	False	DR => A	000010	000000	0	0000	10	101	0	0	0001	10000000
33 LDAB	2	0	0	False	DR => B	000010	000000	0	0000	10	101	0	0	0001	01000000
34 STAA	2	0	0	False	A => MEM	000010	000000	0	0000	10	000	0	0	0001	00000001

35	STAB	2	0	False	B =) MEM	000010	0	000000	0	0000	10	001	0	0	0001	00000001
36	ADDA	2	0	False	A + DR =) A	000010	0	000000	0	0000	00	101	0	0	0001	10000000
37	ADDB	2	0	False	B + DR =) B	000010	0	000000	0	0000	01	101	0	0	0001	01000000
38	SUBA	2	0	False	A − DR =) A	000010	0	000000	0	0000	00	101	1	1	0001	10000000
39	SUBB	2	0	False	B − DR =) B	000010	0	000000	0	0000	01	101	1	1	0001	01000000
40	ANDA	2	0	False	A *and* DR =) A	000010	0	000000	0	0000	00	101	0	0	0010	10000000
41	ANDB	2	0	False	B *and* DR =) B	000010	0	000000	0	0000	01	101	0	0	0010	01000000
42	ORAA	2	0	False	A *or* DR =) A	000010	0	000000	0	0000	00	101	0	0	0100	10000000
43	ORAB	2	0	False	B *or* DR =) B	000010	0	000000	0	0000	01	101	0	0	0100	01000000
44	JMPA	2	0	False	MAR =) PC	000010	0	000000	0	0000	10	110	0	0	0001	00001000
45	JMPB	2	0	False	MAR =) PC	000010	0	000000	0	0000	10	110	0	0	0001	00000000
46	BZEA	2	44	A = 0	NULL	000010	0	101100	0	0001	00	000	0	0	0000	00000000
47	BZEB	2	44	B = 0	NULL	000010	0	101100	0	0101	00	000	0	0	0000	00000000
48	BNZA	2	44	A ≠ 0	NULL	000010	0	101100	0	0010	00	000	0	0	0000	00000000
49	BNZB	2	44	B ≠ 0	NULL	000010	0	101100	0	0110	00	000	0	0	0000	00000000
50	BMIA	2	44	A < 0	NULL	000010	0	101100	0	0011	00	000	0	0	0000	00000000
51	BMIB	2	44	B < 0	NULL	000010	0	101100	0	0111	00	000	0	0	0000	00000000
52	BPLA	2	44	A >= 0	NULL	000010	0	101100	0	0100	00	000	0	0	0000	00000000
53	BPLB	2	44	B >= 0	NULL	000010	0	101100	0	1000	00	000	0	0	0000	00000000
54	LRSA	2	0	False	A ÷ 2 =) A	000010	0	000000	0	0000	01	000	0	0	0000	10000000
55	LRSB	2	0	False	B ÷ 2 =) B	000010	0	000000	0	0000	10	000	0	0	0000	01000000
56	NEGA	2	0	False	(−A) =) A	000010	0	000000	0	0000	10	000	1	1	0000	10000000
57	NEGB	2	0	False	(−B) =) B	000010	0	000000	0	0000	10	001	1	1	0001	01000000
58	INAA	2	11	IN ready	NULL	111010	0	001011	0	1100	00	000	0	0	0000	00000000
59	INAB	2	12	IN ready	NULL	111011	0	001100	0	1100	00	000	0	0	0000	00000000
60	OUTA	2	13	OUT ready	NULL	111100	0	001101	0	1101	00	000	0	0	0000	00000000
61	OUTB	2	14	OUT ready	NULL	111101	0	001110	0	1101	00	000	0	0	0000	00000000
62	END(A)	2	0	False	NULL	111110	0	000000	0	0000	00	000	0	0	0000	00000000
63	END(B)	2	0	False	NULL	111111	0	000000	0	0000	00	000	0	0	0000	00000000

output registers which we do not plan to discuss). The next stage in construction would be to choose components from a manufacturer's catalogue, to design a printed circuit to connect them together, to put the binary microcode into a read-only memory, and to obtain a suitable power supply and cabinet. These activities, however, are in the province of the electrical engineer, and we shall not enter into them here.

Example 10.5

Trace the microinstructions executed by the SNARK when obeying the following program, Use your results to give an approximate instruction speed for the SNARK, assuming that each machine cycle takes 0.4 μs.

```
0    LDA  A   #3
1    LDA  B   #0
2    ADD  B   56A
3    SUB  A   #1
4    BNZ  A   2
5    OUT  B
6    END
57   3
58   7
59   36
```

The solution is set out in the form of a table, with a trace on the left and a list of microinstructions obeyed on the right.

Instruction			Result in: A	B	Out	Microinstructions obeyed
0	LDA A	#3	3			2,3,4,5,10,32
1	LDA B	#0	3	0		2,3,4,5,10,33
2	ADD B	56A	3	36		2,3,4,5,6,7,9,37
3	SUB A	#1	2	36		2,3,4,5,10,38
4	BNZ A	2	2	36		2,3,4,5,6,9,48,44
2	ADD B	56A	2	43		2,3,4,5,6,7,9,37
3	SUB A	#1	1	43		2,3,4,5,10,38
4	BNZ A	2	1	43		2,3,4,5,6,9,48,44
2	ADD B	56A	1	46		2,3,4,5,6,7,9,37
3	SUB A	#1	0	46		2,3,4,5,10,38
4	BNZ A	2	0	46		2,3,4,5,6,9,48
5	OUT B		0	46	46	2,3,4,5,10,61,14
6	END		0	46		2,3,4,5,10,62,62,62, . . .

A count shows that 90 cycles were needed to execute 13 instructions. (This assumes that the output register was ready when the OUT B insttuction was executed, and allows for only one execution of the END microinstruction in location 62.)

Average number of cycles per instructions = 90/13 = 6.92
Average instruction time = 6.92 ∗ 0.4 = 2.77 μs
Instruction speed = 1000000/2.77 ≈ 360000 instructions/s

11 Backing Stores

The main store of a computer is the one which holds the instructions of the program being executed, and the individual items of data — numbers or characters — being manipulated. Main stores are always of the 'random access' variety: each cell can be reached equally quickly in a fraction of a microsecond. In 1979, the cost of main store was about 0.5p per bit, or 8p for a 16-bit word. This makes large quantities of main storage expensive. Even though the price of store may fall in absolute terms, it will remain high in comparison to the cost of the central processor. Computer designers are therefore compelled to use other, cheaper forms of store for data which does not need to be referred to at such short notice. These types are generally called 'backing store'. There exist a number of storage technologies, of which we will discuss only a representative sample. The various techniques fall into one of two broad groupings, depending on the way the stored information is reached.

11.1 SERIAL STORAGE

In a serial store, the information is recorded on magnetic tape, using the method illustrated in figure 11.1. The tape consists of a plastics substrate a few micrometres thick (in figure 11.1 the thickness is greatly exaggerated) and coated with a layer of magnetisable material such as an oxide of iron. The tape is pinched between a rubber idler wheel and a motor-driven capstan, and is pulled mechanically past a read—write head. A pressure pad ensures that the tape stays in contact with the head continuously. The tape moves between two rotating reels, which are not shown in the figure.

To record information, the binary digits are translated, one by one, into varying currents of electricity in the winding round the read—write head. This produces a varying magnetic field in the gap. Some of the magnetic flux spills over into the magnetisable layer of the tape, and magnetises it permanently, in a way which reflects the varying current in the winding. As the tape moves, the recording head leaves a trail of magnetised areas, one for each of the bits being recorded.

Later, the tape is played past the same (or a similar) read—write head. This

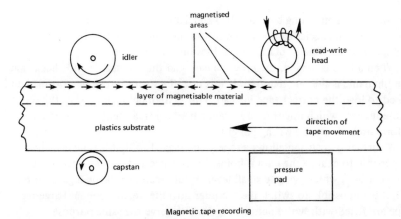

Magnetic tape recording

Figure 11.1

time, the information flow is in the other direction: each magnetised area causes a flux in the read—write head and induces a varying voltage across the winding. This signal is amplified and decoded electronically so as to reconstitute the original information.

The principle of magnetic tape recording is used in a spectrum of devices which covers a wide range of performance. It is feasible to pack information on to a tape at some 800 bits per cm (2000 per inch). Large computers generally use broad tape with several parallel tracks (typically 7 or 9) so that by using a separate track for each bit position, 800 *bytes* per cm of tape can be stored.

The rate at which information can be written and read depends on the speed at which the tape can move. The chief practical limitation lies in the need to start and stop a tape in a short distance without damage. The forces involved can be high: for example, to accelerate a tape from rest to a speed of 2.5 m/s while moving it only 12 mm involves a steady acceleration of over 25g. Complicated and expensive mechanical gear is needed to ensure that the tape is not torn or stretched as it passes through the recorder. The upper limit to reading and writing speed on magnetic tape is about 200 000 bytes per second.

At the other extreme, it is feasible to use domestic cassette recorders, even of the lowest quality. The rate of data transfer is low, because only one track can be used at a time, the speed of the tape is geared to the reproduction of sound, and a different (and less efficient) method of coding binary digits must be used. On the other hand, the cost of each recorder is negligible.

In any computer installation the tapes are kept in a library. When a tape is needed, it must be loaded on to the tape deck by a human operator. People are notoriously unreliable, and often mis-read the labels on the tapes. To help ensure that the correct tape is mounted, all information on a tape is commonly recorded in the form of a *file*. First comes a 'file header', which gives the identity of the file (such as a program name). Next, the body of the file as a sequence of *records*, each containing between 100 and 1000 characters, and finally a 'file terminator', or special record which marks the end of the file. If the tape is long enough, it is possible to place several files on a single tape.

When a tape is loaded, the program can read the file header and check that the file name is the one required. If it is not, the operator can be informed and asked to load the correct tape instead. This system helps to prevent the serious consequences which might arise if, say, a medical treatment plan were based on information about the wrong patient.

A further precaution allows a tape to be tagged so that it is physically impossible to change the data it holds. Every cassette tape has a pair of lugs (one for each side) which operate small levers in the recorder. If the lugs are broken off, it is impossible to switch the recorder into the 'record' mode. Large reels of tape are fitted with 'write permit rings' which serve the same purpose.

Magnetic tapes form the cheapest method of storage, but they suffer from four major snags.

(1) *Access time*: It normally takes up to 10 minutes to run through a tape from one end to the other. If the information on the tape has a natural sequence (as, for example, a list of names and addresses in alphabetic order to be printed out) this presents no problem; the records are read and processed one by one. On the other hand, many types of information, such as libraries of programs, have no natural sequence. If such a library is stored on magnetic tape then, in general, finding and loading a given program will involve a tedious wait of several minutes while the tape is searched. The *average* wait is called the access time.

(2) *Tape wear*: The magnetic layer of the tape runs in contact with the read—write head. If the tape is used frequently the layer wears thin, so that eventually it can no longer hold information reliably. Typically, tapes must be discarded after about 300 passes, and the need to copy them while they are still readable (that is, *before* any errors are detected) causes some administrative difficulties.

(3) *Drop-outs*: When tape is manufactured, it is difficult to ensure that the coating of magnetic material is absolutely uniform: there often remain small bald patches. If the tape is used for sound recording the patches cause minor 'clicks' which are mostly unnoticed by the listener, but in data recording they result in the loss of binary digits with potentially disastrous consequences.

The first defence against a drop-out is the detection that an error has actually occurred. This is done with a 'check sum'. Conceptually, every record in a file consists of a sequence of bytes. As they are recorded, the bytes are also added up as if they were numbers; and after the last data byte the result, which is called a check sum, is also written to the tape.

Later, when the record is read back, the check sum is recalculated from the data bytes and compared with the check sum recorded originally. Any discrepancy must indicate an error in the data. In principle two errors could compensate one another, but in practice this is very improbable, and most errors are in fact detected.

On large computers, each record is read back (by a separate reading head) soon after it has been written. If a discrepancy arises, the record is simply recorded again a little further up the tape. On a cassette unit, a good approach is to write every record twice, in the hope that the drop-outs will not be so close together that they spoil both versions of the same record. With good-quality tape this method gives acceptable results, but decreases the effective speed even more.

(4) *Mechanics*: A tape deck is a mechanical device, and must be kept clean and oiled and adjusted correctly. If a machine uses several tape decks, they have to be adjusted to a common standard so that a tape written on one deck can be read back on any other. This is not always easy to ensure, particularly if multi-track recording is used. Tape decks and cassette recorders have a reputation as the most troublesome components in every computer system.

To summarise, the following table gives figures for tape systems at the extreme ends of the price/performance spectrum. We shall compare a high-speed nine-track deck, as used on a large computer, with a cassette recorder.

	High-speed Deck	Cassette
Unit cost	£20 000	£20
Speed of transfer	200000 bytes/s	40 bytes/s
Cost of one tape	£15	£0.90
Capacity of one tape	10 000 000 characters	400 000 characters
Access time	1 min	5 min
Over-all cost per character (assume 200 tapes in library)	10^{-3}p per character	2.5×10^{-3}p per character

These figures are not directly comparable, since the type of tape deck chosen would depend on the over-all cost and performance of the system being designed, but they indicate, in a rough and ready way, the over-all cost of storage on tape.

11.2 CYCLIC STORAGE

The second main group of storage devices uses the cyclic principle: that is, the information circulates and can be accessed or altered every time it comes round.

A major family of devices is based on the rotating magnetic track, as illustrated in figure 11.2.

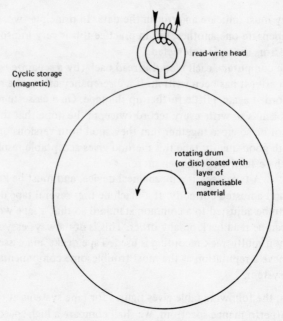

Cyclic storage
(magnetic)

read-write head

rotating drum
(or disc) coated with
layer of
magnetisable
material

Figure 11.2

The store consists of a metal disc or drum, rotating at a high speed and coated with a layer of magnetisable material. The track repeatedly passes under a read–write head, which is close to the surface. The principle of recording is the same as that used on magnetic tape, but data rate can be much higher because the disc spins continuously and is not required to start or stop. The normal rate is about 50 revolutions per second, and each track can hold 50 000 to 100 000 bits of information.

The read–write head must not be allowed to touch the surface of the track, otherwise it would wear it away in a few seconds. It must, however, be kept extremely close (much less than one micrometre) otherwise the magnetic effect disappears. On the earliest cyclic stores the heads were set by screws. The adjustment was an exceedingly delicate one, and any irregularity of the disc would immediately damage the head.

A modern cyclic store let the head determine its own spacing by an aerodynamic principle. Any object moving through the air carries with it a so-called 'boundary layer'. Very close to the object the air moves at almost the same speed, and the further one moves away, the less the speed becomes, until eventually it drops to zero and the air is at rest.

The thickness of the boundary layer depends on the size of the object as well as the speed. (It was supposedly possible to sunbathe comfortably on the tops of airships such as the R101 even though they were moving at speeds of 80 miles/h – the boundary layer must have been several feet thick.)

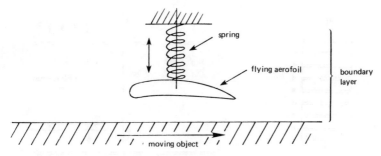

Figure 11.3

When an aerofoil section (that is, a section like the wing of an aeroplane) moves through the air, it experiences a lifting force which is proportional to the square of its speed relative to the air. Figure 11.3 shows an aerofoil fixed in the boundary layer of a moving surface, but free to move up and down. The closer it moves to the surface, the higher the relative air speed, and the more lift is generated. There will be one particular height at which the lift exactly balances the force of the spring, and the aerofoil settles at this height above the surface, automatically riding over bumps and irregularities without changing its distance. A read—write head attached to the aerofoil will also keep to a constant distance over the surface.

A single track does not have a large capacity, and in practice the tracks are always gathered together in groups. There are several ways this can be done, as shown in figures 11.4a–d.

Figure 11.4a shows a drum, which normally has 100 to 200 tracks, with a head for each one. The capacity is about 1 000 000 characters, and the average access time, or latency, is half a revolution time. This is about 10 ms.

Figure 11.4b represents a fixed-head disc. Its behaviour is very like that of a drum, and only the geometry is different. Both sides of the disc can be used, giving a somewhat higher capacity.

Figure 11.4c shows a disc with a single moveable read—write head. The surface may have some 200 concentric tracks, and the head can be moved to any one of them by a mechanical system. The arrangement is cheaper than the fixed-head system, because only one head is needed, and it is also possible to retract the head and replace the disc by another one. This is called an *exchangeable disc store*. The scheme greatly increases the amount of data which can be stored, but at the cost of requiring a 'disc library'.

Figure 11.4d illustrates a common configuration where a number of separate discs are mounted on the same spindle. There is a head for each surface, and the heads are all moved together by the same mechanism. The disc pack is again removable.

In a moving head store the access time depends partly on the speed of head movement between tracks, and partly on the speed at which the disc revolves.

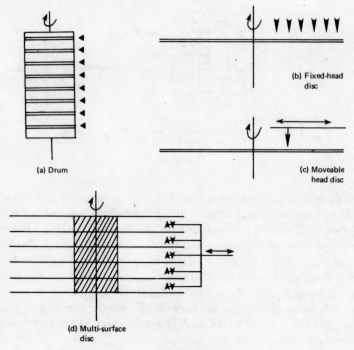

Figure 11.4

Individual access times on the same disc vary widely because the head may or may not have to move a long way. In general, the 'seek time' due to head movement predominates over the 'latency' which is due to the rotation of the disc. Some typical average figures are

Seek time	40 ms
Latency (= ½ a revolution)	10 ms
Total access time	50 ms

Disc systems in general suffer from two difficulties.

(1) *Disc crashes*:　　Sometimes a particle of dust manages to get in between the surface of the disc and the read—write head, and brings the head into contact with the surface. This not only destroys the track so affected; the particles of magnetic material which appear rapidly spread around and destroy other tracks as well. A disc crash is a major catastrophe. It can be made less likely by keeping the store in clean condition, and with a constant temperature and humidity. The only real protection is to copy the discs at regular intervals so that a duplicate is always available.

(2) *Storage allocation*:　　A large disc is likely to be used for many different purposes, by different people. To prevent one person from spoiling

another's data, the allocation of space on the disc must be handled automatically by a *filing system*, a complex program which is held permanently in the computer. The user is not told exactly where on the disc his data is stored, but sees all his information in the form of named files — just like magnetic tape files except that any record can be reached directly without the need to read all the intervening ones first.

Recently, the cyclic principle has been extended to very cheap stores called 'floppy discs'. A 'floppy' is an exchangeable disc store which takes a flexible disc about 180 mm in diameter. The disc rotates at only 6 rev/s and runs in direct contact with the read—write head. It has a specially treated surface which permits several hundred hours' running time before it wears out. The access time of the device is about 0.25 s, and it is cheap — about £400 for the mechanism. Floppy discs are mainly used with microcomputers, where they allow programs to be loaded up to 1000 times faster than from cassette tapes.

Cyclic stores based on non-magnetic technologies are also available. Bubble memories and charge-coupled devices are both purely electronic cyclic stores, manufactured as large-scale integrated circuits. They are fast, and having no moving parts they are more reliable than magnetic discs. However, they are more expensive, and charge-coupled devices are volatile — the information in them disappears if the power is turned off.

A different technology uses a laser beam to impress optical patterns on the surface of a plastics disc. The amount of data which can be placed on one disc is large (at least 5000 million characters) but once written it cannot be altered or erased.

A summary of the different types of cyclic store is given in table 11.1.

Table 11.1

Type	Latency (ms)	Storage Capacity per unit (bytes)	Cost (£)	Typical Cost per Character (p)
Drum	10	10^6	5000	0.5
Fixed-head disc	10	10×10^6	10 000	0.1
Moving-head disc	40	30×10^6	3000	0.01
Exchangeable disc	40	100×10^6	12 000	0.01 (if library has 12 discs)
Floppy-disc	250	0.8×10^6	400	0.005 (if library has 10 discs)

11.3 HIERARCHIES OF STORES

In this chapter we have discussed various types of store, having different characteristics of access time and price per character. The figures can be plotted on a graph, as shown in figure 11.5.

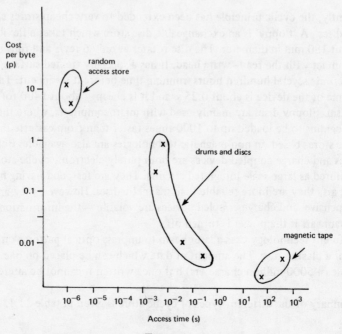

Figure 11.5

In practice, most computers are configured with several types of store, so that each requirement can be handled in the best way. For example, large banks of data are normally kept on discs or tapes, and selected portions are brought into the random access store for scanning or alteration.

It is up to the programmer to ensure that the various types of store at his disposal are efficiently used, but in this he is helped by existing software such as filing systems or database management systems.

12 Peripheral Devices

Peripheral devices allow computers to communicate with the external world. The various devices are classified from the point of view of the computer: thus the machine uses *input* peripherals to collect information about the problems it is to solve, and *output* peripherals to indicate the results of its calculations and decisions.

Peripherals can be divided into two main groups: those which communicate with people, and those used to measure and control systems where no human intelligence is directly involved. There is a third group of devices concerned with punching and detecting holes in paper, but it is an obsolescent remnant of an information technology used before the invention of computers, and is falling into disuse.

Every peripheral must be connected to its parent computer by a link capable of passing information. When a peripheral is at some distance, the need for communication often causes special problems and can be very expensive.

12.1 PERIPHERALS FOR HUMAN COMMUNICATION

People normally communicate by talking, writing and drawing pictures. All these methods can be used with a computer, but with considerable restrictions.

The first method to be developed was communication through writing. The human uses a keyboard, like that on a typewriter, and types the information to be sent to the computer. At present, most of the input from human sources is entered on keyboards, but the method is slow (compared to speech), prone to error, and has to be learned. It cannot be used by people who cannot read and write, and needs a certain familiarity with mechanical devices.

On the output side, a computer has various methods of displaying its results in written form. If a permanent record is not needed, the message can be shown on a 'visual display unit' with a screen like the one on a television set. Other devices produce 'hard copy', which is the name for results printed on paper.

12.1.1 Printers

Keyboards and visual display units show little variety, but printers exist in a wide range of speeds and prices. There are two major ways of classifying them.

Typefaced versus Matrix Printers
Some printers produce written characters by striking type bars against paper, just like a conventional typewriter. This leads to printing which is of good quality and easy to read. Other devices draw each character as a matrix of black dots selected from a grid of 5 x 7 or 7 x 9 positions. Matrix printers are cheaper, but the quality of the print is usually much worse (see figure 12.1).

```
This is an example of a matrix        This is an example of a
printer typeface.                     printer with type-bars.
ABCDEFGHIJKLMNOPQRSTUVWXYZ            ABCDEFGHIJKLMNOPQRSTUVWXYZ
abcdefghijklmnopqrstuvwxyz            abcdefghijklmnopqrstuvwxyz
0123456789 !@#$%^&*()+=~`{}[]          0123456789 !@?$%¾&*()+=¼:;[]
```

Figure 12.1

Character-at-a-time versus Line-at-a-time
Slow devices are designed to print one character at a time, with the printer head moving from side to side along the paper. (It is unusual for the *paper* to move as in a typewriter.) These machines normally run at 30–50 characters per second, although matrix printers are sometimes much faster. A lot of time can be wasted moving the printing mechanism back to the beginning of each line, so some printers use microprocessors (small internal computers) to organise the printing of lines in alternate directions – that is, every second line is printed backwards, although it still *reads* forwards.

Many high-quality printers can use variable horizontal spacing, so that an '1' takes less room than an 'm'. The spacing can also be controlled by the computer to align or *justify* boths ends of each line.

Machines designed to handle larger amounts of output are called line printers. The information is handled a line at a time, and the speed can vary between 200 and 3600 lines per minute.

Two of the main types of line printer are the *barrel* printer and the *chain* printer. In both cases, a set of type bars moves rapidly in front of the paper, separated from it by an inked ribbon. At the instant when any wanted character is exactly in the correct place, the paper is struck against the type bar by a hammer. The impact is fast enough to produce a legible symbol even though the type is in motion.

Diagrams of the barrel printer are shown in figures 12.2 a and b. The rotating barrel has a complete set of types for *each* character position across the page –

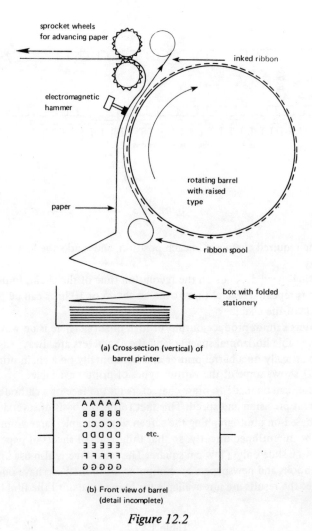

(a) Cross-section (vertical) of
barrel printer

(b) Front view of barrel
(detail incomplete)

Figure 12.2

usually 120 or 160. When the paper is in position for a new line, the control
mechanism simultaneously monitors every character position, and fires the
hammer for that character at the right time. Thus all the As are printed first,
then the Bs, and so on. The entire line is printed within one revolution of the
barrel. In practice, a further revolution is often wasted while the paper is
advanced to the next line.

Figure 12.3 shows the chain printer. The types are carried on a chain which
circulates in front of the paper. The controller keeps track of the position of the

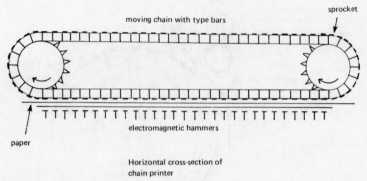

Figure 12.3

chain and the required character in each position, and works the hammer appropriately.

The printing speed depends on the revolution time of the chain. In practice, the alphabet is repeated several times over, so that 5 or 10 lines can be printed for each cycle of the chain.

Line printers cannot produce output of high quality. There is no way to arrange for variable horizontal spacing, and the characters are always slightly smudged – vertically on a barrel printer and horizontally on a chain printer. Table 12.1 shows some of the various types of printer available.

A computer can be made to draw characters on the face of a cathode-ray tube with great precision and speed. This fact forms the basis of several methods of printing based on photographing the screen. For example, large volumes of output can be microfilmed directly, so that thousands of sheets of paper can be replaced by one slide only a few cm square. The technique is also used in typesetting books and newspapers by computer. Both methods have one major disadvantage: the results are not available for human use until the film has been

Table 12.1

	Character Printers	*Line Printers*
Matrix	Tally rolls on cash registers Printers for hand calculators	Cheap slow printers
	Typical cost – £200 to £1000	Typical cost – up to £3000
Type bar	Golf-ball and daisy-wheel printers	Barrel printers Chain printers
	Typical cost – £1000 to £2500	Typical cost – £6000 to £30,000

developed. This introduces a delay of several minutes and limits the possible
areas of use.

Keyboards and character displays are usually paired to make 'terminals'.
This allows instant bidirectional communication between the computer and its
user, and lets each character be displayed as it is typed.

Keyboards are not expensive, and visual display units based on cathode-ray
tubes have much in common with black-and-white television sets. As the quantity
manufactured increases, the price of terminals will drop steadily towards that of
monochrome television receivers, and they will become accepted equipment in
many people's homes.

12.1.2 Graphics

Computers are built to handle information primarily in the form of *symbols*
such as characters or numbers. They are not well suited to manipulate pictures
or other graphic data. Nevertheless, there are important problem areas where
drawings are essential — they include engineering design, architecture, chemistry,
map-making, cartoon animation and flight simulation. Inside the computer
pictures cannot be represented directly but have to be described in an unnatural
and clumsy way by lists of co-ordinates, equations of lines, and so on. Simple
observations — such as whether one object hides another from a given point of
view — have to be replaced by long and complex calculations. Picture processing
is therefore expensive, and can only be used in circumstances where the cost is
justified.

There are several methods of communicating pictures to computers. When a
computer is used to control a machine tool cutting an engineering component,
the geometrical description of the part is converted by hand from the standard
engineering drawing into a set of co-ordinates, and fed to the computer as a
sequence of symbols. A more automatic method is a *graphic tablet*. This is a
flat board, where a picture can be drawn or traced with a special hand-held
'pencil'. In one design the present position of the pencil is determined by timing
pulses of sound which travel between the pencil and strip microphones mounted
along two sides of the board. The computer can 'follow' the pencil as it makes
the drawing, and obtain enough information to reconstruct the picture.

Where a low accuracy is acceptable, a television camera can be directly
connected to the computer. In general, television pictures are very difficult to
analyse because the machine cannot easily distinguish between objects, shadows
and reflections. The method becomes useful when these spurious effects can be
eliminated. Cameras are used to control simple industrial robots. In one medical
application, patients with artificial limbs or other handicaps have small
light-bulbs fixed to their hips, knees and ankles, and then walk across a darkened
room. A computer uses a television camera to record and analyse their move-
ments, and to measure how far they deviate from those of a healthy person.
The results are useful in adjusting the prostheses or monitoring the progress of
illnesses week by week.

For instaneous graphic output, a computer can use a cathode-ray tube. The quality of the drawing depends, among other things, on the *resolution*, or the precision to which any point can be positioned on the screen. 256 positions in each direction give crude but acceptable pictures, while 4096 x 4096 is good enough for an engineering drawing.

Colour pictures can easily be produced by having the computer control a colour television set. Maps can use different colours to shade between contour lines. In complex industrial plants like power stations and oil refineries, the control computer often displays a 'mimic diagram' for the operator in charge. This is a colour picture which displays the state of each major component of the system, and the links between them. Any abnormal condition can be indicated by flashing a different colour over the affected component.

For drawings of three-dimensional objects, the computer can generate two pictures which form a *stereo pair*, and must be looked at with a stereoscope. Alternatively the computer can *model* the object by milling a polystyrene blank.

On some cathode-ray displays the computer can follow the position of a 'light pen' which the user presses against the screen. This allows him to 'draw' pictures directly on the screen, or to point to parts of the picture he wants to remove or change.

12.1.3 Speech

Speech is the most primitive and natural method of communication among people, but it is an area in which little genuine progress has been made with computers.

The basic problem with speech input is that no one knows how it is that humans are able to understand the spoken word. There is therefore no theoretical basis on which to design a mechanical speech recogniser. Nevertheless, some modest results have been achieved by working on purely empirical grounds.

When a person utters a word, he creates a complex sequence of vibrations in the air. These vibrations can be picked up by a microphone and fed to the computer as a sequence of numbers, at a rate of about 8000 per second, giving the instantaneous sound pressure.

In the computer the sequence can be analysed in various ways. For instance, the machine can calculate the length of the word, the relative proportions of low and high-pitched frequencies at various places in the sequence, and so on. This process 'reduces' the thousands of numbers representing the word to a small collection of measurements which form a characteristic pattern.

When a speech-recognising machine is installed it has no vocabulary, but must first be 'trained'. A speaker carefully pronounces some set of words, and indicates the meaning of each one on a keyboard. The machine calculates the characteristic pattern of each word and stores it along with its meaning.

Later, the user will talk to the machine using the vocabulary it was trained with. As each word is spoken the machine works out its characteristic pattern and compares it against all those it has stored away, and chooses the best match as the 'meaning'.

Unfortunately the system has several drawbacks. At best, it has an error rate of one or two words in every hundred, because there is a large variation in the characteristic pattern in different utterances of the same word, even though they may sound identical to the human ear. The number of words in the vocabulary is limited to 30 or fewer, because a larger vocabulary makes the machine confuse different words with similar sounds. Lastly, the machine must be retrained for each individual user, again because two people uttering the same word will generally produce entirely different characteristic patterns.

So far, this system has found use in places where people are using both hands and cannot conveniently operate a keyboard. One such place is the inspection line in a factory, where a suitable vocabulary consists of the decimal digits to identify the part, and such words as 'OK', 'bad' and 'doubtful'. Another area is baggage handling at airports, where cases are put on conveyor belts for automatic distribution to aircraft bound for various destinations. Loss of baggage is now accepted as a common risk when travelling by air, so a low accuracy is entirely adequate.

Spoken output is considerably more advanced. Some systems run by playing continuous recordings of words originally spoken by people. The oldest machine to use this method is the Post Office's speaking clock, which pre-dates the invention of the computer. Other systems generate the speech directly. The mechanics of the human vocal tract are well understood, and can be simulated by an electronic device. A computer can 'say' any word in any language, but it sounds unnatural and takes a little practice to understand. Hardly any progress has been made in making machines sound more like people.

12.2 PUNCHED PAPER

Holes in paper have been used to represent information for many years. There are two basic forms: cards and paper tape.

In certain forms, the use of punched cards can be traced back for centuries. They were used in Victorian times, to control automatic looms and play melodies on fairground organs. The first large-scale systematic application of cards occurred in the 1890s, when Herman Hollerith devised an automatic system to analyse the results of a national census in the United States. All the salient facts about each individual were recorded as holes, in predetermined positions in a card of standard shape. Then a specially designed machine, with probe wires and mercury contacts, was used to process a batch of cards and count the number of holes in each position.

This system gradually evolved over the years. At first the information recorded was purely numerical, but later a convention was devised for letters and other symbols, so that items like names and addresses could be represented as well.

Punched card systems came to be supported by various machines, including

Card punches	to key punch new information on to each card
Card sorters	to sort cards into order, and to pick out groups with different characteristics
Tabulators	to produce printed listings of the information on packs of cards.

One of the major difficulties in designing punched card machinery is to move fragile pieces of paper quickly without tearing them. Many ingenious mechanical solutions were found, and some of these punched card machines ran at speeds as high as 15 cards per second.

In the pre-computer age, many organisations used card systems for various purposes such as stock-keeping, maintenance of mailing lists, personnel records and other routine office jobs. The main drawbacks were that the systems were inflexible, and the cards themselves bulky and liable to damage when being handled or stored.

Punched paper tape has always been associated with transmission of data over long distances. On a paper tape, characters are represented by transverse rows of holes, selected according to a conventional code. Such a tape can be prepared or 'played back' by a 'teleprinter', which is a device with a keyboard and printer.

Two teleprinters can be connected by a telegraph line so that one reproduces material typed on the other. In practice, long-distance transmissions are never made by direct typing, but always by 'playing back' a paper tape which has been prepared beforehand. This allows both teleprinters to run at full speed, and increases the amount of information which can be transmitted for a given cost.

When computers were first constructed, they needed some method of transferring information from the human mind into machine-readable form. It was natural for them to use the well-developed technologies of cards and paper tape, and many computers continue to do so. Such machines use peripherals called 'card readers', 'tape punches' and the like.

The major disadvantage in using cards or paper tape in this context is that the information is not transferred directly from person to computer (as with a terminal) but is stored in an intermediate stage. This inevitably causes a delay and completely prevents direct man/machine interaction.

12.3 LINKS WITH MECHANICAL SYSTEMS

Computers are often used to monitor and control complex systems such as power stations, steel mills, jet engines, lifts and patients in intensive care units. The machine must be supplied with enough information to make correct decisions, and there are many ways this can be done. There are, however, three widely used methods.

(1) Some items of information are simple 'true—false' conditions, such as 'burglar alarm ringing' or 'pressure exceeds safe limit' or 'transmitter switched on'. Variables of this type can be read by the computer as single binary digits.

(2) Some items are represented by the position of a rotating shaft. Good examples are the direction of a weather vane, or the setting of an astronomical telescope. The position is converted directly into binary by a 'coding disc', which rotates with the shaft and has alternate clear and opaque patches.

(3) Some measurements can be made by *transducers* and represented by continuously varying voltages. Thus thermocouples measure temperature, strain gauges measure relative displacement, and piezo-electric crystals measure pressure.

A transducer is normally connected to a computer through an 'analogue to digital converter' which translates the voltage into a binary number. The precision usually lies between one part in 100 to one part in 1000, depending on the application.

On the output side, a computer can control any electrical or mechanical device directly — motors, lamps, valves, industrial robots, telephone exchanges, and so on. The list of devices controlled by computer grows constantly.

12.4 COMMUNICATION

If a peripheral device is close to its parent computer, it can be connected without difficulty by wires. Often, however, the device is remote, and in this case connection is more difficult.

In the United Kingdom, the word 'remote' is easily defined. The law specifies that no privately owned wire may cross a public road, and that all communication across roads must be handled by a Post Office monopoly. The Post Office permits communication through the public telephone network, and also rents out 'private wires' where the communication is expected to be continuous or frequent.

The rules about connecting equipment to Post Office lines are justifiably strict, because of the risk that a fault in the equipment (such as a short-circuit to a mains supply) should be propagated down the line and damage Post Office equipment or injure other subscribers. In practice it is necessary to rent a GPO 'modem' (short for 'modulator/demodulator') at each end of the line. This device translates the binary signals representing the data into a special form which can be handled by Post Office circuits — thus a '1' is represented by a burst of high-pitched tone, and a '0' by a low-pitched tone.

If a 'private circuit' is leased from the Post Office, information can be transmitted at almost any speed (although high-speed links cost more to rent than slow ones). If the ordinary telephone network is used the speed is strictly limited to about 240 characters per second.

There are two types of modem for transmitting data on telephone lines: a fixed one which replaces the ordinary telephone instrument, and an 'acoustic' one which is used together with a telephone. The handset is placed in a special holder, where it picks up sound signals which represent the information to be transmitted.

13 Software

'Software' is a generic term which refers to the various programs a computer needs to do its job. A SNARK machine code program, of the type described in chapters 7–9, is one particular kind of software. In this chapter we discuss the whole topic of software from a more general point of view.

Software can be divided into two categories: user programs and systems programs. A user program is aimed at making the computer do a specific job, such as printing a set of astronomical tables, or keeping personnel records, or controlling a machine tool in a factory. User programs vary in size from just a few instructions to many thousands. Most practical programs are much larger than those you might encounter at the beginning of a computer science course. Many practical systems are built of 'suites' which contain several related programs. The various programs use a common collection of data such as a file. For example, a computerised system for recording student marks can be organised round a file which records each student's name and marks to date. The suite will include a program for setting up the file at the beginning of the academic year, another one for entering weekly marks, one for listing the results in order of merit, and perhaps one for a statistical analysis. Jackson has proposed the following classification for commercial systems

up to 10 000 instructions:	'Small'
10 000 to 100 000 instructions:	'Medium'
over 100 000 instructions:	'Large'

In principle every user program could be written in machine language (like the SNARK) typed into the computer, and run. In practice this would be an impossibly cumbersome and error-prone way of using a machine, and all computers are therefore equipped with *systems* software whose sole function is to provide a better environment for writing, testing, running and storing user programs. Systems programs are usually written by computer manufacturers, and bought together with the machine itself. There is, however, a distinct place for better systems programs written by competent users.

This chapter gives an over-all view of the main types of system program. Subsequent chapters discuss some of these types in greater detail.

13.1 SYMBOLIC ASSEMBLERS

Historically, the first programs were written in machine code. The method worked well for very short programs (up to 40 instructions or so) but rapidly became unusable for anything larger. When writing machine code, the programmer has to allocate addresses to the individual instructions. The address fields of branch instructions cannot be filled in until the allocation is known. This makes it very difficult to make corrections which involve adding or removing instructions, because every change will cause many other instructions in the program to be re-sited, and all the references in branch instructions must be altered accordingly.

Consider a program which cycles indefinitely. For each cycle it reads a value n from the keyboard and displays the sum of the first n numbers $n + (n - 1) + \ldots + 2 + 1$. A first attempt at writing this program is shown below.

```
0    INA  A          ↑ INPUT N TO ACC A
1    STA  A 50
2    ADD  B 50        ↑ ADD ACC TO ACC B
3    SUB  A #1        ↑ TAKE 1 FROM A
4    BNZ  A 1         ↑ JUMP BACK IF ACC A #0
5    OUT  B           ↑ DISPLAY RESULT
6    JMP  0           ↑ JUMP BACK TO START OF PROGRAM
```

A preliminary trace suggests that the program is working correctly. When the program is tried on the machine, however, it gives the following result

```
?        3   ⎫
OUTPUT   6   ⎭   Correct

?        4   ⎫
OUTPUT   16  ⎭   Wrong

?        1   ⎫
OUTPUT   17  ⎭   Wrong
```

The error soon comes to light, and is trivial. We have forgotten to set accumulator B to zero at the beginning of each cycle. The revised version of the program is

```
0    LDA  B #0        ↑ SET ACC B = 0
1    INA  A           ↑ INPUT N TO ACC A
2    STA  A 50
3    ADD  B 50        ↑ ADD ACC A TO ACC B
4    SUB  A #1        ↑ TAKE 1 FROM A
5    BNZ  A 2         ↑ JUMP BACK IF ACC A #0
6    OUT  B           ↑ DISPLAY RESULT
7    JMP  0           ↑ JUMP BACK TO START OF PROGRAM
```

This version now runs correctly, but to fit the new instruction into the program, all the others have been shuffled down by one place. The branch instruction 'BNZ A 2' has had to be altered, even though it was correct in its original context.

As the size of a program increases, so do the difficulty and drudgery of re-allocating addresses after each change. Humans are notoriously unreliable and inaccurate at boring routine tasks, and the size of program is soon reached where each alteration introduces more errors than it cures. The behaviour of the program gets steadily *worse*.

Symbolic assembly overcomes this problem by allowing the programmer to use *names* instead of addresses. The name of an instruction is quite independent of its address, and will stay the same no matter where the instruction is located. In symbolic assembly language, the programs shown above would be written as follows.

```
JACK:   INA  A          JACK:   LDA  B  # 0
JILL:   STA  A  50              INA  A
        ADD  B  50      JILL:   STA  A  50
        SUB  A  # 1             ADD  B  50
        BNZ  A  JILL            SUB  A  # 1
        OUT  B                  BNZ  A  JILL
        JMP  JACK               OUT  B
                                JMP  JACK
```

Here the 'names' are JACK and JILL, but any other names (or distinguishable sequences of characters) would have served equally well. The insertion of a new instruction at the beginning does not involve changing anything later on.

A program written in symbolic assembly language cannot be run directly by a computer. It must first be translated into machine code by a system program called a *symbolic assembler*. The translation process allocates space to each instruction, turns every mnemonic into its corresponding binary pattern, and checks the program for obvious errors such as using the same name for two different instructions. A program must be re-assembled every time it is altered, but the repetitive clerical work can be done quickly and accurately by the computer itself.

The invention of the symbolic assembler was the first major step in simplifying programming. It is quite practical to write large programs in symbolic assembly language, and the method is still used in many commercial computing centres.

13.2 HIGH-LEVEL LANGUAGES

Symbolic assembly has two major disadvantages. First, the programmer has to know the intimate details of the computer he is using such as the order code, the number of accumulators, the store size, and so on. These particulars are totally irrelevant to the problem he is solving, but they nevertheless play a major part in forming the program he eventually produces. Second, a program written for one brand of machine cannot be transferred to another brand, with different internal arrangements; it must be rewritten entirely. Some commercial users have large investments in assembly code programs, and find themselves 'locked in' to obsolete and expensive machines.

These problems are partially solved by the use of high-level languages. A high-level language is a notation for writing algorithms which allows the programmer to express his solution in abstract mathematical terms, without referring to the detailed structure of a machine. Programming in a high-level language is faster, less prone to error, and opens the possibility of moving software from one machine to another.

Programs written in a high-level language cannot be run until they have been converted into machine code. The conversion is done either by a *compiler* or by an *interpreter*, both of which are complex systems programs to be discussed in chapter 14.

There are hundreds of high-level languages. Some are aimed at special problem areas such as commerce, or scientific calculation, or control of mechanical systems. Others claim to be of general-purpose use. There is no agreed way of evaluating the 'goodness' of a language, and the relative merits of the chief contenders are matters of opinion. In practice, nearly all high-level languages share common features which are outlined below. We assume that you are familiar with at least one high-level language (perhaps BASIC or FORTRAN or ALGOL 60 or ALGOL 68 or COBOL or PASCAL or CORAL or . . .), and it is worth noting just how each of the features listed here is provided in the language you know.

(1) *Symbolic names*: Quantities used in calculations, and the storage locations which hold them, are referred to by proper names. In most languages except BASIC, the names can be chosen quite freely, and can serve to remind the programmer of the purpose of the quantity. BASIC names are confined to single letters of the alphabet, optionally followed by single decimal digits. Some typical names are

BASIC: A J K9 X4
Other languages: TEMPERATURE INTEREST X A HEARTRATE

The use of proper names saves the programmer the trouble of assigning locations to his variables, and makes the program more readable.

(2) *Expressions and assignments*: In high-level languages computational sequences are written as expressions, almost in conventional algebraic form. The programmer is freed from the trivial but tedious job of choosing accumulators and storing partial results. New values for variables are written as assignments, indicated by special symbols such as = or :=. Thus, the high-level language statement

$$X = Y + Z - 3$$

is roughly equivalent to the SNARK sequence

LDA	A	50	↑	LOAD Y TO ACC A
ADD	A	51	↑	ADD Z TO ACC A
SUB	A	#3	↑	TAKE 3 FROM ACC A
STA	A	52	↑	STORE NEW VALUE OF X

where store allocations for the variables X, Y and Z have been made arbitrarily.

(3) *Array handling*:   In machine code, the index mode is used to manipulate tables or lists of quantities. In high-level languages, this is formalised as the 'array' facility. Programs which use arrays contain declarations and array references. The declaration gives the name of the array (which can be chosen just like a variable name) and the number and type of its elements. The compiler or interpreter sets aside a group of store cells with consecutive addresses, and allocates this area of the memory to the array.

The most common type of array reference is to a single element. This is normally written as an array name with a subscript, which may be a fixed number or an expression which is worked out every time the reference is used.

Some examples of declarations and array references in two high-level languages are

(BASIC)	(PASCAL)	
DIM X (20)	**var:** a, j;	
	x: **array** [1 .. 20] **of** integer;	(declaration)
A = A + X (J)	a := a + x [j]	(statement: add jth element of x to a)

In machine code (such as used on the SNARK) there are no declarations; the programmer must decide for himself where to locate arrays and other variables. Suppose he has decided on

X: 80 to 99   A: 50   J: 51

then a sequence equivalent to A = A + X (J) (or a := a + x [j]) would be

LDA	A	50	↑	LOAD A TO ACC A
LDA	B	51	↑	LOAD INDEX J TO ACC B
ADD	A	79B	↑	ADD X (J) TO ACC A
STA	A	50	↑	STORE RESULT

(4) *Sequence control*:   The only way of controlling the sequence of events when using machine or assembly code is through branch instructions. This method is primitive and prone to error, and most high-level languages offer improved facilities. The program can test the value of any expression, not merely the sign or zero-ness of an accumulator. There are constructions

for choosing alternative sequences of action depending on the result of a test, and for organising repetition automatically.

Some typical sections with sequence control statements in BASIC and PASCAL are

if x = 6 **then** write ('yes') **else** write ('no');

                                               PASCAL

while $j \langle \rangle k$ **do begin** write $(1/j)$; $j := j + 1$ **end**;

```
FOR J = 1 TO K
    PRINT 1/J                                    BASIC
NEXT J
```

Most high-level languages allow you to attach names to statements and to write unconditional jumps (usually called GOTOs) just as you might write a JMP in assembly code. The practice is now unfashionable, since it is thought to lead to programs which are difficult to read, unreliable and inefficient. Many languages (but not FORTRAN, BASIC or COBOL) allow you to write complete programs without using named statements or GOTOs at all, and this is generally considered to be a better way of programming.

(5)   *Input and output control*:   In most high-level languages complex input and output requirements, which involve many separate values and detailed layout instructions, can be indicated by single statements. The underlying system is often so complicated (particularly in FORTRAN and ALGOL 68) that it may take months to understand. An alternative approach is to provide primitive operations which handle individual characters, and to get the user to program his own input and output functions in terms of these primitives.

(6)   *Program structure*:   Many high-level languages (but not BASIC) offer tools to help with the architecture of large programs. A program can be divided into modules (called procedures, or routines, or paragraphs or sub-programs or subroutines in various languages) which are nearly independent and which interact with one another on well-defined lines. This hierarchic structure, which is the basis of all good engineering design, is essential for the development of all but trivial programs. BASIC's lack in this respect prevents it from even being considered for serious professional use.

(7)   *Error detection*:   All computer languages have strict rules of grammar which govern the construction of programs. The correctness of the grammar in any program can be checked by the compiler or interpreter, and this forms a useful way of catching program errors at an early stage. Unfortunately correct grammar does not guarantee a correct program: there may still be many mistakes which do not emerge until the program is run.

With so many high-level languages, it is sometimes difficult to know which one to use for any application. Often the deciding factors are not technical but depend on tradition, government policy, availability or the programmer's previous background. If an algorithm is well designed, however, the language used for its implementation (so long as it is a high-level language) is only of secondary importance.

13.3 OPERATING SYSTEMS

An operating system is basically a 'layer' of software designed to insulate user programs from the hardware of the machine. It carries out a number of different but interlocking functions, and is therefore usually a large and somewhat unreliable program.

A full discussion of operating systems is given in chapter 16, so here only a brief resume of the most important functions is needed.

(1) *Peripheral control*:   The operating system looks after peripherals and backing store devices on behalf of user programs. This simplifies matters for the programmer (because peripherals often behave in complex ways) but hampers efforts to do anything unusual, such as attaching a new device to an existing computer.

(2) *Provision of multi-access*:   A multi-access computer is one which serves many people at the same time, each one using a console with a keyboard and printer or visual display. The operating system is responsible for sharing the resources, such as the CPU and store, among the users, and protecting them against each other's mistakes. On a well-designed multi-access system each user has the impression that he is the *only* user.

(3) *Job control*:   In general, the running of a 'job' on a computer involves the sequential execution of several distinct programs. For example, a program written in a high-level language must first be translated into machine code, by a compiler. Then the new program must itself be executed.

The job control section of an operating system guides every job through the right sequence of steps, according to a 'job description' submitted by the user.

(4) *File control*:   The operating system controls the backing store, to ensure that every user can store his own information and retrieve it, and that different users cannot interfere with one another's data. The file control system usually involves an 'editor' which allows the filed information to be easily changed.

(5) *Accounting*:   The system keeps track of the resources consumed by each user. This information serves to issue regular bills, or to run a rationing system where the resources are limited.

13.4 THE PROGRAM LIBRARY

Most computers are provided with a 'library' of programs and program modules for common jobs. The library programs can save the user a good deal of time, and they are supposedly written with great care so as to be reliable and efficient. In practice these aims are not always achieved.

The most frequently used library programs are found in the following areas

Commerce: Sorting, merging files.

Mathematics: Various procedures such as solution of simultaneous equations, differential equations, and calculation of common functions.

Operational Research: Critical path analysis, integer programming, etc.

Statistics: Derivation and display of various statistics: averages, means, correlations, and so on.

Graphics: Programs which draw pictures from descriptions supplied by the user.

Linguistics: Programs which construct alphabetic word lists and concordances from literary texts.

14 Translators

This chapter is about compilers and interpreters for high-level languages. This branch of software is very well understood, and research into new and improved languages is now somewhat stifled by the practical need to use established and standardised systems for writing programs. The most widely used languages — COBOL, FORTRAN, BASIC and CORAL — are far from being the best.

In logical order, the first need is for a language to be clearly and rigorously defined. This question is discussed in section 14.1.

Once the rules of a language are established, it is possible to write a compiler or interpreter which processes programs in the language so that they can be run on a computer. The difference is that a compiler translates the complete program into machine code before executing any of it, whereas an interpreter translates and executes each statement as a single unified action. If the statement is inside a loop it will be retranslated many times over.

Compilers and interpreters have many aspects in common. Both of them run in three phases

(1) lexical analysis, where the program is split into a sequence of 'words';
(2) syntactic analysis, where the grammar of the program is checked;
(3) code generation, where the program is turned into a form which can be executed by the computer.

These three phases are described in sections 14.2 to 14.4.

Finally, in section 14.5, the chapter contrasts the properties of compilers and interpreters, and gives circumstances where each type of translator has special advantages over the other.

14.1 LANGUAGE DEFINITION

To be useful for writing algorithms, a programming language must be precisely defined and well understood. The degree of precision and lack of ambiguity must be far better than in a human language, because we often speak of vague ideas, but every step of an algorithm must be well enough defined to allow it to be carried out by a machine.

The description of a language can be considered in two parts — the *grammar* (often called the syntax) and the *meaning* or semantics. The grammar consists of the set of rules which define a 'legal' program, and allow it to be distinguished from any meaningless sequence of characters. For example, you can appeal to the grammatical rules of English to show that the sentence

ALL MEN HAVE THREE NOSES

is grammatically correct, but

SEVENTEEN BLUE HAS GO THRIFT

is not.* Similarly, the grammar of BASIC indicates that

"A = B + C"

is correct, but

"A ⟨ ⟩ = B + −X)2.3.4"

is meaningless.

The grammar of a programming language is usually expressed in a symbolic notation called 'Backus–Naur Form' or 'BNF' for short.

A BNF language definition consists of a collection of formulae. Each formula defines a grammatical unit in terms of simpler units or sequences of them. The notation uses the angle brackets ⟨ and ⟩ to mark the name of the units, ::= to mean 'is defined as', and the vertical bar | to indicate 'or'. Thus the definition

⟨digit⟩ ::= 0 | 1 | 2 | 3 | 4 | 5 | 6 | 7 | 8 | 9

means that a 0, a 1, a 2, . . . , a 9 are all instances of the generic type ⟨digit⟩. Another example is

⟨letter⟩ ::= A|B|C|D|E|F|G|H|I|J|K|L|M|N|O|P|Q|R|S|T|U|V|W|X|Y|Z

Many formulae involve sequences of several units. Thus the majority (not all) of British car registration numbers could be defined as

⟨car number⟩ ::= ⟨letter⟩⟨letter⟩⟨letter⟩⟨digit⟩⟨digit⟩⟨digit⟩⟨letter⟩

This grammar would allow us to recognise HGD652N and UCL908J as valid British ⟨car number⟩s, and to reject 8192GP75.

Some definitions must allow for an indefinite amount of repetition. This can be done with a device called 'recursion', where the element being defined occurs in its own definition. Thus, a ⟨number⟩ can be defined as a sequence of decimal digits of any length from 1 up. This idea is expressed in the formula

⟨number⟩ ::= ⟨digit⟩ | ⟨number⟩⟨digit⟩

---

* That is, not in English. You could always *invent* a language, with its own grammar and semantics, in which the sentence meant something.

which states that

(1) any ⟨digit⟩ is a ⟨number⟩

(2) any ⟨number⟩ *followed by* a ⟨digit⟩ is also a ⟨number⟩.

Given a sequence of symbols and a grammar, you can try to derive a 'recognition tree' which shows exactly how the sequence forms a defined element in the grammar. This process is called *parsing*. For example, the sequence 'GGA 372N' can be parsed with the car grammar to give

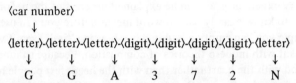

⟨car number⟩
↓
⟨letter⟩-⟨letter⟩-⟨letter⟩-⟨digit⟩-⟨digit⟩-⟨digit⟩-⟨digit⟩·⟨letter⟩
↓ ↓ ↓ ↓ ↓ ↓ ↓
G G A 3 7 2 N

(The downward arrow should be read as 'which is a' and the horizontal dash as 'followed by'.) Similarly, the sequence 471 can be analysed to give

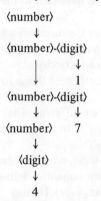

⟨number⟩
↓
⟨number⟩-⟨digit⟩
↓   ↓
↓   1
⟨number⟩-⟨digit⟩
↓   ↓
⟨number⟩ 7
↓
⟨digit⟩
↓
4

Example 14.1
The complete grammar of the SNARK language is given in appendix A. Use it to show that the instruction 'ADD B 45A' is indeed an ⟨item⟩ by forming its parse tree.

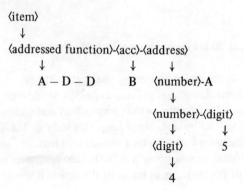

⟨item⟩
↓
⟨addressed function⟩-⟨acc⟩-⟨address⟩
↓   ↓   ↓
A – D – D   B   ⟨number⟩-A
↓
⟨number⟩-⟨digit⟩
↓   ↓
⟨digit⟩ 5
↓
4

The grammars of high-level languages have formulae for expressions, declarations and procedures. The parsing of a purported 'program' can be done automatically, and is normally one of the functions carried out by a translator.

Semantics refers to the *meaning* of a statement which is grammatically correct. Semantics says nothing about any sequence of characters which does not conform to a given grammar; such a sequence is by definition meaningless.

Defining the semantics of a programming language poses a special and difficult problem. In human languages most of the words we use (like 'mouse' and 'house') relate to direct sensory experiences, or can be explained in terms of them. It is hardly ever necessary to know exactly what a word means before you can use it effectively; for example you can empty a building by shouting 'fire!' even if you are not fully conversant with modern theories of combustion. Because so much language is understood with the heart rather than with the head, few people have had much experience in explaining exactly what they mean. (Contrast this with grammar, which has been widely taught for centuries.)

In most computer applications the meaning of the data is irrelevant to the machine. In a mailing list, for example, the titles, MR, MRS, MISS, MS, DR, PROF, SIR, LADY and LORD, which precede the names of the members are just treated as sequences of characters. The machine does not need to be told that they mostly indicate gender and would be arranged in a hierarchy of 'respectability'. (This is just as well, since this word means different things to different people!)

In the translation and execution of a program, matters are different. The various statements must be 'understood' by the machine if it is to carry out the intentions of the programmer.

Definitions of meaning can be written down in various ways, none of them completely satisfactory. Most computer languages have their semantics defined by careful descriptions in English (or some other natural language). Human speech is so imprecise an instrument that this always leads to ambiguities: system designers interpret the definition in different ways. A good example in BASIC is given by the sequence

```
10    FOR J = 1 TO 0 STEP 1
20    PRINT J
30    NEXT J
```

where on some systems statement 20 is executed once, but on others it is skipped entirely.

Such inconsistencies are one of the major barriers to the portability of programs between different systems. Languages defined in English tend to go through a series of 'revisions' made by working parties who collect and remove the ambiguities and inconsistencies one by one. Some languages such as ALGOL 60 are mature enough for ambiguity no longer to be a serious problem.

One group of languages is defined by describing a hypothetical computer and then explaining each construct of the language in terms of the action it would cause this computer to take. This method is used, very loosely, to define the semantics of SNARK. The chief advantage of the method is that it can help to simplify the construction of a translator.

ALGOL 68 is unusual in that its semantics are defined in mathematical terms as well as its syntax. Unfortunately the notation used is so complex that not many programmers have time to learn it; instead they rely on descriptions written in English, with all their faults and inconsistencies.

14.2 LEXICAL ANALYSIS

In its original form a program is made up of a stream of characters, most of which have no meaning when considered in isolation. To be understood they need to be combined into 'words'. The program also includes numerous subjective features such as its use of layout, commentary, and the choice of names, all of which are strictly irrelevant to the meaning and function of the program as a whole, although they can be invaluable to the human reader.

Programs contain four kinds of word, each with its own rules of formation.

(1)   Symbols of constant meaning, including mathematical symbols, punctuation marks, brackets, and certain reserved words such as IF, THEN, GOTO, FOR, and so on. Words in this category may consist of one or several characters.
(2)   Numbers, such as 0 or 777 or 4.12345.
(3)   Strings, or sequences of characters in quote marks.
(4)   Names invented by the programmer and used for variables, arrays and so on.

The first phase of the translation process is called *lexical analysis*. The lexical analyser takes a raw stream of characters, and transforms it into a form more suitable for the next stage of translation. In this new form, the program is arranged as three tables.

(1)   An array giving all the different numbers in the program (as internal values, not sequences of characters).
(2)   An array which gives all the different strings.
(3)   A table which holds a coded version of each word in the program. Each coded word is called a 'token', and is represented by a *pair* of integers. The first integer in each token has the value 1, 2, 3 or 4, and indicates the *kind* of word. The second integer is used to distinguish different tokens of the same kind. A typical coding scheme is as follows

Type a: Symbols of constant meaning. Here the type number is 1, and the identity of the symbol is given by a predetermined code, which might be

Symbol	+	−	*	/	=	⟨	⟩	(	)	,	;	:	.	:=
Code	1	2	3	4	5	6	7	8	9	10	11	12	13	14

Symbol	program	var	begin	end	for	to	do	if	then	else
Code	15	16	17	18	19	20	21	22	23	24

Symbol	or	integer	real	writeln	sin	cos	sqrt	read
Code	25	26	27	28	29	30	31	32

(This example assumes that the source program is written in PASCAL, but you don't need to know this language to understand the discussion).

Type b: Numbers. Here the type number is 2. The actual value is stored in the number table, and the token contains a *pointer* to the element at which the value is recorded. This allows the token to be constructed entirely of integers, even when the number itself is one with a decimal point.

Type c: Strings. The type number is 3, and the token contains a pointer to the place in the string table where the characters are actually stored.

Type d: Names. The type is 4, and the identity is given as '1' for the first name to occur in the program, '2' for the second, and so on.

As an example, consider the PASCAL program

```
program average;
var   n , c : integer;              {n is the number of expected values, all}
      x , y : real;                 { of which must exceed 3.5 and be less}
begin  read (n); x := 0;            {than 49.25}
       for c := 1 to n do
       begin  read (y); if y ⟨ 3.5 or y ⟩ 49.25
              then  writeln (y, 'IS OUT OF RANGE')
              else x := x + y
       end;
       writeln ('AVERAGE = ' , x/n)
end.
```

The lexical analyser would convert this program into three tables, as follows

NUMBER TABLE	
Location	Value
1	0
2	1
3	3.5
4	49.25

STRING TABLE	
Location	Value
1	IS OUT OF RANGE
2	AVERAGE =

Loc.	Values	(meaning)
TOKEN TABLE		
1	1,15	**program**
2	4,1	average
3	1,11	;
4	1,16	**var**
5	4,2	n
6	1,10	,
7	4,3	c
8	1,12	:
9	1,26	integer
10	1,11	;
11	4,4	x
12	1,10	,
13	4,5	y
14	1,12	:
15	1,27	real
16	1,11	;
17	1,17	**begin**
18	1,32	read
19	1,8	(
20	4,2	n
21	1,9	)
22	1,11	;
23	4,4	x
24	1,14	:=
25	2,1	0
26	1,11	;
27	1,19	**for**
28	4,3	c
29	1,14	:=
30	2,2	1
31	1,20	**to**
32	4,2	n
33	1,21	**do**
34	1,17	**begin**
35	1,32	read
36	1,8	(

Loc.	Values	(meaning)
TOKEN TABLE (continued)		
37	4,5	y
38	1,9	)
39	1,11	;
40	1,22	**if**
41	4,5	y
42	1,6	⟨
43	2,3	3.5
44	1,25	**or**
45	4,5	y
46	1,7	⟩
47	2,4	49.25
48	1,23	**then**
49	1,28	writeln
50	1,8	(
51	4,5	y
52	1,10	,
53	3,1	'IS OUT OF RANGE'
54	1,9	)
55	1,24	**else**
56	4,4	x
57	1,14	:=
58	4,4	x
59	1,1	+
60	4,5	y
61	1,18	**end**
62	1,11	;
63	1,28	writeln
64	1,8	(
65	3,2	'AVERAGE = '
66	1,10	,
67	4,4	x
68	1,4	/
69	4,2	n
70	1,9	)
71	1,18	**end**
72	1,13	.

The meaning of the program is still present in these tables. For example, the token table shows that the first 'word' in the program is a word of constant meaning, with code number 15. In the standard code this stands for *program*. Likewise the 43rd word is a number, with its value stored at cell 3 of the number table. Word 23 is a user name, the fourth one to be mentioned in the program. The actual name cannot be retrieved from the table (for the 'meaning' column is not actually present in the translator but is only included as a guide to the reader), but the sense of the program is in no way affected. All that matters is that the name should be identified correctly wherever it occurs.

The process of lexical analysis has removed all the unnecessary information about layout, comments, and names chosen by the user. To illustrate this point, consider the program shown below. It will give precisely the same set of tables as the one we have discussed, for it is essentially the same program.

> **program** history; **var** antony, cleopatra: integer;
> caesar, octavius: real; **begin** read (antony); caesar := 0;
> **for** cleopatra := 1 **to** antony **do begin** read (octavius);
> **if** octavius ⟨ 3.5 **or** octavius ⟩ 49.25 **then**
> writeln (octavius, 'IS OUT OF RANGE') **else** caesar := caesar + octavius
> **end** ; writeln ('AVERAGE = ', caesar / antony) **end**.

To recognise user names, the lexical analyser has to maintain a table where the names are recorded as character strings. Whenever the analyser recognises a sequence of characters as forming a name, it attempts to look it up in this table. If it is not found the analyser deduces that it must be a new name, and enters it into the table beneath all the others. It then constructs a token which gives the identity of the name in terms of its position in the name table. The name tables for the two programs we have just discussed would be

loc	value
1	average
2	n
3	c
4	x
5	y

loc	value
1	history
2	antony
3	cleopatra
4	caesar
5	octavius

The name table is private to the lexical analyser, and is not passed on to the next stage of translation. When the lexical analyser has finished its job the name table can be thrown away.

14.3 SYNTACTIC ANALYSIS

The main task of the syntax analyser is to check that the program being translated conforms to the rules of grammar. There are many different algorithms for this purpose, all of which are based on the formulae of the BNF language definition or on some transformation of them. One useful and simple method relies on a 'state-symbol' table.

Suppose that you are scanning a program, word by word, to check its grammar. Imagine that you have already examined a certain number of words, and found them to be grammatically correct. Your attention is focused on the next word in sequence, as shown below

| words already scanned | word being examined | rest of program |

The correctness of the next word depends on its *context*, which is determined by the words already scanned. For example a '+' would be acceptable if it followed a number in an expression, but not if it came directly after another '+'. In general every possible context defines a subset of all possible words, such that only a member of this subset are acceptable as the next word.

Once the next word has been found correct, then it joins the words already accepted and defines a new context for the word which follows.

In practice it would be impossible to list all the acceptable words for even one context, let alone all possible contexts. Fortunately these hypothetical lists can be replaced by a set of rules.

First, words can be arranged in families or groups, where all the members of the group behave in the same grammatical way. For example, all numbers could form one group, and all names another. These groups are somewhat confusingly called 'symbols'.

Second, the various contexts can also be arranged in groups, or 'states' which have the same properties. A typical state might represent the context reached whenever the '=' in an assignment statement has just been accepted.

The grammar of a language leads to a finite number of symbols and states.

The state-symbol table is a two-dimensional array of cells. The columns are numbered 1, 2, 3 . . . and each one of them corresponds to a different state. By convention, state 1 is the context which applies when the *first* word of the program is being examined.

The rows of the table are labelled with the various symbols. The table therefore comprises one cell for each combination of state and symbol.

The contents of each cell depend on the grammar of the language. If the symbol is an acceptable one in the current state, the cell contains a tick and the number of the state to be used in checking the next symbol, or if this symbol completes the sequence correctly, a '0'. Otherwise the cell is left blank.

To illustrate the use of the state-symbol table, consider the grammar of declarations in PASCAL (this example is greatly simplified and ignores many features of actual declarations in this language). For our purposes, we assume that a declaration is made up of a sequence of one or more names (separated by commas if necessary), followed by a colon and a *type*.

The type may indicate a scalar variable, in which case it is simply one of the *mode* words integer, real boolean or char. Alternatively the type can specify an array, and takes the more complicated form

    array [⟨lower bound⟩ . . ⟨upper bound⟩] **of** ⟨mode word⟩

where **array** and **of** are system words, ⟨lower bound⟩ and ⟨upper bound⟩ are numbers, and the ⟨mode word⟩ is one of integer, real, boolean or char. Every declaration ends with a semicolon.

To illustrate this description, here are some possible declarations

    joe : real ;
    susan, jane, mary : integer;
    henry, george, james, alexander : **array** [1 . . 20] **of** boolean ;

The state-symbol table which corresponds to this definition is shown below.

	State											
Symbol	1	2	3	4	5	6	7	8	9	10	11	12
name	√2											
,		√1										
:		√3										
array			√5									
[					√6							
number						√7			√10			
.							√8	√9				
]										√11		
of											√12	
mode word			√4									√4
;				√0								

The table uses eleven symbols, which between them cover all possible words in this context. Most of the groups (like , **array** and]) have only one member.

The table shows that in state 1, which corresponds to the beginning of a declaration, the only acceptable word is a name. If a name is found the next state is 2.

State 2 follows a name. There is some choice of possible symbols : thus a comma signifies that another name is expected and a colon indicates that a type follows immediately.

State 3 is the beginning of a type. It can either be a mode word or the system word **array**.

The scanning of any sequence with a state-symbol table can be described by a simple flow chart (figure 14.1).

This process is easily automated, because the lexical analyser has already split the source program into words.

The state-symbol table as we have described it indicates if a program is grammatically correct, but stops as soon as the first error is detected. In practice it is useful to have the syntactic analyser go on and find as many errors as it can. To do so it must first re-establish a context, and this will involve special actions after a mistake such as searching for a specific symbol like a semicolon.

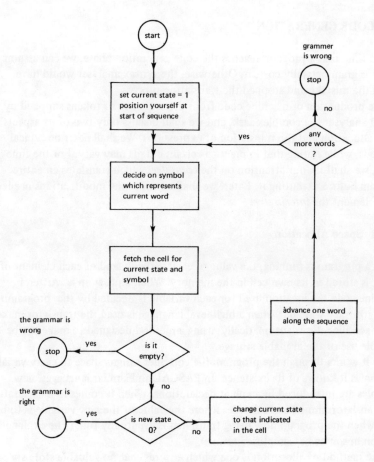

Figure 14.1

Example 14.2

Using the state-symbol table on p. 156, check the sequences

      kate, john : **array** [5 . . 57] **of** real;

and   paul : **array** : [1:10] **of** integer;

for correct grammar. Write down the cells you visit as you check, as (state/symbol)

(a)   (1/name), (2/,), (1/name), (2/:), (3/**array**), (5/[), (6/number), (7/.), (8/.),
       (9/number), (10/]), (11/**of**), (12/mode word), (4/;). This cell ends the
       process, and finds the first sequence correct.

(b)   (1/name), (2/:), (3/**array**), (5/:). This cell is blank, so the second sequence
       is wrong.

14.4 CODE GENERATION

By the time that a program reaches the code generation phase, we can assume that it is grammatically correct. Otherwise, the syntax analyser would have found the mistake and stopped the translation process.

The production of machine code from the sequence of tokens supplied by the lexical analyser is a complex task, and we shall discuss only two of its aspects : space allocation and the translation of expressions. We shall describe typical methods, while noting that in practice certain details may vary. For the time being, we shall fix our attention on the *compiler*, which translates an entire program before executing it. Later, we shall consider the modifications needed to implement the *interpreter*.

14.4.1 Space Allocation

When a program is running, the value of each variable, and of each element of an array, is stored in its own cell in the memory. When a program is written in machine code the location used for each variable is decided by the programmer in an arbitrary way, but when a high-level language is used the translator makes the space allocations automatically, using a method designed to make the best possible use of the available storage.

As it works through the program, the compiler assigns space to every variable as soon as it knows of its existence. In PASCAL and similar languages, new variables are introduced by explicit declarations. When it comes to a declaration, the translator immediately decides *where* the value of the new variable is to be kept when the program now being translated is eventually run. (The explanation is given in somewhat simplified terms.)

The method of allocation is one which ensures that no valuable store space is wasted. It is assumed that the instructions will start from word 0 and work up, as the variables are assigned space at the top of the store downwards thus

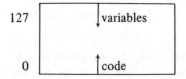

To allocate space correctly, the code generator maintains a table which gives the properties of each variable name, and the space allocated to it. It also remembers the next free location address available.

Consider a PASCAL program which starts with the following declaration

   a, *b*: integer;
   x: **array** [1 . . 10] **of** integer;   (this declares an array of 10 elements)
   y: integer;

and suppose that the computer has 128 store locations numbered 0 to 127. The variables will be allocated as follows: *a* to 127; *b* to 126; *x* to the block 116 to 125; *y* to 115. At the end of this process the table will say

Variable name	Type	Address
1	integer	127
2	integer	126
3	**array** [1 . . 10] **of** integer	116
4	integer	115

$$\boxed{114}$$

Next free address

(Remember that the lexical analyser will have re-named the variables 1, 2, 3, and 4.)

If, later, another integer is declared it will be given address 114 and the next free address will be set to 113.

Some languages, notably FORTRAN and BASIC , permit variables to be used without declarations. For these languages the compiler must be programmed to keep a watch for names used for the first time, and go through the space allocation process whenever it finds one.

Finally, every compiler must continually check that space has not been allocated for more than one purpose. As the translation proceeds, the code area and the 'variable' area grow from opposite ends of the store. If they should meet, the program is too big for the machine and cannot be run.

14.4.2 The Translation of Expressions

The aim of expression translation is to convert algebraic expressions like

$a + b * (c - d)/f$

into sequences of code which work out their values. Since machine code is remote from algebraic notation, this is a process which requires several stages.

The first problem is that in the conventional algebraic notation the various operations such as addition and multiplication are not written in the same order as they are executed. In our example, the order of evaluation is first the −, then the *, then the /, and finally the +.

In general, the order of evaluation is governed by the rule of *precedences*. Every arithmetical operator has its own numerical precedence, and in the absence of brackets the operators with higher precedence are used *first*. When precedences are the same, the order is from left to right. Brackets raise the precedence of every operator inside them.

These rules lead to an order of evaluation which is the same as the conventional one used by mathematicians. If we take the following precedence values

    +, − : 1
    *, / : 2
    ( ) : raise precedence of operators inside them by 2

we can assign absolute precedences to each of the operators in our example. (Precedence of − is 3: 1 of its own plus 2 for being inside a pair of

$a +_1 b *_2 (c -_3 d) /_2 f$

The order of precedence is now correctly indicated. The brackets are no longer necessary (because they have already been used in assigning a precedence to the −) and can be discarded

$a +_1 b *_2 c -_3 d /_2 f$

Once the absolute precedences of the operators have been worked out, the expression can be re-arranged so that the order of the operators is the same as the order of evaluation. We need a new notation, called reverse Polish (or 'RP') after the nationality of its inventor Lukacziewicz. In RP, the operator is placed not between its operands, but following them. Thus '$a + b$' becomes '$ab+$' in RP, and $x + y * z$ becomes $xyz*+$.

Expressions in RP are evaluated strictly from left to right. The expression is scanned and the values of variables are 'remembered' until an operator is encountered. The operator is then applied to the last *two* values, and replaces them by a single result, which may be used as a value for operators still to come.

Using this rule, '$ab+$' is worked out as the sum of a and b. '$xyz*+$' is scanned until the * is met. This is applied to y and z, giving a single product. Then + is applied to x and the product of y and z.

We can clarify the order of evaluation by using a horizontal bar to link each operator with its operands, thus

$\overline{a\ \ b\ \ +}$ or $x\ \overline{\overline{y\ \ z\ \ *}\ \ +}$

Example 14.3
Use the bar notation to clarify the following RP expression

$a\ b\ c + d\ e - * /$

We add the bars in the following order

$a\ \overline{b\ c} + d\ e - * /$

$a\ \overline{b\ c} + \overline{d\ e} - * /$

$a\ \overline{\overline{b\ c} + \overline{d\ e}} - * /$

$\overline{a\ \overline{\overline{b\ c} + \overline{d\ e}} - *} /$

Example 14.4
Convert the RP expression of example 14.3 into conventional notation.

We note that '*xy*−' means '*x* − *y*', and '*xy*/' means '*x*/*y*'. By going through the evaluation symbolically we find

$$b + c$$
$$(b + c)\,(d - e)$$
$$(b + c) * (d - e)$$
$$\frac{a}{(b + c) * (d - e)}$$

The conversion of conventional notation in to RP is best done by Dijkstra's algorithm.

(1)   Imagine that the elements of the expression are trucks arranged on the right-hand branch of a railway network as shown below.

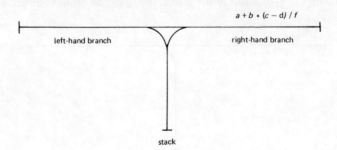

(2)   Attach absolute precedences to all the operators, and discard the brackets.

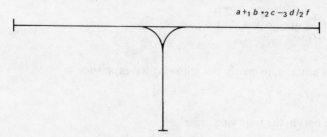

$$a +_1 b *_2 c -_3 d /_2 f$$

(3)   Move the elements over to the left-hand branch, one at a time. If the element is a value, move it straight across. If it is an operator, move it down into the siding. The fundamental rule is that the precedences of operators in the siding must be in *increasing* order (working from the buffers), and if necessary any operators already in the siding which would cause this rule to be violated must be moved out to the left-hand branch first.

(4)   When the right-hand branch is empty, the siding is also emptied out to the left-hand branch. The resulting train is in RP.

In our example, the application of these rules is straightforward until the / is reached. At this stage the position is as follows

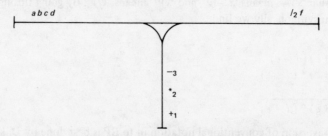

At present, the operators in the siding have increasing precedences, but if the $/_2$ were brought down this would no longer be true. Following the algorithm the siding is emptied out, sending the − and the * up to the left-hand side. As the operators move up, they lose their precedences which are no longer needed

When only the $+_1$ remains in the siding, the $/_2$ can be brought down. This gives

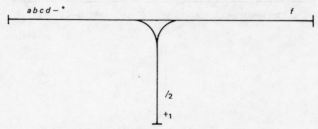

Finally, the *f* is moved across and the siding emptied out. This gives

$a\ b\ c\ d - * f / +$

which is the correct form of the expression in RP.

Example 14.5
Convert the following expression into RP

$$((a + b) * (d + e - c)) * (a - b) / (c + d)$$

Dijkstra's algorithm gives

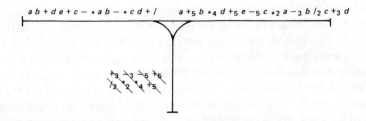

Note the effect that nested brackets have on absolute precedences.

Once an expression has been converted to RP, it can be evaluated directly from left to right by using a 'stack'. This is an array of registers, with the rule that new values can only be added at the top. When a value is transferred to the stack, it does not replace previous values, which are still 'concealed' underneath.

The elements in a RP expression can be interpreted as instructions for a computer with a stack. Every operand in the expression is a command to put the corresponding value on to the stack, and every operator instructs the machine to do the appropriate arithmetic on the two top elements of the stack, replacing them by the result. When the end of the expression is reached the stack will be left with just one value, which is the required result.

Consider the expression $a * b + c$, for which the RP equivalent is $ab*c+$. The evaluation would go like this

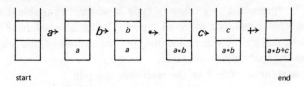

Initially the stack is empty.

a Puts the value of *a* into the bottom of the stack.
b Puts the value of *b* into the stack, 'over' that of *a*.

*   The top two values (*b* and *a*) are multiplied, leaving a single number (*a*b*) in the stack.

c   Puts the value of *c* into the stack, 'over' the value already there.

\+   The top two numbers are added, leaving the result (*a*b+c*) in the stack.

To work correctly, the operator − must be interpreted as (second top element *minus* top element), and / must be taken as (second top element *divided by* top element). This rule sometimes seems contrary to one's intuition.

In our example, we only used two places in the stack. In practice a stack with ten elements or so is enough for any normal expression.

Some computers are built with a ready-made stack mechanism, and the conversion of RP expressions into sequences of machine code is extremely straightforward. Unfortunately many machines do not have this facility, but, like SNARK, are obliged to evaluate expressions using one or two accumulators.

Where there is no true stack, expressions can still be worked out by 'simulating' a stack, or making the machine behave as if it had a stack after all. This is done by designating an area of store to represent the stack, and keeping a special variable, called a *stack pointer*, which keeps count of the number of values in the stack at any time. We arrange that this pointer be *incremented* every time a new value is moved to the stack, and *decremented* for every arithmetic operation which uses two values to give one result. The stack pointer is kept in an accumulator, where it also serves to help us refer to the top of the stack by index modification.

In our example, we shall assume a machine identical with the SNARK except for two new instructions

MUL   which *multiplies* the selected accumulator by the operand
DIV   which *divides* the selected accumulator by the operand.

We begin by choosing an area of store to represent the stack. We take cells 90 to 100, which is a completely arbitrary decision. We also decide to use accumulator *B* to hold the stack pointer. We set ACC *B* to 0 at the beginning of every expression.

We can now lay down simple fixed rules for translating RP expressions into machine code.

Operands occur in two varieties: constants and variables. A constant is a number, and is represented by a token of type 2, whereas a variable is a user-defined name represented by a token of type 4. The variable will have been allocated a store cell by the space allocator, and the address of this cell will be available from the space allocation table.

To put a constant of value *k* on the stack, we compile

```
LDA   A   #k        ↑ GET K INTO ACC A
STA   A   90B       ↑ STORE IN TOP OF STACK
ADD   B   #1        ↑ INCREMENT STACK POINTER
```

Similarly, to load a variable which has been allocated cell q, we put

```
LDA   A   q        ↑ GET VALUE FROM CELL Q
STA   A   90B      ↑ STORE IN TOP OF STACK
ADD   B   #1       ↑ INCREMENT STACK POINTER
```

The four arithmetic operations can also be translated by fixed sequences of code, thus

```
SUB   B   #1              SUB   B   #1
LDA   A   89B             LDA   A   89B
ADD   A   90B             SUB   A   90B
STA   A   89B             STA   A   89B

       (+)                       (−)

SUB   B   #1              SUB   B   #1
LDA   A   89B             LDA   A   89B
MUL   A   90B             DIV   A   90B
STA   A   89B             STA   A   89B

       (*)                       (/)
```

The index-modified addresses 89 and 90 have been chosen so that the operations are always done on the top two elements of the stack wherever it may be.

To give a full example, consider the evaluation of the expression $10 * x + y$. We suppose that the variables x and y have been allocated cells 122 and 117 respectively.

The RP equivalent of the expression is $10x*y+$, and the corresponding code is

```
LDA   B   #0       ↑ INITIALISE STACK POINTER
LDA   A   #10      ↑ LOAD CONSTANT 10
STA   A   90B
ADD   B   #1
LDA   A   122      ↑ LOAD VALUE OF X
STA   A   90B
ADD   B   #1
SUB   B   #1       ↑ MULTIPLY
LDA   A   89B
MUL   A   90B
STA   A   89B
LDA   A   117      ↑ LOAD VALUE OF Y
STA   A   90B
ADD   B   #1
SUB   B   #1       ↑ ADD
LDA   A   89B
ADD   A   90B
STA   A   89B
```

If you work carefully through these instructions, you will see that they do genuinely leave the value of the expression in cell 90, the lowest cell of the stack. In summary, we have presented a completely mechanical way of translating an expression in conventional algebraic form into a sequence of instructions to evaluate that expression.

However, it is worth having another look at the sequence. It is very long for what it does; in this case, the same result could have been achieved by the shorter sequence

```
LDA   A   122
MUL   A   #10
ADD   A   117
STA   A   90
```

In practice, a compiler will often attempt to improve or 'optimise' the code it generates. The best compiler can produce code which is nearly as good as that written by a skilled human programmer. Unfortunately we do not have the space to describe any of the methods of optimisation.

14.5 COMPILERS AND INTERPRETERS

When a source program is being handled by a compiler, it passes through two distinct phases

(1)   it is first translated in its entirety into a machine code program;
(2)   this program is then executed.

If an interpreter is used, the two stages are closely interwoven. As the interpreter translates each statement, it immediately executes it, and discards the machine code version.

At first sight, the compiler would seem to have considerable disadvantages.

(1)   The translation of a statement is usually much more laborious than its subsequent execution, so the interpreter is significantly slower than the compiler. This is most in evidence when the source program has loops which are repeated a large number of times, because the interpreter has to translate the statements in the loop every time round.
(2)   The interpreter program has to be present in the store *at the same time* as the program being executed. If the store capacity is limited this puts severe restrictions on the size of program which can be run.

The arguments, however, are not all on one side. The interpreter is a simpler and less expensive program than a compiler (for it does not need to optimise its code), and it offers a much more 'friendly' interface to the programmer. It is easier to make changes in programs because the interpreter does not need to retranslate the whole program after every change. Furthermore all the tables produced by the lexical analyser and code generator phases are present when the program is being run, and this allows the user to stop his program and enquire about the present values of his variables, referring to them by his own names. This facility would not be impossible with a compiler, but would be an expensive 'extra'.

Interpreters are usually run on 'interactive' systems, where the user has direct contact with the computer through a terminal, but the advantages described here have no direct relation to interaction, which is often used for running compiler-based systems as well.

In summary, the compiler and the interpreter form useful alternatives to one another. Conditions favouring each of them are set out below.

Use a *compiler* when:	Use an *interpreter* when:
The program you are writing will be run many times	The program you are writing will be used only once or twice
You have plenty of time to develop and debug it	You wish to get the program running as quickly as possible
You haven't got an interpreter	You haven't got a compiler

15 The History of Computers

When asked why their subject is important, historians often say that a study of the past helps to explain many strange and unaccountable aspects of the present. This is certainly true of the history of computing. This chapter is placed here, rather than the customary place at the beginning of the book, because so much of the development of computing is tied up with various technical advances. Computer history could not be well understood by a reader who had never encountered gates or high-level languages.

The ancestry of the computer can be traced back to the clock-maker's art, which emerged in the fifteenth and sixteenth centuries. The clock-builders invented the principles on which all mechanical devices are built, and laid the foundation of our mechanistic civilisation. It is only recently that some mechanical devices have begun to be replaced by electronics.

By the end of the eighteenth century, mechanisms of various types were already in widespread use. Two particular types are of special interest to us: calculators and automata.

Blaise Pascal (1623–62) was a philosopher only in his spare time. By profession he was a collector of taxes, and to help with this task he invented a table-top calculator based on gear-wheels and ratchets. Pascal's machine could only add and subtract, but some 50 years later Leibnitz made the essential modification which allowed multiplication and division as well. Calculators based closely on Leibnitz's model were built and used for hundreds of years, until they were suddenly and completely superseded by electronic calculators in the 1970s.

An automaton is a machine which carries out some predetermined and often complex sequence of actions. Machines of this kind were first built in the eighteenth century. There was a proliferation of musical boxes and barrel organs (some 'programmed' by Mozart), and several engineers specialised in building and exhibiting dolls with life-like characteristics. Among the best known are a flute-player, a chess player (although this machine is rumoured to have had a midget chess master inside it) and a mechanical duck which reputedly mimicked all the actions of its natural counterpart with complete accuracy.

Although the early automata were mainly meant for entertainment, there was a notable exception. The Jacquard loom was capable of weaving complex patterns and tapestries. Its automatic action was controlled by a long chain of punched cards, each of which specified the lie of one thread in the material.

The basic principle of the computer was invented by Babbage (1791–1871) who combined mechanical arithmetic with automatic control by a sequence of stored commands. Babbage was a mathematician and engineer, who had a lifelong interest in mechanical computation. With government help, he tried to build an 'analytical engine' which would have been the first true computer. He failed because the standards of engineering in the nineteenth century were not high enough to make the large number of identical components needed with sufficient precision.

After Babbage's death little happened until the early 1940s. A few sequenced calculating machines were built based on electromagnetic relays, but they hardly count as new developments because they were *less* versatile than Babbage's design.

The practical development of computers was triggered by the Second World War (1939–45). At least three workers or groups developed computer-like devices independently, and it is difficult to ascribe precedence to any one of them.

(1)   In Nazi Germany Konrad Zuse developed a machine which ran in binary, and used a drum store. Fortunately its potential was not recognised by the authorities.

(2)   In the United States, Eckert and Mauchly designed and built the ENIAC, a machine intended to make ballistic calculations for the army. This computer was completed in 1946 and used for several years.

(3)   In the United Kingdom, the war-time government soon realised the supreme importance of 'military intelligence' if the country was to survive the attacks of the strong forces at Germany's disposal. One of its most successful projects was the 'Colossus' series of machines, which were successful in decyphering the coded messages used by the Germans.

The Colossus project was so secret that only recently has its existence become known publicly, and even now some of the details are still classified. It is widely accepted that the ability to read the enemy's signals was a key factor in the eventual outcome of the war. For example, Rommel was defeated in North Africa because few of the supplies despatched in great secrecy from Sicily ever reached him: the Allied bombers knew exactly where and when to lie in wait and sink the German convoys.

The war-time machines were dedicated to particular military purposes, and their programs could not easily be changed. Soon after the war ended several general-purpose computers were constructed. The arrangement of store, arithmetic unit and control in all these machines followed the 'Von Neumann' configuration, named after the American mathematician who first described it. The machines had all the essential features of any modern computer, including the ability to execute any program. The first machines to run successfully were in the United Kingdom, and their designers were

Mark I   (Kilburn and Williams, Manchester University)
EDSAC I   (Wilkes, Cambridge University)
Pilot ACE   (Turing, National Physical Laboratory)

These early machines were designed for 'scientific' calculation, and produced some useful results, mainly in crystallography (the science of the structure of crystals) and in mathematics. However, their potential in commerce was soon recognised, and the first machine intended for business processing was sold by UNIVAC in 1951. IBM (which previously had concentrated on typewriters and office machinery) began to take an interest in computers at about this time.

All these early computers were based on thermionic valves like those still to be seen in some television sets and hi-fi amplifiers. Each logic gate was constructed with a valve and about twelve other components, soldered together by hand and mounted on a metal 'chassis'. The machines were consequently huge in physical size, and dissipated hundreds of kilowatts of heat which had to be removed by special cooling plant. The machines were also grossly unreliable; the valves were always failing like light-bulbs, and among the several hundred thousand hand-soldered joints there were inevitably some which gave intermittent trouble.

Using an early computer was a frustrating experience: the machine would often be out of order, and when it was apparently working, it was difficult to decide whether an unexpected result was due to a program error or a momentary breakdown. This led to constant and unproductive tension between the programmers and the maintenance engineers, each of whom blamed the other for the machine's faults. In spite of these difficulties, many present-day computer techniques originated on the early valve machines. Symbolic assemblers, high-level languages and program libraries can all be traced back to this era.

A major development which took place in the late 1950s was the application of the transistor to computing. The transistor had been invented in 1948 at the Bell Telephone Company Laboratories, and had undergone continuous refinement. After 10 years it reached the stage where it could replace the valve, while being 1000 times smaller, cheaper and far less prone to frequent random failure. Transistors were so obviously suited to computers that they quickly replaced valves entirely. Machines of this new, 'second' generation were more compact than the old, and somewhat less expensive, but above all they were incomparably more reliable. The computer ceased to be an interesting and temperamental scientific curiosity and became a usable tool in science, commerce and engineering design. The manufacture of computers grew into a sizeable industry.

The use of a computer was still a frustrating matter, but now for a different reason. On the early machines the users had been allowed to operate the control panel themselves, and could load, modify and run their own programs. When the demand for use began to grow this method was seen as inefficient, because users would sometimes fumble with the unfamiliar machinery or pause to think while the expensive computer lay idle. The computer management was forced to ban direct user access, and to employ teams of professional operators who would do nothing but run programs written by other people. The outcome was the imposition of an opaque layer of bureaucracy between the user and his machine. There was a general failure of communication between programmers and operating staff, and a rigid imposition of fixed and often inadequate procedures. No one had yet realised that programmers' time is a valuable and expensive resource, and users often had to wait a week to get the results of a single computer run.

In some enlightened places the management encouraged the use of 'batch monitors' — primitive operating systems which looked after the running of the machine and gave priority to programs being developed or tested. This eased problems considerably but still kept users distant from the machine. It must be remembered that the barriers to providing direct access were not technical but economic: with computers costing £100 000 or more no organisation could afford to give each user his own machine.

As the hardware of machines improved over the years, it was closely followed by the software. The first computers were all programmed in machine code, a method which was only satisfactory if the user was a skilled and strongly motivated scientist or engineer. It was soon realised that to extend the advantages of computing more widely a better method of programming was urgently needed. IBM, which had just entered the field, had the corporate wisdom to establish a working party to solve this problem. In 1956, after a gestation period of some 15 months, the party published a description of FORTRAN, a primitive high-level language, A little later IBM supplied the first FORTRAN compiler to its users, having invested 100 man-years in its production.

By modern standards FORTRAN is clumsy, illogical and archaic. In its own time it was a striking innovation, and its introduction was a major advance in computer science. After 20 years FORTRAN is still the most widely used language for science and engineering, and all attempts to replace it by a better system have failed.

FORTRAN was never designed to handle large volumes of non-numeric data, such as arise in many commercial computer applications. In 1960 a new language called COBOL was introduced to handle problems in this area. Like FORTRAN, COBOL has won itself a permanent place in computing. It is probable that adherence to two such ancient languages is restricting the development of the subject; this is a price which must be paid for standardising too early.

Until the mid 1960s, computer users were forced to run their programs remotely, by giving written instructions to operators. Then it was realised that individual access could, after all, be organised if one machine were made to look after the needs of many users at the same time. In such a system each user had his own terminal, and the computer switched itself rapidly between the various users, so that each one had the impression of being the only person using the machine.

The implementation of this idea, called 'multi-access', turned out to be extraordinarily complex and led to the vast operating systems used on many computers today. Techniques of supporting large numbers of terminals by a single computer are still not fully understood, and may never be worked out since the whole scheme is being overtaken by other developments.

While these ideas were being explored, semiconductor technology was also progressing fast. In the late 1960s the first integrated circuits were introduced. In these devices discrete components such as transistors and resistors are replaced by patterns etched on to the surface of a slice or 'chip' of silicon. The manufacturing process is a complex one but has close affinities with printing; the initial design tends to be expensive and the subsequent production of each unit is very cheap.

This development led to a further drop in the size and cost of computers, and an increase in reliability. At first, only a few dozen components could be put on one chip, but the number increased steadily with improving production methods and today (1980) the limit is about 100 000. This is enough for a complete small computer. Such a chip is called a microprocessor and can be bought for the cost of a ticket to the opera.

Modern computers are all built of integrated circuits. Some of them are still very expensive, but the price is no longer related to the cost of the components; it is more likely to depend on what customers will pay.

15.1 A CLASSIFICATION OF COMPUTERS

The evolution of computers has split them into three broad streams. The boundaries between them are indistinct, but the main trends are clear. Each type is defined briefly here, and will later be described in a chapter of its own.

15.1.1 The 'Main-frame' Machine

A 'main-frame' is a large and expensive computer, typically used by many people for a variety of different purposes. The earliest machines were all main-frames in this sense, even though their speed and versatility were greatly inferior to that of a modern microcomputer.

Many main-frames nowadays are used in universities and research establishments, where they supply general-purpose computing facilities. Others are used by commercial organisations such as banks, where large amounts of information have to be collected, sorted, stored and distributed.

The distinguishing marks of a main-frame are

(1)   costs over £100 000
(2)   uses air-conditioned room

(3)   has professional management and operating staff — users not allowed
      direct access except through remote terminals
(4)   is designed to get the best possible performance out of the hardware, even
      at the cost of great complexity
(5)   is sold in small numbers — usually less than 100.

15.2.2 Minicomputers

Up to the mid 1960s all manufacturers concentrated on large machines, and
vied with one another to claim the 'fastest' or 'biggest' on the market. In 1965,
however, the Digital Equipment Corporation began to sell the PDP-8, a minimal
computer in which reliability, small size and low cost were given priority over
sheer performance. The first PDP-8 could be bought for a small fraction of the
cost of the next cheapest computer. The result was to open up a huge market for
applications where a main-frame would have been too expensive or unusable
because it took up too much space. Some obvious applications were in instru-
mentation and control, and teaching, where 'hands-on' experience, or direct
interaction between student and computer, again became a feasible proposition.
   The PDP-8 was the first of many brands of minicomputer. They tend to have
the following characteristics in common.

(1)   costs less than £50 000 (for the whole system)
(2)   often dedicated to a single purpose
(3)   often operated by programmers; no complex management structure
(4)   can be used in ordinary office conditions
(5)   number sold: over 10 000 of the most popular models.

15.1.3 Microprocessors

Microprocessors are so cheap that they can be used to control all types of
domestic, office and industrial machinery. When a microprocessor is connected
to a few simple peripherals (like a keyboard, television screen and cassette
recorder) it becomes a 'microcomputer'. These machines are cheap enough for
private ownership and for mass purchases by colleges and schools; they are being
sold on a huge scale and have done more than any other device to bring the
benefits of computing to the individual user.
   The main characteristics of a microprocessor are

(1)   costs less than £10
(2)   usually built-in to a complete system or machine
(3)   can be operated by completely unskilled people
(4)   can be used in extreme conditions: cars, under water, etc.
(5)   numbers sold: over 1 000 000 each of the standard types.

A complete microcomputer can cost between £500 and £3000, depending on
the peripheral devices supplied.

16 Main-frame Computers

Main-frame computers are large and expensive machines. They are normally housed in air-conditioned rooms, surrounded by security measures, and run by teams of professional operators. It is widely but falsely believed that main-frames are far more powerful than all other computers; there is a substantial overlap, and some of the smaller main-frames are out-performed by minicomputers which cost one-tenth as much.

Under these circumstances it seems surprising that large organisations continue to buy so many main-frames. There are two possible reasons for such a decision. Firstly, the organisation may indeed have data processing problems so massive that only the largest computer can handle them. Secondly, and far more often, the organisation may be 'locked-in' to the use of a main-frame by tradition and investment. Many organisations bought their first computers a long time ago, when all computers were main-frames. They will have set up 'computer departments', with large staffs all various points on a career structure; and they may have put up special air-conditioned buildings which are symbols of the organisations' involvement with modern technology.

Furthermore, all the programs in regular use will have been prepared to run on the main-frame of a particular manufacturer, and would cost a great deal to transfer to a different type of machine. When the present computer wears out, or can no longer cope with a growing load of work, the decision to replace it by another main-frame bought from the same manufacturer can be successfully defended as sensible and safe. It is, after all, hard for a non-technical management to accept that the ultra-modern department of 10 years ago is already obsolete.

In the sections which follow we shall discuss three important applications of main-frame computers.

16.1 FILE MAINTENANCE

Modern civilisation depends on the keeping of records. Every person in the country has a health record, and millions of people have social security records, driving licences, bank accounts, credit card accounts, employment records, or mailing list entries. Records are not necessarily concerned with people: many organisations keep records of stock items, library books which have been lent out, and so on.

A collection of records is called a *file*. Once a file has been set up, there are four possible operations or *transactions* which can be done with it. Consider a file of bank accounts.

(1) The information in a specified record can be looked up: for example, 'What is Mr J. B. Snooks' bank balance?'

(2) The information in a given record can be changed: for example, 'Mr J. B. Snooks has paid in a cheque for £123.45'.

(3) A new record can be added to the file: for example 'Ms S. Q. Snooks has opened a new account with £5.00'.

(4) An existing record may be removed: for example 'Mrs. D. Snooks has closed her account'.

The cost of maintaining files by human labour is immense, and there are obvious advantages in using a computer instead. The files are normally kept on a backing store, and the data in them can be listed on a line printer or displayed on a terminal whenever it is needed.

There are two basic modes of file maintenance. In a *transaction processing system* the computer is fitted with a number of terminals, and the file is kept on a medium such as a magnetic disc, which has a low access time. Users can type requests for information which are answered immediately, and they can also make changes to the file which are then straightaway reflected in the answers given to other queries. A good example of a transaction processor is an airline booking system. Here each record represents a particular flight on a specified day, and contains the number of passenger seats still for sale. The user is the travel agent, who can find out immediately whether a flight has any seats left. If so, he can reserve them for his clients and alter the record so that they will not be sold to anyone else.

Transaction processing is useful where many users need to access and change information on a minute-by-minute basis, but it is susceptible to errors due to machine failure, and above all it is very expensive: costs of 40p *per transaction* have been quoted. This is perhaps the reason why transaction processing has been most successful in the area of airline booking where the price of the commodity sold is high enough to mask the cost of the booking system, and where no error lasts for ever, but disappears as soon as the journey it relates to is completed.

The other type of file maintenance is based on batch processing. Here the details of various transactions are collected over a period (usually a day or a week) and used to update the file in one concentrated burst. This mode of working can be organised efficiently with the file stored on magnetic tape. This is far cheaper than magnetic discs, and very large files are invariably processed in this way. A large file may consist of 10 million records and be subject to a million amendments a day.

Both transaction and batch based files have an essential requirement: any specified record must be easy to find. Suppose the records were stored in some random order. Then to answer any query a transaction system would have to search the whole file, from beginning to end, until it found the record concerned. The position with a batch system would be just as bad: every single amendment would make the system scan through an entire magnetic tape, taking about 10 minutes to do so. How could such a system handle a million amendments in a day of 24 hours?

To avoid this difficulty, records in a computer file are always stored in a pre-defined order — usually that determined by a unique identifier such as a bank account number or social security code. (Names are a poor choice for defining order because they are not unique.) On a transaction processing system the file is divided into 'buckets', each of which hold a few dozen records with adjacent identifiers. There is an index which enables the system to select the right bucket for any record without scanning the rest of the file. In a batch system, all the amendments can be made in *one* pass through the file, provided that the various amendment instructions are also in their predefined order. To illustrate this point, think of a file on tape as a telephone directory in a vat of golden syrup, where you can only turn one page at a time, and slowly. If you want to make a large number of corrections, insertions and deletions, it pays to put the list of alterations into alphabetic order before you start.

Unfortunately the process of sorting is far from trivial. There are two distinct contexts.

(1) If the *n* records to be sorted can all be fitted into the immediate access store of the machine at the same time, the best algorithms give a sorting time proportional to $n \log_2 n$.

(2) When there are too many records to go into the immediate access store simultaneously, the time needed for sorting is very much larger. The method used is to split the records into small batches, each of which can be sorted in the immediate access store. The sorted batches are temporarily recorded on tapes, which are then merged to create the final sorted set of amendments.

Let the number of records to be sorted be *n*. Suppose that the size of one batch is *b* (which is much smaller than *n*, so that there are many batches), and that the system has *c* tape decks all capable of simultaneous operation. It can be shown that the sorting time is proportional to

$$\left[\frac{n}{b}\right] \log_{(c-1)} \left[\frac{n}{b}\right]$$

From this expression it is clear that with other factors being equal, the sort will run most quickly on a machine with the largest possible immediate access store and the most tape decks.

In many commercial systems, sorting takes more time than any other activity. Banks generally update their account files overnight, using large main-frames with millions of words of store and dozens of tape decks. The amendment records (mostly cheques and pay-in slips) are keypunched in the early evening, and transmitted from the branch banks to the computer centre over telephone lines.

The sorting process may start at 10 p.m. and continue until 6 the following morning; only then is it possible to update the master account file.

16.2 PHYSICAL AND ENGINEERING PROBLEMS

The basic properties of matter, such as heat conductivity, elasticity and plasticity of solids, and the viscosity and density of fluids, are all well understood in physical and mathematical terms. Any physical system, whether it be the atmosphere of the Earth, or the concrete shell of a large building, can be described by a set of partial differential equations which relate the various properties and their rates of change at each physical point of space and time in the system. The over-all behaviour of the system depends partly on these equations, and partly on the starting state and the constraints imposed from outside. These are collectively knows as the 'boundary conditions'. To give an example, the pattern of flow of water past the hull of a ship depends partly on the intrinsic properties of the water itself, and partly on the shape of the hull an and the speed it is moving.

In principle our mathematical understanding of these systems should permit us to predict how they will behave. Meteorologists could analyse the Earth's atmosphere to give accurate weather forecasts; aircraft designers could find out exactly how well their planes would fly before a single component were made, and bridges and buildings could be constructed with great economy — exactly strong enough to withstand the heaviest possible load and no more.

In practice, however, matters are not so convenient. It turns out that the differential equations which describe a system can only be solved exactly for the simplest boundary conditions. Thus eclipses and other astronomical events can be predicted with great accuracy because the heavenly bodies can be regarded as 'point masses'. In most other cases of practical interest, engineers and scientists have had to make predictions by using rules of thumb, or statistics, or models (such as those used in wind-tunnels) or guesswork.

Where exact mathematical solution is not feasible, it is often possible to get an approximate solution by using a *numerical method*. These methods generally work by taking the state of the system at various known points along the boundary, and simplifying assumptions to calculate the states at a whole network of points throughout the system. The values are not exact, but their accuracy increases if the points are close together — which means there are more of them. The calculation involves the solution of large sets of simultaneous equations, and other laborious mathematical processes.

Methods of this general type have been studied extensively by mathematicians specialising in numerical analysis. There are ways of deciding in advance just how many points are needed to achieve a given precision. In most practical cases you have to take a very large number of points, and before the invention of the computer the process of solution was not practicable; it would have taken too long. To give a vivid example, it might have taken 3 years to calculate the weather 1 day ahead.

Now that computers are available, useful solutions can be found for many of these problems. For example, a 24-hour weather forecast can be worked out in about 1 hour; the performance of ships, submarines and subsonic aircraft can be predicted quite accurately; and the forces acting inside a metal component such as a crankshaft can be determined precisely; this allows the design to be 'tuned' for the best possible performance.

The main-frames used for these problems tend to have at least a million characters of store, and special hardware for floating-point arithmetic.

Some important problems (in particular the analysis of supersonic flight) are still beyond the power of even the largest conventional present-day computer. To advance in this area a number of special-purpose machines have been built, all of which have multiple arithmetic units and allow many of the calculations involved to run at the same time. The earliest of these computers is the ILLIAC IV, which has 64 processors arranged in an 8 x 8 array. In the United Kingdom ICL's Distributed Array Processor has 4096 extremely simple arithmetic units, again arranged in a square array. The fastest machine currently being designed has a target speed of 2 gigaflops (2 000 000 000 floating-point arithmetic operations per second).

16.3 OPERATING SYSTEMS

In universities and scientific research establishments main-frames are used to provide 'general-purpose' computing facilities. These systems provide an extremely wide range of services, and support users in different branches of science, engineering, the humanities, or administration; they are intended as 'all things to all men'. In a typical case there may be a choice of 20 different programming languages, and a large library of 'packages', or special pre-written programs to solve problems in areas as diverse as electrical engineering and linguistics.

The hardware of a general-purpose main-frame is entirely conventional, although it is often built on a massive scale, and the architecture may use complicated methods to improve the over-all instruction execution speed. The entire gamut of facilities for the users is the responsibility of the *operating system*, which is a large and complex program.

The traditional way of putting work into a main-frame is to use punched cards, but most machines now also support a number of multi-access terminals as well. The terminals give access to all the facilities mounted on the machine.

One of the most important features of a computing service is the *file store*. This is a repository for information which belongs to the users, and which is kept on a backing store so that it is immediately accessible to the machine. The information is not restricted in type, and may be a source program, a compiled program, a set of data, a file, the results of a program, or anything else which can be represented in a computer. In most systems the basic unit of storage is the *document*, which is a sequence of characters of arbitrary length. Every document in the file store has a name chosen by the user. The names which belong to any one user are collected into a 'directory', which is normally accessible only to that user. Above this level, the file store can be made to reflect the structure of the organisation which uses it. Thus the directories which belong to a group of associated users (such as the members of a research team) can be linked into a 'meta-directory' which belongs to the team leader. He is given automatic access rights to any of the documents of his subordinates.

This structure can be extended upwards through as many layers as may be needed. The top meta-directory belongs to the managing director, who can read or alter any document in the entire system (should he want to).

In a well-designed system, a user can treat a document just like a stream of characters from a peripheral device. For example he can specify that his source program is to come from the file store instead of a pack of cards, and he can direct the results of computation into the store as a named document instead of (or as well as) having them printed out. Such a document can be used as input for the next program.

A vital aspect of the system is to provide a way of entering new documents and correcting mistakes in them. On a multi-access system documents can be typed directly on to a terminal. There is always an 'editor', which allows corrections and other alterations to be made to existing documents. When the editor program is entered, it begins by asking the user to name the document to be edited. When this document has been found, the user makes his changes by giving a series of commands, which are fundamentally of four sorts.

(1) FIND '*xxx*' : The computer searches through the document until it finds an occurrence of the string '*xxx*' which represents any sequence defined by the user.

(2) INSERT '*yyy*' : The computer inserts the string '*yyy*' at this point. The string may again by any arbitrary sequence of characters.

(3) DELETE *n* : The computer removes the previous *n* characters

(4) END : The computer ends the editing process and restores the newly corrected document to the file store.

To give an example, consider a badly typed document, as follows.

Document name: WILLIAM

> YOU ARE OLDE, FATER WILLIAN, THE JUNG MAN SAID,
> AND YOUR HAIREM HAS BECOME VERY WHITE;
> AND YET YOU PERSISTENTLY STAND ON YOUR HEAD —
> DO YOU THINK, AT YOUR AGE, IT IS RIT?

The editing sequence could be

> EDIT WILLIAM
> FIND "OLDE"
> DELETE 1   (i.e. from the *end* of the sequence OLDE)
> FIND "FAT"
> INSERT "H"   (i.e. after the *end* of the sequence FAT)
> FIND "J"
> DELETE 1
> INSERT "YO"
> FIND "HAIREM"
> DELETE 2
> FIND "PERSISTENTLY"
> DELETE 12
> INSERT "INCESSANTLY"
> FIND "RIT"
> DELETE 1
> INSERT "GHT"
> END

The corrected version of the document will be

> YOU ARE OLD, FATHER WILLIAM, THE YOUNG MAN SAID,
> AND YOUR HAIR HAS BECOME VERY WHITE;
> AND YET YOU INCESSANTLY STAND ON YOUR HEAD —
> DO YOU THINK, AT YOUR AGE, IT IS RIGHT?

In sharp contrast to the state of affairs with programming languages, there is no standardisation among editors — every manufacturer or designer of an operating system makes up his own variant. Thus many editors combine searching, deletion and replacement into one command, like

> "JUNG MAN" = "YOUNG MAN"

The organisation of a file store is a complex task. For example, the length of any document is unknown in advance and may change as material is inserted or taken away during editing. Files often embody a great deal of work by their owners, and must be protected against loss by sudden machine failure, or interference by other users. These factors combine and interact with one another, so that the section of program which looks after the file store is one of the largest in the whole operating system.

Another major responsibility of the operating system is to control the use of resources. The main-frame computer is expensive and has high running costs, and it is seen as important for the management to decide who is allowed to use the machine and how much.

Resource control is usually done on the basis of maintaining accounts for registered users. Any person who has received permission to use the computer will be assigned a unique 'job number', a secret 'password' and a 'computing allowance', which is usually measured in notional money. This information is stored in an accounting file inside the computer.

When a piece of work is submitted to the machine, or when a user attempts to 'log on' through a terminal, the system first checks that the job number and password correspond to an entry in the accounting file, and that the computing allowance has not all been used up. If work is allowed to proceed, then the resources used are 'charged' against the user's allowance on a scale which is set at so much per second of CPU time, so much for each minute of terminal time, so much per page printed, and so on. To encourage even use of the machine the management may offer cut-rate computing during the night, and charge a premium during popular times.

Although the accounting is apparently done in financial terms, it is really a method of rationing a scarce resource amongst a community of users. 'Real' money (that is, money which could be spent anywhere without restriction) rarely changes hands.

The main channel of communication between the user and the operating system is the *job control language* or JCL. Each statement in JCL is an instruction for the operating system to take some action on behalf of the user, so that a JCL itself is a special kind of programming language. As in BASIC, a JCL instruction can be obeyed as soon as it is given, or a complete set of JCL commands can be stored and executed later.

Possible JCL statements can be divided into several groups.

(1)   Statements dealing with the use of resources. In the first statement of any job, the user identifies himself with his job number and password. He may also lay down maximum limits to the resources he expects *this* job to use, so that if there is a program error the machine will not loop indefinitely or print miles of wallpaper (thereby using up all his precious allowance) but will stop automatically when the stated resources have been used.

(2)   Statements requesting the execution of programs. The user can ask the system to execute any program in its library on his behalf.

(3)   Statements which indicate the source of an input stream and the destination of an output stream. Thus the user can say where any program is to find its input data; this could be a peripheral device such as a card reader or a terminal, or a named document in the file store.

(4) Statements which detect exception conditions and allow special action to be taken.
(5) Instructions to tell the computer operator what to do.
(6) Statements to
(7) A statement to end a particular job.

The examples which follow are written in an 'idealised' JCL instead of a real one, because most existing JCLs (with a few notable exceptions) have strange and obscure grammatical rules which make them incomprehensible without detailed explanation.

The first example relates to a commercial job. A file called OLDMASTER is to be updated by a series of amendments in a file called CHANGES. The new version of the file is to be called NEWMASTER. Finally, the names and addresses in the amended file are to be printed on sticky label stationery.

The job uses three library programs, the first of which is needed to sort the amendments into their predefined order. The sorted amendments are recorded in a 'temporary' file called TEMP which is automatically discarded at the end of the job. The JCL commands to run this job would be

USER KR17/XXXX	(User's job number and password)
INPUT1 = CHANGES	Run the SORT program, using document
OUTPUT1 = TEMP	CHANGES as input and TEMP as output
RUN SORT	
INPUT1 = TEMP	Run the UPDATE program using TEMP
INPUT2 = OLDMASTER	and OLDMASTER as inputs and
OUTPUT1 = NEWMASTER	NEWMASTER as output
RUN UPDATE	
OPERATOR: "LOAD LABELS"	Tell the operator to load special stationery on the line printer, and stop the job until they have done so
INPUT1 = NEWMASTER	Run the LABELPRINT program using
OUTPUT1 = LINEPRINTER	NEWMASTER as input and the line
RUN LABELPRINT	printer as output
DELETE TEMP	Discard temporary file
OPERATOR: "LOAD ORDINARY STATIONERY"	
ENDJOB	End the job

These commands could be given, one by one, by a user seated at a terminal. Alternatively they could be typed in advance and stored in the file store as a document in its own right. The user could then instruct the operating system to obey the commands in this document. Such a stored JCL program is called a 'macro' or a 'catalogued procedure'.

The second example shows the compilation and possible execution of a program written in a high-level language such as PASCAL. This job again consists of a sequence of three programs.

First, the PASCAL compiler reads a source program from cards, and generates two outputs: a listing on the line printer, and a machine code version of the program on a temporary file called OBJECT. It also generates an internal flag which is set 'true' if the program was not translated successfully and syntax errors were found.

Second, a program called a *link editor* combined the translated program with the appropriate library subroutines for input, output and various mathematical functions. The result, called TEMPROG, is temporarily placed in the program library.

Finally, the newly created program is run, using cards for its data, and the line printer for its output.

The various job steps are

```
USER KR19/YYYY
INPUT1 = CARD READER          Run PASCAL compiler
OUTPUT1 = LINE PRINTER
OUTPUT2 = OBJECT
RUN PASCAL
IF FLAG THEN GOTO             Abandon if errors found
INPUT1 = TEMP                 Run link editor
INPUT2 = LIBRARY
OUTPUT1 = TEMPROG
RUN LINKEDITOR
INPUT1 = CARD READER          Run object program
OUTPUT1 = LINE PRINTER
RUN TEMPROG
DELETE TEMPROG                Discard TEMPROG
CLOSE: DELETE TEMP            Discard TEMP
ENDJOB                        Stop
```

This set of JCL instructions is needed to run even the simplest high-level program. One has only to consider the needs of beginners in programming to appreciate the importance of macros or catalogued procedures.

The chief drawback of a main-frame computer supporting a general-purpose facility is that it is very expensive for what it provides. The decision to handle every kind of user requirement without restriction leads to an inordinately complex operating system with massive organisational overheads, and heavy maintenance costs. The high price of the system generally causes the organisation to surround the machine with a bureaucratic barrier which further cuts its effectiveness and increases costs. It is felt imperative to run the machine for 24 hours a day, a policy which is not only expensive but leads to labour troubles which can paralyse the machine for many months. In the next chapter we shall discuss some low-cost alternatives for the general-purpose facility.

17 Minicomputers

17.1 GENERAL APPLICATIONS

Minicomputers are cheaper, smaller and easier to install than main-frame
machines, but need be very little inferior in raw computing power.
Minicomputers are therefore increasingly used for all the same purposes as
main-frames. In addition there are several areas of application for which the
minicomputer is particularly suitable because of its low cost, reliability and
simplicity of operation. These applications are all 'dedicated'; that is, the
minicomputer is installed for one purpose only, and is not switched from
program to program like a general-purpose computer.

17.2 PLANT CONTROL

The operations of a modern industrial plant are complex, and conditions must
be controlled exactly if the product is to come up to its specification. For
example, the mixture of raw materials and the temperature in a steel-making
furnace must both be right to within narrow limits or else the steel will be weak
and brittle.

The control of industrial processes has passed through a sequence of
evolutionary steps. The earliest processes relied on the intuitive judgment of a
skilled and experienced artisan. Old Jim — who had been at the works for 30
years — would spit in the air, screw up one eye, peer at the furnace through a bit
of blue glass from a broken bottle, and say, 'She ain't hot enough. Give her
another half ton of coke.'

Unfortunately Old Jim was unable to explain the way he arrived at his
decisions, and when he retired it was necessary to replace him with a measuring
instrument connected to a dial. The operator no longer needed to make any
judgement, but was simply told to add more coke until the pointer on the dial
reached a certain mark. To everyone's surprise (except Old Jim) this 'scientific'
system did not work nearly as well and reliably as the old intuitive method. Jim
subconsciously took into account all kinds of other factors — such as the ambient
atmospheric conditions — which would not be indicated on a single instrument.

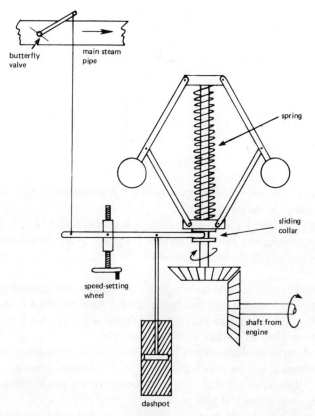

Figure 17.1

The next stage in the development of control systems was to bypass the human operator and make the instrument control the process directly. In our simple example the machine which fed coke to the furnace would be stopped *automatically* when the temperature was high enough. In a more complex process, where conditions had to be kept steady for a considerable length of time, the reading of the instrument would determine the corrective action to be taken. Such a system is called a 'servo mechanism'. The earliest known example is the centrifrugal governor on Watt's steam engine, as sketched in figure 17.1. The aim is to keep the engine running at the same speed irrespective either of the load or the pressure of steam in the boiler. The governor consists of two spinning weights, arranged so that the faster the engine runs, the further they swing out by the action of centrifugal force.

The weights drive a system of levers connected to a butterfly valve in the main steam pipe, and the system is designed so that when the weights rise they *cut down* the supply of steam to the engine, and vice versa. As a result the engine

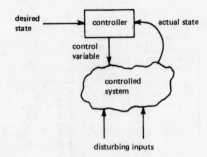

Figure 17.2

speed is nearly constant because any deviation is immediately compensated by a corrective change in the steam supply.

A generalised view of a servo mechanism is shown in figure 17.2. A system is to be kept running in a particular state. It is subject to several influences or inputs, only one of which can be controlled: the others are called 'disturbing inputs'.

The controller receives two main inputs: one signal which represents the desired state of the system, and another which indicates its actual state. It uses this information to derive a control input to the system, in such a way as to keep its state as close as possible to the desired value.

In general, servo mechanisms can be implemented mechanically, electrically or with electronics, and they are widely used in all industrial processes. The main role of the human operator is to start the system up and to monitor it, taking emergency action if it goes wrong.

In a large industrial plant there are often hundreds of variables to be controlled, and it is possible to program all the rules for controlling them into a single minicomputer which then runs the whole plant. The centralisation of control also means that the computer can make strategic as well as tactical decisions: that is, it can decide the best values for the controlled variables as well as ensuring that these values are maintained. This is best illustrated by an oil refinery which converts crude oil into various products — petrol, paraffin, heating oil, tar, and so on. The relative yield of these products is not constant, but depends on the temperature and pressure used at various points in the distillation process.

If the minicomputer were used simply as a tactical control system, then its responsibility would be limited to keeping the process conditions to the values specified by the human manager. In practice, however, the machine is often kept informed of the current demand for the various oil-based products, and of the market prices as they fluctuate from hour to hour. It can then calculate whether the plant is being run in the most profitable way. If not, it can change the process conditions so as to make more of a product currently in demand at the expense of another which may already be in plentiful supply.

In a steel-rolling mill the minicomputer can be used in quite a different way. One important job is to cut standard lengths of steel from the rolling mill into the odd-sized girders ordered by the customer. This inevitably results in 'off-cuts' which are wasted and can only be used as scrap.

Suppose the plant minicomputer is given the complete list of orders to be filled, as it stands at the beginning of any day. It can then plan a cutting scheme which groups girders from various orders so that they fit more tidily into standard lengths. This allows the wastage to be reduced.

The improvement in plant efficiency brought about by this kind of strategic planning is of the order of 1 to 3 per cent. This seems small until it is expressed in money terms, for the over-all production of a modern plant is so great that the whole minicomputer system can often recoup its own capital cost in weeks.

One major drawback to the use of a centralised computer for plant control is its vulnerability to breakdowns or malicious damage. If everything is controlled by one machine, then one faulty component or a saboteur with a pair of wire cutters can stop the entire plant.

To overcome this problem most plants have secondary, localised control systems for each of the important variables. These servo mechanisms take over automatically if the main controller breaks down, and allow the system to keep running, possibly at reduced efficiency, until the central machine is repaired.

17.3 X-RAY TOMOGRAPHY

X-rays were a major medical discovery and have proved invaluable in diagnosing illness and guiding the work of surgeons. However, an X-ray plate is a two-dimensional picture of a three-dimensional object, and lacks important information about the depth of the various structures seen. Furthermore the features on an X-ray are only visible because different body tissues absorb X-rays by different amounts — thus a dense organ such as the heart absorbs more radiation than the surrounding tissues and appears as a lighter patch on the X-ray negative. It happens that bone absorbs far more than any other kind of tissue, so that X-rays taken through a layer of bone show little detail of anything else.

A clear case in point arises in diseases of the head. A surgeon who plans to remove a brain tumour must know exactly where to cut open the patient's skull, but the conventional X-ray is a poor guide: the image of the tumour is faint and blurred because the X-rays have to pass through two layers of bone, and further-more it is not at all obvious whether the tumour is at the front or the back of the picture. Even two X-rays taken at right angles barely convey enough information.

The recently developed technique of X-ray tomography allows a far clearer picture to be made. The 'brain scanner', designed and marketed by EMI Ltd, is shown diagrammatically in figure 17.3.

The patient lies on a couch with his head inside a massive rotating bracket. On one side of the bracket an X-ray tube generates a fine 'pencil' of X-rays

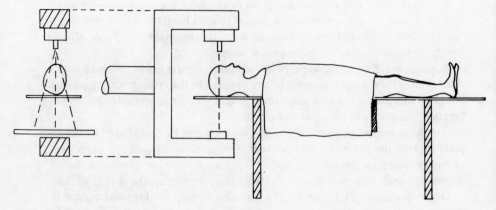

Figure 17.3

which can be swung from side to side, as shown in the end-on view. On the other side of the bracket there is an X-ray detector which can measure the intensity of the X-ray beam after it has passed through the patient's head. The whole bracket can rotate (without, of course, touching the patient).

For a single 'pass', the pencil is positioned at one extreme of its travel and then moved steadily across to the other. A continuous record is made of the beam strength reaching the detectors, and stored in the controlling minicomputer. This is illustrated in figure 17.4, where the curve is drawn on the assumption that normal brain tissue, tumour and bone absorb X-rays in the ratio 1:2:4. The sharp bumps at the ends of the curve (a and c) are clearly due to the beam passing through a lot of bone, but the more diffuse bump at b is caused by the tumour. However, this curve *by itself* conveys little information except that the two sides of the head are in some way different.

To make a complete brain scan, the bracket starts in one position – say with the X-ray tube vertically above the patient – and a pass is made and recorded. The bracket is then turned by one or two degrees and another pass is made. This process is repeated some hundreds of times until the bracket returns to its starting position. All this takes only a few minutes.

When all this data has been collected the minicomputer sets to work to analyse the readings. It uses a mathematical technique called Fourier synthesis to build an image of the structures which can best explain the various readings. This involves heavy computation, but after a few minutes the computer prints a cross-section of the patient's head which is as clear as a drawing in a book of anatomy. One such picture showing a tumour can be seen in figure 17.5.

This technique has recently been extended to make cross-sections of the body as well as the head. This is much more difficult because the body contains organs which move continuously and confuse the picture, but useful information can still be obtained.

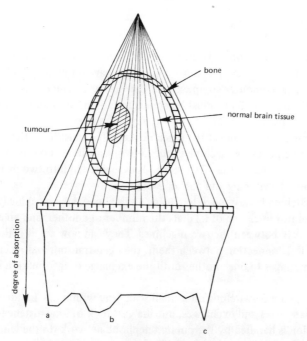

Figure 17.4

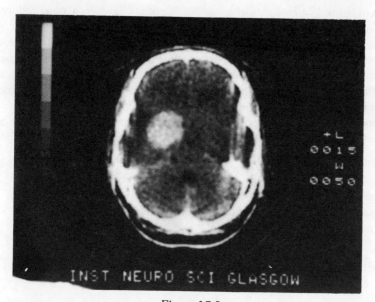

Figure 17.5

17.4 PACKET SWITCHING

Many computer applications rely on networks of computers scattered over large geographical areas. For example, most banks now have terminals which are all linked to a central computer complex, and the various machines used for air traffic control and air defence must be connected to one another in order to have a complete picture of the situation at any moment.

The systems used to connect the machines together must be as flexible as possible; in principle every machine in the network must be allowed to communicate with every other. The methods available fall into two main categories: circuit switching and packet switching.

Circuit switching is very much like using a telephone. One machine (or sometimes the operator in charge of it) dials the number of another, and an exchange establishes a 'call' between the two machines. They can now act as if there were a direct physical connection between them: they can transmit and receive a dialogue of messages to one another until the exchange of information is complete.

In practice, circuit switching on a small scale (say within one building) is done by private wires and exchanges, but the vast bulk of long-distance communication is handled by the public telephone network. In the United Kingdom, the Post Office offers its 'DATEL' service for circuit-switched data transmission, with a maximum communication speed of about 400 characters/s.

Packet switching, the other main method of communication between computers, is much more like the letter post. A 'packet switched network' (shown in figure 17.6) consists of a number of nodes (N_1 to N_5) connected by links (L_1 to L_6). Each node is a minicomputer, and the links can be wires, or microwaves or satellite communication channels. Most of the nodes also service some local 'subscribers' which are the customers of the network. The subscribers are usually computers (although they could be special-purpose machines such as typesetters or industrial robots) and each subscriber is allocated its own unique number (T_1 to T_{16} in our example) which is its *address*.

In operation, a subscriber posts a 'packet' of information addressed to some other subscriber. The packet has a fixed format, and generally includes

The destination address
The sender's address   (only used if delivery is impossible)
A message   (usually some thousands of characters)
A check sum   (used to detect errors, like the check sum on a block of
    magnetic tape − see chapter 11).

Once in the system, the packet is sent from node to node, until eventually it is delivered to the destination. For example, if T_3 sends a packet to T_7, it is transmitted four times in all

T_3 to N_1 : N_1 to N_2 : N_2 to N_4 : and N_4 to T_7

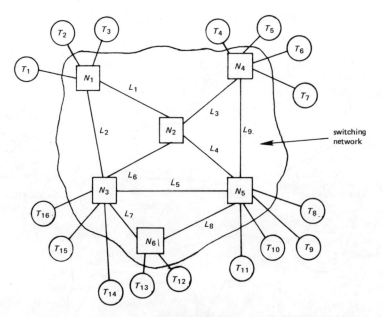

Figure 17.6

The action of each node is somewhat like that of a sorting office. One part of the control program receives packets and places them in a special area of RAM called a 'buffer'. Another part examines the packets in the buffer and decides what (if anything) to do with them. The decision is governed by a table which specifies a link to be used for every possible destination. For N_1 in our example this table could be

Destination	1	2	3	4	5	6	7	8	9	10	11	12	13	14	15	16
Link	T_1	T_2	T_3	L_1	L_1	L_1	L_1	L_1	L_1	L_1	L_1	L_2	L_2	L_2	L_2	L_2

The links between the nodes can carry information in both directions, and a node can simultaneously receive and transmit packets on every line connected to it. This does not necessarily prevent queues from building up; for example if T_4, T_5, T_6 and T_7 all simultaneously send packets to T_{16} then queues will form for links L_3 and L_6, and for the connection between N_3 and T_{16}. Fortunately queues are extremely simple to manage. The node continually scans all the packets in its buffer. If the link needed for a particular packet is free then it transmits the packet and removes it from the buffer. Otherwise it does nothing, for the line will eventually become free and the packet will be dealt with on a later scan.

In general, packet switching networks form a resilient method of communication. If the connections between the nodes are rich enough the system can work

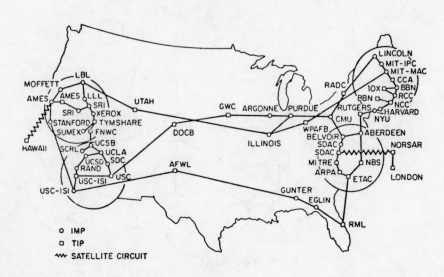

Figure 17.7

even though some of the nodes and links are broken. Alterations are necessary in the control table of the remaining nodes, but they can be made automatically by software.

The first widely used packet switching system was ARPA network organised by the United States Department of Defense (see figure 17.7). It was installed in 1970 and connects some hundreds of computers in universities and government research establishments.

It is interesting to compare circuit switching and packet switching.

	Circuit switching	Packet switching
Flexibility:	High: messages can be as short as 1 character and replies come immediately	Low: Message length is fixed, and replies may take several seconds to arrive
Ease of use:	Calls must be 'dialled', and destination may be 'engaged'. Connection can never be guaranteed in advance	A packet can be posted at any time

	Circuit switching	*Packet switching*
Cost of connection	Low	Rather high
Reliability:	Poor. Data is often corrupted	Good. Correct delivery is practically guaranteed
Speed of transmission:	Low if public telephone systems used	High (because links are special high-speed circuits)

In summary, packet switching is superior where the subscribers are machines, but when humans are involved — say, as users of terminals — circuit switching is cheaper, more responsive and convenient.

18 Microprocessors

A microprocessor is a complete central processor on a single integrated circuit. From a computer scientist's point of view, it is distinguishable from other types of computer only by its extremely low price and high reliability. It is sometimes said that microprocessors are 'less powerful' or 'less versatile' than minicomputers and main-frames. It is true that the first microprocessors to be offered for sale did have clumsy and inadequate instruction codes, and were handicapped by very short word lengths (such as 4 bits). At that time the number of gates which could be etched on to one chip of silicon was still severely limited, and the uncomfortable architecture of the first microprocessors resulted from the need to 'shoehorn' the design into this limit. Recently, the technology of chip production has improved and these restrictions no longer apply. Modern microprocessors have excellent order codes and for certain tasks are effectively just as fast as many minicomputers and main-frames. Some of them incorporate immediate access stores and peripheral control circuitry as well as a CPU, and this variety is said to be a complete 'computer on a chip'. Others include all the mechanisms for giving efficient support to high-level languages, and for controlling very large stores. There is a tendency among manufacturers to put microprocessors into sealed boxes and to market the result as 'main-frames'. The microprocessor is chosen with the same order code as the machine to be replaced, so that the software can be transferred directly. The customer is well pleased, since he is unaware of any change except a massive reduction in price.

In the near future, microprocessors will replace nearly all minicomputers and main-frames except those which are specially designed for a particular purpose. This effect, however, represents only a miniscule fraction of the total impact of the microprocessor, because its cheapness opens up a huge field of applications where the use of other kinds of computer, although technically feasible, would have not have been justifiable on economic grounds. Microprocessors can be built in to cheap, mass-produced equipment, and used in locations where they only do useful work for a small fraction of the time. In this chapter we shall discuss only a small range of current applications. There are of course many others, and the list will grow rapidly over the next few years.

18.1 TOYS AND GAMES

One of the first large-scale uses of microprocessors was in the production of electronic toys and games. The reader will probably have seen TV game kits in the shops, and various new types of pintable and other automats in amusement arcades. People have always delighted in toys which behave in complex ways, and demand some measure of skill and judgement. In the past, the 'complexity' of these games has depended on electrical relays which are expensive and unreliable, but if the relays are replaced by microprocessors, then any amount of complexity can be built in at almost no extra cost. On a TV games box, six different games effectively cost no more to produce than one.

Many of these 'electronic pastimes' exercise mainly manual skills, but some are genuinely intellectual. One can already buy chess-playing machines which offer a reasonable game for novices (although they are easily beaten by good players). Computer scientists have always been interested in chess-playing programs, and many of them are working to improve the standard of play. The leading chess program at present can beat all but the best human players. It runs on a large main-frame computer, but in all probability programs of this standard will be available on microprocessors in a short time. It is worth mentioning that the better class machines allow the user to select a standard of play appropriate to his own level, so as to avoid the depressing experience of losing every time.

18.2 WORD PROCESSING

In our information-centred civilisation, a huge amount of effort is devoted to writing, typing, editing, storing and reproducing words. Every organisation spends a large proportion of its resources on typists, filing clerks and secretaries to do this work.

It has been known for a long time that most information-handling tasks could be automated, but until recently this was prevented by the high cost of computers. The microprocessor has changed the picture completely; from now on, office procedures will be progressively mechanised.

A typical word processing system for a small office might be assembled from the following components

(1) a microprocessor CPU with 16—32K bytes of RAM
(2) a 'floppy disc' store, where each removable disk can hold some half-million characters
(3) a good-quality printer, similar to an electric typewriter
(4) a terminal with a large screen and a keyboard which has all the conventional keys and a row of special 'function buttons' with appropriate labels.

Each function button activates a program permanently stored in the system. In use, the various office procedures are made up from sequences of the appropriate functions, much as a complex sum is worked out on a hand calculator. Some of the most frequently used functions are as follows.

(1) *Enter*: This allows the typist to enter a new document (which may be a letter, a legal agreement, an exam paper, a poem or anything else) on the keyboard. As the document is typed it is displayed on the screen, and any corrections can be made by using the 'delete' key and other keys which allow existing material to be altered. This is much faster than using white paint on a conventional typewriter! The 'enter' function also permits the typists to insert 'standard paragraphs' which have been previously typed and stored on the floppy disc. This is invaluable when legal documents are being prepared.

(2) *Justify*: This function takes the document in the system and re-arranges it so that both margins are straight lines. Justification is done by inserting extra spaces between words and sometimes by hyphenation, and it makes the text look like printing rather than typing. The rules for automatic hyphenation are rather complex. Even these rules sometimes give unfortunate results with words like 'therapist', and a large dictionary of exceptions is also required. Automatic hyphenation programs use a lot of random access store and are therefore available only on more expensive word processing sets.

(3) *Print*: The document in the system is sent to the printer, where it may appear at the rate of 60 characters per second (that is, about 10 times as fast as a human typist at full speed).

(4) *File*: The document is sent to the floppy disc store, together with the current date and a name chosen by the typist. This name serves to identify and retrieve the document if it is needed later.

(5) *Retrieve*: Given a name (and possibly a date), this function will fetch the corresponding document from the floppy disc and bring it into the system. The document will be displayed on the screen as if it had just been typed, and can be changed or edited as necessary.

Perhaps the simplest task in an office is that of typing a letter from shorthand, manuscript or dictaphone. Here the word processing system confers very little advantage except that of making it easier to correct typing errors. In more complicated tasks, however, the word processor confers major benefits.

(1) If a letter contains standard paragraphs, they can be inserted literally by the touch of a button.

(2) If a similar letter is to be sent to several people, there is no need to type each copy individually; one 'master copy' can be re-edited and printed for each recipient.

(3) Documents with an extended life — such as a catalogue, or a syllabus or a set of lecture notes — often undergo frequent changes. With a word processor, there is no need for such a document to be retyped by hand

every time it is altered; once the document is on file, the changes can be inserted on the screen and the new version printed whenever it is needed.

(4)   There is no longer any need for a bulky physical filing system. All documents can be kept on a small collection of floppy discs, and displayed or printed whenever they are needed.

The system we have described is suitable for a small office, employing one secretary. In a larger organisation, the word processing system would consist of a number of 'work stations', each consisting of a CPU, terminal and printer. The work stations would all be served by a central file store, with a large capacity, so that every work station has access to material typed on any other. In addition, the system might be equipped with extra terminals (without printers) so that managers and other executives could retrieve and enter documents without direct recourse to the secretarial staff.

When seen in prospect, the installation of a word processor in an office often alarms the existing staff, who fear that they will be reduced to unthinking machine minders. Actual experience suggests that this is not so; word processing seems to enhance job satisfaction because the papers sent out by the office are always perfectly typed and laid out, important documents are always up to date, and the filing is always well organised. Furthermore, word processors offer unlimited scope for imaginative layout of tables and other documents, and can give their users great pride in their work.

18.3 MICROCOMPUTERS

A microcomputer is essentially a complete computer system small enough to be portable, and cheap enough to be bought by private individuals, schools, or in large quantities by universities and colleges.

There are many different brands of microcomputer, but they all share the same basic configuration

a microprocessor CPU with 8K (or more) of RAM
a keyboard
a display screen
a backing store (either tape cassette or floppy disc)

In some models all these components are built into one box, while in others the display screen, keyboard and backing store may well occupy different units connected to each other and to the mains power supply by cables. In the author's view the integral construction method is much the better, since trailing cables and the plugs and sockets which go with them form a weak and dangerous aspect of any design.

Microcomputers are normally sold with interpreters for the BASIC language, which is simple to learn and highly popular even though it does not reflect modern advances in the design of programming languages. Microcomputers are also increasingly being equipped with PASCAL compilers or interpreters, and nearly all of them can be programmed in the machine code of the central microprocessor as well.

This basic configuration is enough to support many interesting applications. The user can program the machine in BASIC, he can store programs and data on the backing store, and he can exchange programs with other users (either personally or through published magazines) and he can buy them on cassettes or floppy discs from dealers. Nevertheless all microcomputers are designed to be expandable. More store can be added so that large programs can be run, and peripheral devices of any type can be plugged in to a standard interface.

Microcomputers were originally designed for the 'home market', and this remains a major area of use, particularly in the United States. A home micro-computer is advertised as being useful for financial planning, menu control, the maintenance of the family diary and birthday lists. The effectiveness and importance of these applications is not self-evident, and in most cases the microcomputer is used for playing games and learning to program. The greatest impact of a home computer is on children, who can gain familiarity with programming and information handling machinery long before they would have the opportunity to do so at school or university. In the United Kingdom, personal owners of microcomputers are rare, and most machines are used for business and teaching.

In its 'business' configuration, the microcomputer is fitted with a printer and a floppy disc store. It can now fulfil a number of tasks: word processing, financial control, stock control, maintenance of address lists, production planning and various technical design calculations. Standard programs for these functions can be bought from software firms, and cost much less than the equivalent programs for main-frame machines, because the supplier can rely on selling a far greater number of them.

In teaching, microcomputers fulfil three aims.

First, they can be used to teach the art of programming without exposing the student to the misery of using a main-frame computer through its operating system. If BASIC is the only language available, the course can only cover the more primitive aspects of programming, but this is enough for many students who do not plan to specialise in computer science.

Second, a microcomputer can be used as a sophisticated teaching machine. It can administer quizzes, score the answers, and adapt the level of questioning and the rate of progress to the student's ability. Although the machine cannot replace the human teacher, there are several 'formal' areas — such as arithmetic, algebra and differential calculus — where it can form a useful adjunct.

Third, the microprocessor can be used to teach by simulation. Consider a person in charge of a complex system such as an aircraft, a badly injured patient, or an army fighting a battle. The person has to be aware of all the relevant facts about the system from moment to moment, and to make complex decisions based on these facts. In training someone for this role, the most important factor is experience. Realistic practice sessions are expensive or even impossible to provide, and training depends on lengthy periods of 'apprenticeship'.

In many cases the behaviour of the system being controlled is well understood in mathematical terms. It is then possible to write a program which makes the computer behave in the same way as the system might be expected to do. The student can then practise on the 'pretend' system, and gain his experience quickly and cheaply.

This approach has been used for some time in aircraft simulators for training pilots and 'war games' systems for military officers. The introduction of the microprocessor now allows the idea to be extended to many more students by modelling activities such as running small businesses, or examining the effect on the environment of alternative fishing or energy policies.

18.4 CONCLUSION

The steam engine caused the first Industrial Revolution, but it took the petrol engine to make its benefits widely and directly available to everyone by providing fast personal transport and instant portable power. The microprocessor stands in the same relation to the main-frame computer: we as individuals can now begin to benefit from the revolution in information handling. If history is a reliable guide, the changes brought in by the microprocessor may well continue for a century or more. In 2080 this book should make interesting historical reading!

Appendix A: SNARK–An Abstract Teaching Machine

INTRODUCTION

This abstract machine is designed for use in an elementary computer science course. It aims to teach the elements of machine code programming, and is implemented in BASIC on a PET computer with at least 8K of writable store.

THE MACHINE

The machine consists of a CPU with two 16-bit accumulators, a 9-bit program counter, and a memory with a maximum of 512 words of immediate access store. In the present version only 128 words are available.

The CPU has a repertory of 16 instructions, of which 4 are addressless. The general format is shown below

FUNCTION	ACCUMULATOR	MODE	ADDRESS
4 bits	1 bit	2 bits	9 bits

Each instruction specifies an accumulator (either A or B), and all instructions with addresses also indicate operands.

The various functions, with their mnemonics, are as follows.

a: Functions with Addresses

LDA	Load operand to accumulator
STA	Store contents of accumulator
ADD	Add operand to accumulator
SUB	Subtract operand from accumulator
AND	Logical 'AND' operand with accumulator
ORA	Logical 'OR' operand with accumulator
JMP	Jump unconditionally to stated address
BZE	Jump if selected accumulator = 0
BNZ	Jump if selected accumulator $\neq$ 0
BMI	Jump if selected accumulator $<$ 0
BPL	Jump if selected accumulator $\geqslant$ 0

b: Functions without Addresses

LRS	Shift accumulator one place right logically
NEG	Negate accumulator
INA	Input a number from the keyboard and put it into the selected accumulator
OUT	Print the number in the selected accumulator, on a line by itself
END	Stop

The mode field has four possible values

00 :	Immediate mode. The address part is taken as the operand
01 :	Direct mode. The operand is taken from the store location specified by the address
10 :	Index by accumulator A. The operand is taken from the cell pointed to by the *sum* of the address part and the current contents of accumulator A.
11 :	Index by accumulator B. The description is similar to the one above, except that accumulator B is used to calculate the address.

Note that STA and the jump instructions do not allow the immediate mode.

THE ASSEMBLY LANGUAGE

SNARK programs are entered from the keyboard using the following syntax

⟨CR⟩   ::= 'return' key
⟨digit⟩   ::= 0|1|2|3|4|5|6|7|8|9
⟨number⟩ ::= ⟨digit⟩|⟨number⟩⟨digit⟩
         e.g. : 5,   47,   123
⟨address⟩ ::= ⟨number⟩|#⟨number⟩|⟨number⟩A|⟨number⟩B
         e.g. : 14,   #0,   51A,   47B

These examples illustrate the direct, immediate, index A and index B modes respectively.

⟨acc⟩ ::= A/B/⟨empty⟩
     e.g. A,   B

If ⟨acc⟩ = ⟨empty⟩, then A is implied by default

⟨addressed function⟩ ::= LDA|STA|ADD|SUB|ORA|AND|JMP|BZE|BNZ|BMI|BPL
⟨addressless function⟩ ::= LRS|NEG|INA|OUT|END
⟨item⟩ ::= +⟨number⟩|−⟨number⟩|⟨addressless function⟩⟨acc⟩|
        ⟨addressed function⟩⟨acc⟩⟨address⟩
   e.g. : +4,   −15,   NEG B,   LDA A 74A

⟨comment⟩ ::= ↑⟨followed by a sequence of any characters⟩|⟨empty⟩
⟨return⟩ ::= ⟨comment⟩⟨CR⟩
⟨labelled item⟩ ::= ⟨number⟩⟨item⟩⟨return⟩
  e.g.: 0   +44
          1   −123   ↑MINUS ONE TWO THREE
        46   ADD B #7
⟨c line⟩ ::= C⟨number⟩⟨followed by a sequence of any character⟩⟨CR⟩
⟨preamble⟩ ::= ⟨preamble⟩⟨c line⟩|⟨empty⟩
⟨text⟩ ::= ⟨labelled item⟩|⟨text⟩⟨labelled item⟩
⟨program⟩ ::= ⟨preamble⟩⟨text⟩

An example of a ⟨program⟩ is shown below.

```
C0    PROGRAM TO READ, SORT AND PRINT A SET OF N
C1    NUMBERS, PRECEDED BY N
C2    STORAGE ALLOCATION:
C3      N IN 49
C4      FLAG IN 48
C5      NUMBERS IN 50 ONWARDS
 0    INA  A
 1    STA  A  49              ↑ STORE N IN 49
 2    BZE  A   7              ↑ JUMP IF ALL NOS READ
 3    INA  B                  ↑ READ NEXT
 4    STA  B  49 A            ↑ STORE
 5    SUB  A  #1              ↑ DECREMENT A
 6    JMP  2                  ↑ JUMP BACK
 7    LDA  A  #0              ↑ SET FLAG = 0
 8    STA  A  48
 9    LDA  A  #2              ↑ SET COUNT
10    LDA  B  49 A            ↑ COMPARE PAIRS OF VALUES
11    SUB  B  48 A
12    BPL  B  20
13    STA  B  48              ↑ SWAP IF NEED BE
14    LDA  B  49A
15    STA  B  47
16    LDA  B  48A
17    STA  B  49A
18    LDA  B  47
19    STA  B  48A
20    SUB  A  49              ↑ SEE IF ARRAY EXHAUSTED
21    BZE  A  25
22    ADD  A  49
23    ADD  A  #1              ↑ IF NOT, ADD 1 AND JUMP BACK
24    JMP  10
```

```
25   LDA  A  48          ↑ GO BACK IF FLAG #0
26   BNZ  A  7
27   LDA  A  49          ↑ OUTPUT RESULTS
28   LDA  B  49A
29   OUT  B
30   SUB  A  #1
31   BNZ  A  28
32   END
```

PRACTICAL DETAILS

The SNARK simulator can be loaded into the PET from a cassette tape. When started, the system will accept comment lines, program lines or any of a number of 'directives' which control the SNARK operating system.

(1) *Comment lines* A comment line starts with a C followed by a number in the range 1 to 20 and some arbitrary text. Comment lines are stored in the sequence of their numbers irrespective of the order in which they are typed. A comment line with a particular number will replace a previously entered comment with the same number.

(2) *Program lines* A program line consists of a labelled item, as defined in the previous section. Each item is sent to the SNARK store cell whose address is given at the start of the program line, so that, for example, the item in the program line

   7 LDA B #46

is sent to cell 7.

   A program line with a particular number will replace a previously entered line with the same number. A line can be deleted by typing its number and nothing else.

   Note that program lines will generally have consecutive numbers. Unlike BASIC, new program lines may not in general be inserted between existing ones without rewriting the entire program. This is because the numbers represent *addresses*, not labels as in BASIC.

(3) *DUMP* This command will write all the material (comment and program lines) typed so far on to a cassette tape, whence it may be retrieved later by a LOAD directive.

(4) *LOAD* The LOAD directive will read a SNARK program back from a cassette tape. As it is read, the program is listed.

(5) *WIPE* All comment and program lines are deleted.

(6) *LISTALL* All comments and program lines are displayed.

(7) *LC* All comment lines are listed and displayed.

(8) *LIST n−m* m and n are integers in the range 0 to 127. Program lines n to m (inclusive) are listed.

(9)   *RUN*   The present program is translated from its source into binary and
run. The details of the run are elicited by a brief dialogue.
- (a)   DISPLAY ON?   If the reply is 'YES', (or Y) then each instruction
   and its results are displayed as the instruction is obeyed.
- (b)   SINGLE SHOT?   If the reply is 'YES', the program is executed one
   instruction at a time. Each instruction is initiated by typing any key
   except 'B'.
- (c)   START ADDRESS?   The reply (which should be an integer)
   indicates the address at which execution should start.

   Execution can be stopped at any time by typing 'B' (for 'break').
   The translation runs at about 2 program lines per second. It is
omitted if the source program has not been altered since the last
translation.
   Provided that no translation has taken place, a program can safely
be restarted after a break by specifying the start address '−1'.

(10) *TRANSLATE*   This directive forces the translation process. It is useful
in circumstances where a new translation is necessary but would have
been omitted by the RUN directive. A possible case in point would be the
initialisation of a self-modifying program.

(11) *PM m−n*   This directive generates a post-mortem dump of registers *m−n*
of the SNARK store. Each cell is displayed (a) as an instruction, and (b) as
a decimal number.

PRACTICAL HINTS

(1)   Cursor editing is *not* available.
(2)   Under certain rare conditions, pressing the return key by itself can lead to
a jump back to the BASIC monitor. The machine types

   READY.

It is now rather easy to corrupt both the SNARK program *and* the
underlying simulator. The only correct response is

   GOTO 100

If, at this stage the user does something else, he should reload the
simulator from its cassette and restart the session.

Appendix B: The SNARK Simulator Program

```
100 REM   COPYRIGHT C ANDREW COLIN 1978
110 REM SNARK SIMULATOR FOR COMMODORE PET
120 REM   ******************
130 REM   CP MARKS NEED TO RECOMPILE
140 REM   EF IS NUMBER OF ERRORS IN SOURCE
150 REM   GH IS SET=1 IF "END" OBEYED
160 REM   SS MARKS "SINGLE-SHOT"
170 REM   PC IS CONTROL COUNTER
180 REM   ******************
190 DIMC$(20)
200 DIMT$(127)
210 DIMT(127)
220 DIM M$(16)
230 CP=1
240 REM   ******************
250 REM READ MNEMONICS
260 FORJ=0TO15:READM$(J):NEXT
270 DATALDA,STA,ADD,SUB,AND,ORA,JMP,BZE
280 DATABNZ,BMI,BPL,LRS,NEG,INA,OUT,END
290 REM   ******************
300 REM   READ CODES TO BE IGNORED
310 FORJ=1TO10
320 DATA18,146,141,19,147,17,145,29,157,148
330 REM   ******************
340 REM   MAIN CONTROL POINT
350 GOSUB 1040
360 REM   LC IS "LIST COMMENTS"
370 IFX$="LC"THEN720
380 IFX$="LISTALL"THEN820
390 REM   TEST FOR "LIST A - B "
400 IF LEFT$(X$,4)="LIST" THEN 740
410 IFX$="RUN"THEN 510
420 IFX$="WIPE"THEN 860
430 IF X$="DUMP" THEN        1550
440 IF X$="LOAD" THEN        1720
450 IFX$="TRANSLATE"THEN910
460 IF LEFT$(X$,2)="PM"THEN 960
470 PRINT"DIRECTIVE NOT RECOGNISABLE"
480 GOTO350
490 REM   ******************
500 REM   RUN SEQUENCE
510 IF CP=0THEN 550
520 PRINT"TRANSLATION NEEDED.":GOSUB2370
```

```
530 IFEF=0THENPRINT"COMPILATION CORRECT":CP=0:GOTO550
540 PRINTEF;"ERRORS IN TRANSLATION":GOTO350
550 INPUT"DISPLAY ON   ";Q$:LF=1:SS=0
560 IFLEFT$(Q$,1)="N"THEN LF=0:GOTO590
570 INPUT"SINGLE SHOT";Q$
580 IFLEFT$(Q$,1)="Y"THENSS=1
590 INPUT"START ADDRESS";PX
600 IF PX=(-1)THEN 630
610 PC=PX
620 IF PC<00RPC>127THEN590
630 GH=0
640 GOSUB2630
650 IF GH=1THEN 350
660 IFSS=1THEN690
670 GETQ$:IFQ$<>"B"THEN640
680 GOTO350
690 GETQ$:IFQ$=""THEN690
700 IFQ$="B"THEN350
710 GOTO640
720 GOSUB 1390: GOTO350
730 REM   *******************
740 X$=MID$(X$,5):GOSUB3210:REM GET PARAMETERS FOR LIST A-B
750 IF AB=1THEN780
760 GOSUB 1470
770 GOTO350
780 PRINT"LIST PARAMETERS WRONG"
790 GOTO 350
800 REM   *******************
810 REM   "LISTALL"
820 GOSUB 1390:A=0:B=127:GOSUB1470
830 GOTO350
840 REM   *******************
850 REM   "WIPE"
860 FORJ=0TO20:C$(J)="":NEXTJ
870 FORJ=0TO127:T$(J)="":NEXTJ
880 GOTO350
890 REM   *******************
900 REM   "TRANSLATE"
910 GOSUB2370
920 IFEF=0THENPRINT"COMPILATION CORRECT":CP=0: GOTO350
930 PRINTEF;" ERRORS":GOTO350
940 REM   *******************
950 REM   "PM"
960 X$=MID$(X$,3):GOSUB3210
970 IF AD=1THEN   1000
980 GOSUB3330
990 GOTO350
1000 PRINT"POST-MORTEM PARAMETERS WRONG
1010 GOTO350
1020 REM   *******************
1030 REM   READ SOURCE FROM KEYBOARD
1040 PRINT"?";:X$=""
1050 GETY$:IFY$=""THEN1050
1060 K=ASC(Y$)
1070 FORJ=1TO10
1080 IFK=C(J)THEN1050
1090 NEXT
```

```
1100 IFK<>20THEN1130
1110 IFX$=""THEN1050
1120 X$=MID$(X$,1,LEN(X$)-1):PRINT"▌ ▌";:GOTO1050
1130 PRINTY$;:IFK=13THEN1150
1140 X$=X$+Y$:GOTO1050
1150 IF X$=""THEN 1040
1160 IF LEFT$(X$,1)<>"C" THEN 1230
1170 Z=VAL(MID$(X$,2))
1180 IF Z>=0 AND Z<=20 THEN 1210
1190 PRINT"WRONG COMMENT NUMBER.RANGE IS 1-20"
1200 GOTO1040
1210 C$(Z)=X$
1220 GOTO1040
1230 Z$=LEFT$(X$,1)
1240 IF ASC(Z$)>57 OR ASC(Z$)<48 THEN 1360
1250 Z=VAL(X$)
1260 IF Z>=0 AND Z<=127 THEN 1300
1270 PRINT   "WRONG DESTINATION ADDRESS.
1280 PRINT"   RANGE IS 0 TO 127"
1290 GOTO1040
1300 X$=MID$(X$,2,LEN(X$)-1)
1310 IF X$="" THEN 1340
1320 IF LEFT$(X$,1)=" "THEN 1300
1330 IF ASC(X$)<=57AND ASC(X$)>=48THEN1300
1340 T$(Z)=X$:CP=1
1350 GOTO1040
1360 RETURN
1370 REM ******************
1380 REM LIST COMMENTS
1390 FORJ=1TO20
1400 IFC$(J)=""THEN1420
1410 PRINTC$(J)
1420 NEXTJ
1430 PRINT
1440 RETURN
1450 REM ******************
1460 REM LIST SOURCE TEXT
1470 FOR J=A TO B
1480 IFT$(J)=""THEN1500
1490 PRINT J;T$(J)
1500 NEXTJ
1510 PRINT
1520 RETURN
1530 REM ******************
1540 REM "DUMP"
1550 GOSUB 1910
1560 OPEN 1,1,1
1570 FORJ=1TO20
1580 IF C$(J)=""THEN 1610
1590 PRINT#1,C$(J)
1600 GOTO1620
1610 PRINT#1,"X"
1620 NEXTJ
1630 FOR J=0TO127
1640 IFT$(J)="" THEN 1660
1650 PRINT#1,T$(J):GOTO1670
1660 PRINT#1,"X"
```

```
1670 NEXTJ
1680 CLOSE 1
1690 GOTO350
1700 REM ******************
1710 REM "LOAD"
1720 GOSUB1910
1730 OPEN1
1740 CP=1
1750 FORJ=1TO20
1760 INPUT#1,C$(J)
1770 IF C$(J)="x" THEN 1790
1780 PRINTC$(J): GOTO 1800
1790 C$(J)=""
1800 NEXT
1810 FORJ=0TO127
1820 INPUT#1,T$(J)
1830 IF T$(J)="x" THEN 1850
1840 PRINT J;T$(J):GOTO1860
1850 T$(J)=""
1860 NEXT
1870 CLOSE 1
1880 GOTO 350
1890 REM ******************
1900 REM OPEN CASSETTE FOR READING OR WRITING
1910 PRINT"REWIND TAPE AND PRESS A KEY"
1920 GETX$:IFX$=""THEN1920
1930 RETURN
1940 REM    ******************
1950 REM COLLAPSE X$ INTO Y$
1960 Y$=""
1970 FORJ=1TOLEN(X$)
1980 Z$=MID$(X$,J,1)
1990 IF Z$="↑"THEN RETURN
2000 IFZ$=" "THEN2020
2010 Y$=Y$+Z$
2020 NEXT
2030 RETURN
2040 REM    ******************
2050 REM DECODE INSTRUCTION IN Y$
2060 E%=0:M%=0:D%=0
2070 IFLEN(Y$)<3THEN E%=1:RETURN
2080 FORJ=0TO15
2090 IFLEFT$(Y$,3)=M$(J)THEN2120
2100 NEXT
2110 E%=2:RETURN
2120 F%=J
2130 Y$=MID$(Y$,4)
2140 A%=0
2150 IF J>=11 AND LEN(Y$)=0THEN RETURN
2160 IF J<=10THEN 2200
2170 IF LEFT$(Y$,1)="A"THEN RETURN
2180 IF LEFT$(Y$,1)<>"B"THEN E%=3:RETURN
2190 A%=1:RETURN
2200 REM ADDRESSED INSTRUCTION
2210 IF LEN(Y$)=0THEN E%=4:RETURN
2220 IF LEFT$(Y$,1)="A"THEN2250
2230 IF LEFT$(Y$,1)<>"B"THEN2270
```

```
2240 A%=1
2250 Y$=MID$(Y$,2)
2260 IF LEN(Y$)=0THEN E%=4:RETURN
2270 M%=1
2280 IF LEFT$(Y$,1)<>"#"THEN 2310
2290 M%=0
2300 Y$=MID$(Y$,2)
2310 D%=ASC(Y$)
2320 IF D%<480RD%>57THEN E%=4:RETURN
2330 D%=VAL(Y$)
2340 IF RIGHT$(Y$,1)="A"THEN M%=2
2350 IF RIGHT$(Y$,1)="B"THENM%=3
2360 RETURN
2370 REM INSTRUCTION TRANSLATOR
2380 EF=0
2390 FORH=0TO127
2400 IFT$(H)=""THEN2600
2410 X$=T$(H):GOSUB1950
2420 IF ASC(Y$)=430RASC(Y$)=45THEN2570
2430 GOSUB2050
2440 IFE%<>0THEN2480
2450 T(H)=D%+512*M%+2048*A%+4096*F%
2460 IFT(H)>32767THEN T(H)=T(H)-65536
2470 GOTO2600
2480 EF=EF+1
2490 PRINT"ERROR IN LINE ";H
2500 PRINTH;T$(H)
2510 IFE%=1THENPRINT"TOO SHORT":PRINT
2520 IFE%=2THENPRINT"UNKNOWN MNEMONIC":PRINT
2530 IFE%=3THENPRINT"WRONG ACC DESIGNATION":PRINT
2540 IFE%=4THENPRINT"ADDRESS PART MISSING":PRINT
2550 IF E%=5THENPRINT"ADDRESS OR VALUE TOOLARGE":PRINT
2560 GOTO2600
2570 T=VAL(Y$)
2580 IFABS(T)>32767THENE%=5:GOTO2480
2590 T(H)=T
2600 NEXTH
2610 RETURN
2620 REM  ****************
2630 REMSINGLE INSTRUCTION CYCLE
2640 IR=T(PC):PC=PC+1
2650 D=IRAND511:M%=(IRAND1536)/512
2660 A%=IRAND2048:F=INT(IR/4096)
2670 IFF<0THEN F=F+16
2680 IFLF=0THEN2760
2690 PRINTPC-1;M$(F);:IFA%>0THENPRINT"#B ";:GOTO2710
2700 PRINT" A ";
2710 IFF >10THENPRINT"        ";:GOTO2750
2720 IFM%=0THENPRINT"#";
2730 PRINTD;:IFM%=2THENPRINT"A";
2740 IFM%=3THENPRINT"B";
2750 PRINT"    ",
2760 CA=A0:IFA%=2048THENCA=A1
2770 IFF>7THEN2790
2780 ONF+1GOTO2810,2800,2820,2830,2840,2850,2860,2870
2790 ONF-7GOTO2890,2910,2930,2950,2960,2970,2980,2990
2800 GOSUB3090:T(D)=CA:GOTO3040
```

```
2810 GOSUB3150:CA=D:GOTO3000
2820 GOSUB3150:CA=CA+D:GOTO3000
2830 GOSUB3150:CA=CA-D:GOTO3000
2840 GOSUB3150:CA=CA ANDD:GOTO3000
2850 GOSUB3150:CA=CA OR D:GOTO3000
2860 GOSUB3090:PC=D:GOTO3040
2870 GOSUB3090:IFCA=0THENPC=D
2880 GOTO3040
2890 GOSUB3090:IFCA<>0THENPC=D
2900 GOTO3040
2910 GOSUB3090:IFCA<0THENPC=D
2920 GOTO3040
2930 GOSUB3090:IFCA>=0THENPC=D
2940 GOTO3040
2950 CA=INT(CA*0.5):GOTO3000
2960 CA=-CA:GOTO3000
2970 INPUTCA:GOTO3000
2980 PRINT"OUTPUT IS ";CA:RETURN
2990 GH=1:GOTO3040
3000 IFCA>32767THEN CA=CA-65536:GOTO3000
3010 IFCA<-32768THENCA=CA+65536:GOTO3010
3020 IFA%=0THENA0=CA:GOTO3040
3030 A1=CA
3040 IFLF=0THEN RETURN
3050 PRINT"A=";A0,"B=";A1
3060 RETURN
3070 REM   ****************
3080 REM   GET ADDRESS OF OPERAND
3090 IFM%=2THEND=D+A0
3100 IFM%=3THEND=D+A1
3110 IFD>=0ANDD<128THENRETURN
3120 PRINT"ADDRESS VIOLATION IN LINE";PC-1:D=127:GH=1:RETURN
3130 REM   ****************
3140 REM   GET OPERAND
3150 IFM%=2THEND=D+A0
3160 IFM%=3THEND=D+A1
3170 IFM%=0THENRETURN
3180 IFD>=0ANDD<128THEND=T(D):RETURN
3190 GOTO3120
3200 REM   ****************
3210 REM   GET PARAMETERS FOR LIST OR PM
3220 Y$=X$:AB=1
3230 IF Y$=""THEN RETURN
3240 Y$=MID$(Y$,2)
3250 IF Y$=""THEN RETURN
3260 IF ASC(Y$)<>45THEN3230
3270 Y$=MID$(Y$,2)
3280 A=VAL(X$):B=VAL(Y$):IF A<0ORA>127THEN RETURN
3290 IFB<0ORB>127THEN RETURN
3300 IF B<ATHEN RETURN
3310 AB=0:RETURN
3320 REM   ****************
3330 REM   INSTRUCTION CODE AND LISTING
3340 FORJ=ATOB
3350 PRINTJ;:IR=T(J):D%=IR AND 511
3360 M%=(IR AND1536)/512:A%=IRAND2048
3370 F%=IR/4096
```

```
3380 IF F%<0THEN F%=F%+16
3390 PRINTM$(F%);
3400 IFA%>0THEN PRINT" B ";:GOTO3420
3410 PRINT" A";
3420 IFF%>10THENPRINT"  ",:GOTO3460
3430 IFM%=0THENPRINT"#";
3440 PRINTD%;:IFM%=2THENPRINT"A";
3450 IFM%=3THEN PRINT"B";
3460 PRINT" ",IR
3470 NEXTJ
3480 RETURN
READY.
```

Assignments

ASSIGNMENT 1 (Chapters 1 and 2)

Part A. Multiple Choice Questions

1.   The use of an alphabet with a fixed number of letters limits the number of different ideas we can express: true / false.

2.   The less expected a message is, the more information it carries: true / false.

3.   When the number of possible messages from a source is fixed, the probabilities of the various messages add up to: less than 1 / exactly 1 / more than 1 / any of these.

4.   Answer without using calculator or tables: $\log_2(1/7)$ is about: 0.14 / −0.5 / −2.8.

5.   Answer without using calculator or tables: $\log_2(1)$ is about: −1 / 0 / 3.322.

6.   In an ergodic message source the average message length is: always greater than the entropy / never less than the entropy / sometimes less than the entropy.

7.   Is the following code ambiguous? If not, what is the average message length?

Message	Probability	Code
Blue	0.6	101
Black	0.1	110
Green	0.2	0
Red	0.1	111

Ambiguous / 2.4 / 2.6 / 2.85.

8.   Is the following code ambiguous? If not, what is the average message length?

Message	Probability	Code
One	0.25	1
Two	0.25	10
Three	0.25	11
Four	0.25	100

Ambiguous / 0.25 / 2.0 / 2.5.

9.   The binary system can be used to write down: a limited selection of numbers (like '101' or '111011') / any number whatever.

10.   In two's complement notation there are exactly as many negative numbers as positive ones: true / false.

11.   In two's complement notation, if you add two numbers of different sign the answer is always correct: true / false.

12.   Octal and hexadecimal numbers are chiefly useful to: programmers and engineers / computers / both people and computers.

13.   In an 8-bit 2's complement system, the hexadecimal representation of every negative numbers starts with 8, 9, A, B, C, D, E or F: true / false.

Part B. Problems

1.   A game is played with tetrahedral (four-sided) dice. The two numbers thrown are added together, and the probability of each result is as follows

Result	2	3	4	5	6	7	8
Prob.	1/16	1/8	3/16	1/4	3/16	1/8	1/16

Calculate the entropy of this method of throwing the dice, when seen as an information source.

2.   Devise a constant-length code for the dice throws in question 1.

3.   The following coding scheme has been proposed for the dice throws in example 1.

Result	2	3	4	5	6	7	8
Code	000	001	01	100	1010	1011	11

Calculate the average message length.
  Decode the following sequence of messages

 010001100100101010110010010100010111111010100101101

4.   Write down the binary numbers from 0 to 19.

5.   Convert the following decimal numbers into their binary equivalents: 34, 10, 317, 296.

6.   Convert the following binary numbers into decimal: 101011101, 11, 10101010, 1111101000.

7.   Complete the following sums in binary

11010100	10101101	10101	1011010
10110101 +	1010011 +	101 x	1101 x

8.   What size of binary number (i.e., how many bits) would you need to represent all the whole numbers between zero and one million?

9.   Convert the following 8-bit two's complement numbers into decimal: 01010101, 11010100, 10000000, 10111111.

10.   Convert the following decimal numbers into 8-bit binary, using the two's complement notation: 120, −5, 77, −100, 127.

11.   Carry out the following additions in two's complement arithmetic, and state whether the answers are right

01011110	01111010	11010111	10001001
00010101 +	10001001 +	01111101 +	11101101 +

12.   Assuming 8-bit words, what are the octal equivalents of the decimal values: 36, 100, −5, −59.

13.   The hexadecimal form of certain two's complement binary numbers are given below. What are the decimal equivalents? 17, 7C, BA, FF, 99.

Part C. Open-ended Problems

1.   Identify the source, the code, the medium, the destination and the time delay in each of the following information systems: A daily newspaper, A digital clock, A fire alarm system, An inscription in an Egyptian tomb, A traffic light.

2.   Derive a formula which gives the *largest* number that can be stored in a binary word of n bits (assuming the smallest is zero).
    What would be the largest numbers in words of: 4 bits, 6 bits, 10 bits?

ASSIGNMENT 2 (Chapters 3 and 4)

Part A. Multiple Choice Questions

1.   The inverter is a NAND gate with only one input: true / false.

2.   In a two-input NAND gate one input is 1 and the other is 0. The output is: 0 / 0.5 / 1.

3.   In one second the number of nanoseconds is: a million / a thousand million / a million million.

4.   The speed of a typical modern logic gate is 100 million operations per: second / minute / hour / day / year.

5.   A logic network with four inputs needs a truth table with how many lines? 4 / 8 / 16.

6.   Serial transmission of data is faster and cheaper than parallel transmission: true / false.

7.   In binary addition $(1 + 1 + 0)$ equals: 0 carry 1 / 1 carry 0 / 2 carry 0 / 0 carry 2.

8.   In a full adder, X and Y inputs can be interchanged without ill effect: true / false.

9.   In a full adder, the sum and carry outputs can be interchanged without ill effect: true / false.

10.   A multiplexer with 16 inputs needs how many control lines? 4 / 8 / 16.

Part B. Problems

1.   Derive truth tables for the following networks

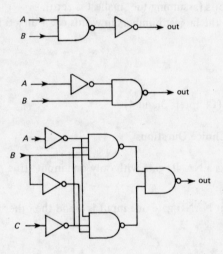

2.   Draw networks corresponding to the following truth tables.

A	B	Out
0	0	1
0	1	0
1	0	0
1	1	0

A	B	Out
0	0	1
0	1	0
1	0	0
1	1	1

A	B	C	Out
0	0	0	0
0	0	1	0
0	1	0	1
0	1	1	1
1	0	0	0
1	0	1	1
1	1	0	0
1	1	1	1

3.   In a calculator each decimal digit is represented as 4 binary digits, with straightforward binary coding. For example, '3' is '0011'. The combinations 1010 to 1111 are never used.

Consider a seven-segment display, as shown in chapter 1, and complete the truth table for segment e, using '1' to mean 'this segment should light up'. The truth table begins

A	B	C	D	Out	
0	0	0	0	1	(since '0' uses segment e)
0	0	0	1	0	(since '1' does not use it)
0	0	1	0		
0	0	1	1		
0	1	0	0		
0	1	0	1		
0	1	1	0		
0	1	1	1		
1	0	0	0		
1	0	0	1		

Translate your truth table into a logic network.

4.   Some computers do not subtract by complementing and adding, but use 'full-subtractors', which are analogous to full-adders. A full-subtractor has three inputs: a digit of X, the minuend (i.e. the number being diminished), a digit of Y, the subtrahend (i.e. the number being subtracted), a 'borrow' from the previous stage. It has two outputs: a 'difference' digit (analogous to a 'sum' digit), and a 'borrow' digit (analogous to 'carry' digit). Draw up truth tables for a full subtractor, and design a logic network for the 'borrow' section only.

X	Y	Previous Borrow	Difference	Borrow
0	0	0		
0	0	1		
0	1	0		
0	1	1		
1	0	0		
1	0	1		
1	1	0		
1	1	1		

5.   A binary subtractor is constructed according to the pattern shown in figure 4.5. If the numbers are 20 bits long, and the gate propagation time is 10 ns, what is the maximum propagation time of the whole subtractor? Assume that the propagation delays of a full adder are: sum digit : 3δ, carry digit : 2δ.

6.   Consider the two-input multiplexer shown in figure 4.6. What is the maximum propagation delay: (a) with respect to the inputs A and B, (b) with respect to the control line X? Do these figures hold for multiplexers with greater numbers of inputs?

7.   An arithmetic unit, shown below, has three control inputs: X, Y and C. Complete the table of its functions.

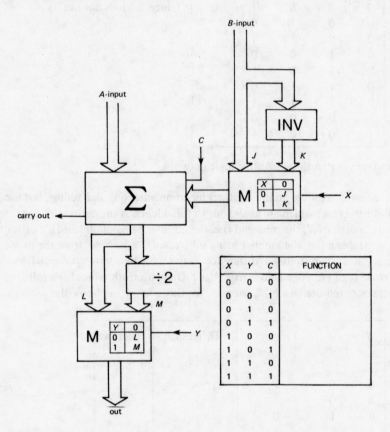

Part C. Open-ended Problems

1.   A safety device to be fitted to a car receives inputs from three sources: A = bonnet shut, B = driver's door shut, C = passenger's door shut. A safety interlock is designed so that under normal circumstances it only allows the engine to be started if the bonnet and *both* doors are shut. For testing, it also allows the engine to be started if both the bonnet and the driver's door are open — and in this case the state of the passenger's door is immaterial.

Draw up a truth table for this interlock, assuming that an output of 1 means 'it is safe to start the engine'. Show how the device could be implemented with inverters and NAND gates.

2. Most computers are fitted with 'logic' instructions, which operate on whole words, but treat each bit as an independent value (i.e., not as part of a number). The main operations are as follows

Name	*Truth Table*			*Example on 8-bit words*

Name	*Truth Table*			*Example on 8-bit words*
NOT	A		Out	NOT 11001001
	0		1	= 00110110
	1		0	

AND	A	B	Out	11001001
	0	0	0	10100111 AND
	0	1	0	10000001
	1	0	0	
	1	1	1	

OR	A	B	Out	11001001
	0	0	0	10100111 OR
	0	1	1	11101111
	1	0	1	
	1	1	1	

EQ	A	B	Out	11001001
	0	0	1	10100111 EQ
	0	1	0	10010001
	1	0	0	
	1	1	1	

NEQ	A	B	Out	11001001
	0	0	0	10100111 NEQ
	0	1	1	01101110
	1	0	1	
	1	1	0	

Design a 'logic unit' (by analogy with an arithmetic unit) which has two input highways for words A and B, one output highway Out and three control lines

X, Y, Z. The function of the unit is defined by the following table

X	Y	Z	FUNCTION
0	0	0	Out = A
0	0	1	Out = B
0	1	0	Out = NOT(A)
0	1	1	Out = NOT(B)
1	0	0	Out = A AND B
1	0	1	Out = A OR B
1	1	0	Out = A EQ B
1	1	1	Out = A NEQ B

Hint: Begin by designing a network for each of the functions. Then define a symbol for a network which operates on all the bits of a word at the same time, and finally connect all the networks to a parallel multiplexer.

ASSIGNMENT 3 (Chapters 5 and 6)

Part A. Multiple Choice Questions

1.   The output of a flip-flop depends on its past history as well as on the current inputs: true / false.

2.   When a reset signal is applied to a flip-flop in the '1' state, it changes instantaneously to the '0' state: true / false.

3.   In a synchronous computer, the clock ensures that: all the flip-flops change at the same time / all the flip-flops which need to change in any one machine cycle change at the same time / the operator can tell the time of day.

4.   Logic networks which pass through a number of states are called: combinatorial / sequential.

5.   A register with n flip-flops can store 2^n different patterns of binary digits true / false.

6.   Propagation delay: can be ignored by the computer designer / is a minor nuisance / is a major factor in computer design.

7.   In a parallel machine, a 'bus' carries: 1 bit at a time / 1 word at a time / more than 1 word at a time.

8.   In any one cycle, a bus allows information to be passed: from one register to one other / from one register to any number of others / simultaneously from many registers to many others.

9.   In general (although there are exceptions) a given register: is always a bus master / is always a bus slave / can be either — master for one cycle, and slave the next.

10.   An error in design causes two tri-state buffers driving the same bus to be on at the same time. On a particular signal line one buffer tries to transmit a '1', while the other attempts to send a '0'. What will happen? The '1' wins / The '0' wins / The signal is indeterminate and there is a risk of the machine catching fire.

11.   A memory has 8K words of 8-bits each. How many bits in its MAR? 8 / 13 / 8192.

12.   The MAR is always a bus slave: true / false.

13.   The address selection mechanism is combinatorial: true / false.

14.   Suppose you have just recorded the wrong information in a fusible-link ROM chip. Your best course of action would be: wipe the chip clear and record the information again, getting it right / send the chip back to the manufacturer for repair / throw the chip away and start with a new chip.

15.   In a RAM chip the contents of all the cells can be accessed equally easily: true / false.

Part B. Problems

1.   Show how a register and a parallel adder can be connected so that each clock pulse increments the contents of the register by 1 (i.e., adds 1).

2.   A computer consists of nine registers arranged on a horizontal line at 10 cm intervals. Calculate the total length of highway cabling needed if (a) every register is connected to every other (i.e., cables in both directions); (b) all the registers drive a bus through a multiplexer sited in the middle of the line; (c) each register drives the bus through a tri-state buffer. (Consider only horizontal cabling.)

3.   Referring to figure 5.11, tabulate the signals needed for the following transfers: ACC => MAR, ACC − DATA => ACC, 0 => ACC, 2*ACC => MAR, −1 => MAR.

Part C. Open-ended Problems

1. Write very short notes (not more than 50 words) on the following: flip-flop, D flip-flop, RAM, ROM, volatility.

2. (This question taken from University of Strathclyde, B.Sc in Computer Science, paper 52.101 for June 1979.) Describe the following components: parallel adder, parallel inverter, parallel multiplexer, register. Show how they can be connected together to form a multi-function arithmetic unit. The circuit you design should have two accumulators A and B, and be capable of the following operations

$$A := B \qquad\qquad B := A$$
$$A := (-B) \qquad\quad B := (-A)$$
$$A := A + B \qquad\quad B := A + B$$
$$A := A - B \qquad\quad B := A - B$$
$$A := B - A \qquad\quad B := B - A$$
$$A := A + 1 \qquad\quad B := B + 1$$

ASSIGNMENT 4 (Chapter 7)

Part A. Multiple Choice Questions

All questions refer to the SNARK computer

1. SNARK has a store with 512 cells numbered 0 upwards. The 'address' of the last one is: 511 / 512 / 65535.

2. The LDA instruction destroys the previous contents of the accumulator used: true / false.

3. The LDA instruction destroys the previous contents of the store location used: true / false.

4. What is the result, in accumulator B, of the following sequence?

```
LDA   B   #3
ADD   B   #5
SUB   B   #2
END
```

$B = 6 / B = 3 / B = 8.$

5. Two instructions are in cells 34 and 35. Can you put another instruction between them without moving at least one of the two instructions first? yes / no.

6. What are the results of the following program?

    ```
    0  LDA  A    35
    1  LDA  B   #17
    2  END
    17 +63
    35 +39
    ```

$A = 35, B = 17 / A = 35, B = 63 / A = 39, B = 17 / A = 39, B = 63.$

7. What would be the results of the following?

    ```
    0  LDA  A    4
    1  STA  A    2
    2  LDA  A   #3
    3  END
    4  +2100
    ```

$A = 2100, B = 3 / A = 4, B = 3 /$ something else.

8. What is displayed by the OUT instruction?

    ```
    0  LDA  A  #31
    1  ADD  A   #3
    2  OUT  A
    3  END
    ```

31 / 34 / something else.

9. What is displayed by the OUT instruction?

    ```
    0  LDA  B  #47
    1  LDA  A   #5
    2  ADD  A    12
    3  OUT  B
    4  END
    ```

47 / 17 / something else.

10. What should be typed to make the machine print '+102'?

    ```
    0  INA  A
    1  STA  A  50
    2  ADD  A  50
    3  OUT  A
    4  END
    ```

50 / 51 / 100 / 102.

Part B. Problems

Answers to problems in this section should be checked out on the SNARK simulator.

1.   Write a SNARK program which calculates $(361 - 153 + 7)$ and leaves it in accumulator A.

2.   Write a program which calculates $(1 + 2 + 3 + 4)$ and leaves the result in cell 2. (Hint: Do not start your program in cell 0!)

3.   Write a SNARK program which accepts two numbers from the keyboard and outputs their sum (i.e., the two numbers added together).

4.   Write a SNARK program which accepts three numbers from the keyboard and outputs them in the opposite order.

Part C. Open-ended Problems

Your assignment is to describe the exact operation of the AND and ORA instructions of the SNARK. Write a program which inputs two values from the keyboard, does the AND operation on them, and displays the result. Run your program with various pairs of values, keeping notes on your results, until you can explain how the results are obtained and predict the outcome of operations which you have not yet tried. Repeat this procedure for the ORA instruction. (Hint: Look at the *binary* representations of your values.)

ASSIGNMENT 5 (Chapter 8)

Part A. Multiple Choice Questions

1.   The SNARK uses two's complement notation. it is correct to say that the BMI instruction jumps if (and only if) the most significant bit in the selected accumulator is 1? yes / no.

2.   0 INA   A
      1 BZE   A 5
      2 BMI   A 4
      3 NEG   A
      4 OUT   A
      5 END

What will this program output if the input is 3?
3 / −3 / something else / nothing.

3. What will the program in question 2 output if the input is 0?
0 / something else / nothing.

4. What will the program in question 2 output if the input is −4?
4 / −4 / something else / nothing.

5. Which of the following could occur in a properly constructed flow chart?

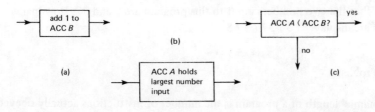

6. Which of the following could occur in a properly constructed flow chart?

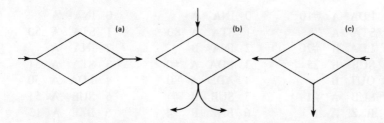

7. Which of the following could occur in a properly constructed flow chart?

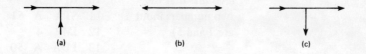

8. In a flow chart a line links block *A* to block *B*, with the arrow pointing towards *B*. The line implies: *B* follows logically as a consequence of *A* / *B* is never started until *A* is finished / when the action specified in *A* is complete, proceed to **B**.

9.   0 LDA A #10
      1 OUT A
      2 SUB A #2
      3 BPL A 1
      4 END

How many numbers are displayed by **OUT**?   5 / 6 / 10.

```
10.   0   INA   A
      1   STA   A   50
      2   INA   A
      3   OUT   A
      4   SUB   A   50
      5   BPL   A   3
      6   END
```

Suppose that the two numbers input to this program are 5 and 37. How many numbers are displayed? 5 / 37 / 7 / 8.

Part B Problems

The 'dynamic' length of a program is the number of instructions actually obeyed when it is executed. Thus if each instruction takes one unit of time, the dynamic length is equal to the total time needed for the program to run. Give the dynamic lengths of the following programs.

```
0   LDA   A   #10          0   INA   A                0   INA   A
1   STA   A   75           1   STA   A   80           1   STA   A   50
2   LDA   B   #20          2   INA   B                2   INA   A
3   SUB   B   75           3   LDA   A   #0           3   STA   A   51
4   OUT   B                4   ADD   A   80           4   LDA   A   50
5   SUB   A   #1           5   SUB   B   #1           5   SUB   A   51
6   BNZ   A   1            6   BNZ   B   4            6   BZE   A   13
7   END                    7   OUT   A                7   BMI   A   10
                           8   END                    8   STA   A   50
                                                       9   JMP   4
                     (Assume that the                10   NEG   A
                     two numbers input               11   STA   A   51
                     are 7 and 5)                     12   JMP   4
                                                      13   LDA   A   50
                                                      14   OUT   A
                                                      15   END
```

(Assume that the two numbers used are 35 and 14)

2.   The following program is designed to read ten numbers from the keyboard and to display their sum. Add the missing orders

```
0   LDA   A   #10
1   LDA   B   #0
2   STA   B   47
```

```
 3  INA  B
 4  ADD  B    47
 5
 6  SUB  A    #1
 7
 8  LDA  B    47
 9  OUT  B
10  END
```

3.   Draw a flow chart for the following program.

```
 0  INA  A
 1  BZE  A    10
 2  LDA  B    #0
 3  BMI  A    8
 4  STA  A    50
 5  ADD  A    50
 6  ADD  B    #1
 7  JMP  3
 8  OUT  B
 9  END
10  LDA  B    #16
11  OUT  B
12  END
```

What does this program do? (Hint: consider the *binary* form of the number used.)

Part C. Open-ended Problems

All answers should be thoroughly checked on the SNARK simulator.

1.   Write a program which reads a number n and displays the sum of the first n numbers: $1+2+3+ \ldots + n$.

2.   Write a program which reads 10 numbers and displays the value of the largest.

3.   Write a program which reads two numbers a and b, and calculates and displays (a) the quotient and (b) the remainder when a is divided by b. Use repeated subtraction. Assume both numbers are positive.

ASSIGNMENT 6 (Chapter 9)

Part A. Multiple Choice Questions

1.   In the store of the SNARK, numbers and instructions are distinguished from each other because: they always occupy different 'blocks' of store / they have distinctive formats / there is no distinction; the machine obeys anything pointed to by its program counter.

2.   In SNARK, every possible combination of 16 bits represents a valid instruction: true / false.

3.   In SNARK, every combination of 16 bits represents an instruction with a different effect: true / false.

4.   The index modes are used chiefly for manipulating arrays and tables: true / false.

5.   In an index modified instruction, the contents of the modifier register is: added to the address field when the instruction is translated into machine form / added to the address field when the instruction is executed / added to the result when the instruction has been obeyed.

6.   In an index modified instruction, the modifier register and the accumulator must be different: true / false.

7.   Consider the sequence

```
LDA  A  #47
LDA  B  #59
ADD  B   45A
```

The effective address of the ADD instruction is: 47 / 59 / 45 / 92.

8.   Consider the program

```
0  LDA  A  #3
1  LDA  B   3A
2  OUT  B
3  END
4  +4
5  +7
6  +11
7  +13
```

What is displayed? 4 / 6 / 7 / 11 / 13.

9. What area does the following sequence clear?

```
0  LDA  B  #0
1  LDA  A  #17
2  STA  B   59A
3  SUB  A  #1
4  BNZ  A   2
5  ....
```

60 − 76 / 59 − 75 / 59 − 76 / 60 − 77.

10. What is displayed?

```
0  LDA  A  #3
1  JMP      2A
2  LDA  B  #2
3  OUT  B
4  END
5  LDA  B  5
6  JMP   3
```

2 / 5 / 2 and 5 / something else.

Part B. Problems

1. Give the binary equivalents of the following SNARK instructions

```
LDA  B  #0
SUB  A  50B
BMI  B  40
OUT  A
ORA  B  77B
```

2. Give the instructions represented by the following binary values

```
1001001000010000
0111111111111111
0000000000000000
0011001100110011
0001010100000000
```

3. Translate the following numbers into SNARK instructions: −6144, +11311.

4. Translate the following SNARK instructions into denary numbers:
BMI A 35, END

5.   The following program is designed to read a number in the range 0 to 3, and display '0' if the number is even, and '1' if it is odd. Fill in the missing instruction

```
0  INA  A
1
2  OUT  B
3  END
4  +0
5  +1
6  +0
7  +1
```

6.   The following program is designed to display the contents of 15 cells of store-cells 74 to 60 (in that order). Fill in the spaces.

```
0  LDA
1  LDA  B
2  OUT  B
3  SUB  A  #1
4
5  END
```

7   Write a program which inputs a number in the range 1 to 15 and displays its highest prime factor. (Hint: use a table.)

8.   Write a fragment of program which counts *how many* of the words in the store between cells 20 and 50 (inclusive) are different from zero. Illustrate your reply with a flow chart.

Part C. Open-ended Problems

1.   Write and run a program to read 10 numbers, sort them into ascending order and display them. Use a method different from the one in appendix B, and similar in outline to the one in example 9.5. Organise a series of passes, of decreasing size, in which the largest remaining number is found and moved to the end of the table.

ASSIGNMENT 7 (Chapter 10)

Part A. Multiple Choice Questions

1.   In a single cycle a machine can execute: a microinstruction / a machine instruction / neither of these.

2.   Professional programmers are often expected to write microinstructions for the machines they use: true / false.

3.   The 'sequence' field of a microinstruction ensures that the successor to the microinstruction is chosen correctly: true / false.

4.   Microinstructions that are to be obeyed in sequence must normally be in consecutive locations of the ROM: true / false.

5.   Every microinstruction must specify a successor: true / false.

6.   Every microinstruction must specify a register transfer: true / false.

7.   Any microinstruction can specify a transfer and a conditional jump: true / false

8.   Any microinstruction can specify a transfer and a conditional jump which depends on the outcome of the transfer: true / false.

9.   The number of machine cycles taken for the SNARK to fetch and execute the instruction ORA B 57A is: 1 / 6 / 7 / 8 / 10.

10.   The number of machine cycles taken to fetch and execute the instruction NEG B is: 1 / 5 / 6 / 7.

Part B. Problems

1.   Using the configuration in figure 10.1, write down the shortest transfer sequence you can find to multiply the number in A by each of the following: 11, 31, 63, 64.

2.   Using the configuration in figure 10.5, give a sequence of three transfers which interchanges the values in X and Y. (Hint: It can be done if you use Z as an intermediate store. Some arithmetic is necessary.)

3.   The 'bit count' of a binary word is the number of 1s in it. For example, the bit count of 0011111001 is 6. Use the configuration given in example 10.2 to write a microcode sequence which generates a bit count. The sequence is to start with the word to be bit-counted in register X, and the result is to be placed in register Y. The value in X need not be preserved, and Z can be used if necessary. The first microinstruction of your sequence should be in location 14, and on completion control is to be transferred to location 37. Give your answer both in symbolic and in binary form. (Hints: Remember that the '$X < 0$' condition is true if the most significant digit of X is a 1, regardless of the other

digits. Note that when a binary number is added to itself, it is effectively shifted one place left, and the previous most significant digit disappears. Use the following microflow chart. The '0 => Z' transfer has been included since, with the given configuration, it is not possible to increment Y by 1 except by addition.)

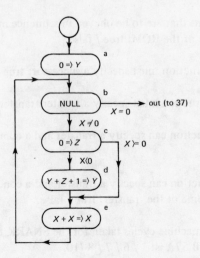

Part C. Open-ended Problems

1.   'Exclusive OR' is a logical operation which uses two operands and generates one result. Each bit in the result is a '1' if and only if the corresponding bits in the operands are *different*. For example 00110100 ⊕ 01010110 = 01000010 (where ⊕ means 'exclusive OR'). The order code of SNARK is to be altered so that the NEG A and NEG B instructions are replaced by two new instructions

EOR   A   A ⊕ B => A
EOR   B   A ⊕ B => B

Design appropriate changes to the microcode.

ASSIGNMENT 8 (Chapters 11, 12 and 13)

Part A. Multiple Choice Questions

1.   Computer memories and public libraries are both stores of information. In computing terms, is a large library: a random access device / a cyclic device / a serial device?

2.   Answer question 1 for a travelling library (i.e., one which is housed in a van and visits your village at regular intervals): a random access device / a cyclic device / a serial device.

3.   What is the latency of a store? The time needed to gain access to any item of information it contains / the time needed to extract and copy *all* the information it contains / the time that the information can be expected to remain stored accurately and reliably.

4.   How can the information on a magnetic tape best be preserved safely? by keeping the tape in suitable air-conditioned rooms / by making sure that the tape deck mechanism is well maintained / by copying the information to another tape.

5.   What is a filing system? A system for organising data on a backing store / a system for ensuring that information is preserved even though disc crashes and other accidents may occur / a system for preventing unauthorised access to information by people who have no right to it / a system which is responsible for all three of these functions.

6.   The best quality of print is produced by a matrix printer: true / false.

7.   In the context of document production, what is 'justification'? Getting the margins straight on both sides / getting the spelling right / marking up the text for the printer.

8.   The chief advantage of a symbolic assembler is that: it simplifies transfer of programs to other machines / it simplifies alterations to programs / Programs written in symbolic assembly language use the computer more efficiently than those written in machine code.

9.   A 'compiler' for a high-level language is: a machine ('hardware') / a program ('software') / a person ('liveware').

10   The prime aim of a multi-access system is: to allow its users to communicate with one another / to allow a large number of people to use the same program at the same time / to allow a large number of people to use the computer simultaneously and independently.

Part B. Problems

1.   A magnetic tape store has the following characteristics: length of tape: 3600 feet; recording density: 2000 bytes per inch; reading speed: 100 inches per second; gap between records: 1 inch; time needed to start tape moving or to

stop it: 10 milliseconds. If the record size is 1000 characters, and the tape has to be stopped between each record, how much information can be stored on the tape? How long will it take to read through the entire tape? (Give your answers to the nearest megabyte and minute, respectively.)

2.   Repeat question 1, assuming a block size of 10 000 characters.

Part C. Open-ended Problems

1.   List the types and capacities of the various storage systems on the computer you are using for your present course.

2.   Find out as much as you can about the system software on your local computer and write short notes under each of the following headings: Operating system(s); Languages available; Accounting system and resource control; Other facilities.

3.   Write a short essay (1 page) on input and output. Use examples with which you are personally familiar.

ASSIGNMENT 9 (Chapter 14)

Part A. Multiple Choice Questions

1.   Consider the grammar

⟨var⟩ ::= X|Y|Z
⟨exp⟩ ::= ⟨var⟩|⟨exp⟩+⟨var⟩|⟨exp⟩−⟨var⟩

Which of the following sequences is an ⟨exp⟩? −X+Y / XYZ / X+Y−Z.

2.   Consider the grammar

⟨var⟩ ::= A|B|C|(⟨exp⟩)
⟨exp⟩ ::= ⟨var⟩|−⟨var⟩|⟨exp⟩+⟨var⟩|⟨exp⟩*⟨var⟩

Which sequence is an ⟨exp⟩? (A+B)*(A+(A*B)+C) / −(A+B)(A+C) / −A+−B.

3.   It is easier to define the semantics of a language than its syntax: true / false.

4.   Assuming the rules given on p. 160, what is the precedence of the + in '$a*(b+c)$'? 1 / 2 / 3 / 4.

5.   Which is the valid reverse Polish expression? $(a+b)$ / abc+++ / ZC+I+W*E/I+C−AKUL+*+ / .

6.   Consider the reverse Polish expression '*abc*/+'. Which diagram best describes the stack after the evaluation of the '/'?

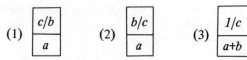

(1) | *c/b* |
    |-------|
    | *a* |

(2) | *b/c* |
    |-------|
    | *a* |

(3) | *1/c* |
    |--------|
    | *a+b* |

7.   What is the largest number of stack cells in use at any one time when the following reverse Polish expression is evaluated: '*ab+cde—*x/—*': 1 / 2 / 3 / 4 / 5 / 6.

8.   Which of the following expressions is equivalent to the one in question 7? *cde—*x/ab+—   ade—c*x/—b+   ab+xcde—*/—*.

9.   In general, an interpreter is cheaper to produce than a compiler: true / false.

10.   In general, an interpreter generates more efficient machine code than a compiler: true / false.

Part B. Problems

1.   Use the SNARK grammar given in appendix B to draw parse trees for each of the following items: OUT A, BZE A 35, LDA B ≠107, +346.

2.   In the following state-symbol table, ⟨digit⟩ ::= 0|1|2|3|4|5|6|7|8|9.

		STATE					
SYMBOL	1	2	3	4	5	6	7
⟨digit⟩	11 √3	16 √3	21 √3	26 √4	31 √7	36 √7	41 √7
	12	17	22 √4	27	32	37	42
+ or −	13 √2	18	23	28	33 √6	38	43
E	14	19	24 √5	29 √5	34	39	44
;	15	20	25 √0	30 √0	35	40	45 √0

To help you answer the question, each cell in the table carries a *label*, which is a number in the range 11 to 45. Consider each of the following strings, and decide whether it conforms to the grammar defined by the table. Give a list of the cells visited for string, as shown in the example.

	Cells visited	Correct?
345;	11, 21, 21, 25	Yes
+35.73;		
−12.19.7;		
44.;		
−1E7;		
−3E+;		

3.   Convert the following into reverse Polish using Dijkstra's algorithm: $A+B$, $X+(Y-3)$, $(A+B)*(C-D)$, $\dfrac{A+B*C}{X+2} + \dfrac{A-B/C}{X-2}$, sqrt$(X+Y-5)$. (Note that in reverse Polish operators with only one argument, like sqrt, are written after their operands.)

4.   The reverse Polish equivalent of the expression $(A-B)/(C+D)$ is $AB-CD+/$. Suppose that variables A, B, C and D have been allocated cells 100, 101, 102 and 103 respectively. Write down the SNARK code obtained by compiling the above expression, using the automatic method described in chapter 14.

5.   Write down the shortest code sequence you can think of to evaluate the expression in question 4. Use location 90 as a workspace if necessary.

Part C. Open-ended Problems

1.   (This question taken from University of Strathclyde, B.Sc in Computer Science, paper 51,101 for June 1979.) In a certain programming language declarations are written in one of three forms

⟨identifier⟩;
or   ⟨identifier⟩ := ⟨number⟩;
or   [⟨number⟩] ⟨identifier⟩;

where   ⟨identifier⟩ ::= ⟨identifier⟩⟨digit⟩⟨identifier⟩⟨letter⟩|⟨letter⟩
and   ⟨number⟩ ::=⟨number⟩⟨digit⟩|⟨digit⟩

for example

    x;
    why := 123;
    [99] zed3;

Assuming that the symbols in the language have been categorised into the classes letter digit := [ ] ; and 'other', draw up a state-symbol table which checks the grammar of a declaration.

ASSIGNMENT 10 (Chapters 15 to 18)

1   It is the year 2000. You have been asked to revise this textbook. Write a section to be added to chapter 15, outlining the history of computers between 1980 and 2000. A list of suggested 'keywords' for your answer is: VLSI, multi-computer systems, distributed data bases, communication, home computing, Josephson effect, automated office, robotics, artificial intelligence, ultra-reliable and self-repairing systems.

Sample Solutions

ASSIGNMENT 1

A1 false; **A2** true; **A3** exactly 1; **A4** −2.8; **A5** 0; **A6** never less than the entropy; **A7** 2.6; **A8** ambiguous; **A9** any number whatever; **A10** false; **A11** true; **A12** programmers and engineers; **A13** true

B1 2.656

B2

Result	2	3	4	5	6	7	8
Your code	000	001	010	011	100	101	110

(Any unambiguous 3-bit code will serve.)

B3 $3\frac{1}{8}$, 4283344455634886574; **B4** 0, 1, 10, 11, 100, 101, 110, 111, 1000, 1001, 1010, 1011, 1100, 1101, 1110, 1111, 10000, 10001, 10010, 10011; **B5** 100010, 1010, 100111101, 100101000; **B6** 349, 3, 170, 1000

B7 110001001   100000000   1101001   10010010010

B8 20; **B9** 85, −44, −128, −65; **B10** 01111000, 11111011, 01001101, 10011100, 01111111; **B11** 01110011 correct, 00000011 correct, 01010100 correct, 01110110 incorrect; **B12** 044, 144, 373, 305; **B13** +23, +124, −70, −1, −103

C1 reporter − English − newsprint − reader − 1 day, etc.
C2 $2^n − 1$, 15, 63, 1023

ASSIGNMENT 2

A1 true; **A2** 1; **A3** a thousand million; **A4** second; **A5** 16; **A6** false;
A7 0 carry 1; **A8** true; **A9** false; **A10** 4

B1   **B2**

A	B	Out
0	0	0
0	1	0
1	0	0
1	1	1

A	B	Out
0	0	1
0	1	0
1	0	1
1	1	1

A	B	C	Out
0	0	0	1
0	0	1	0
0	1	0	1
0	1	1	0
1	0	0	0
1	0	1	0
1	1	0	0
1	1	1	0

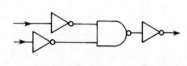

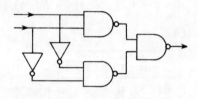

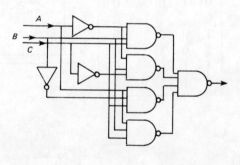

B3   10001010

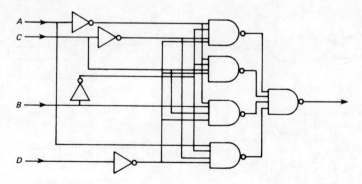

B4   difference: 01101001, borrow 01110001

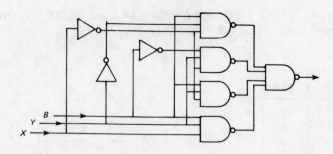

B5   410 ms; **B6** $2\delta, 3\delta$, yes; **B7** $A + B, A + B + 1, \frac{1}{2}(A + B), \frac{1}{2}(A + B + 1),$
$A - B - 1, A - B, \frac{1}{2}(A - B - 1), \frac{1}{2}(A - B)$

C1

A	B	C	Out
0	0	0	1
0	0	1	1
0	1	0	0
0	1	1	0
1	0	0	0
1	0	1	0
1	1	0	0
1	1	1	1

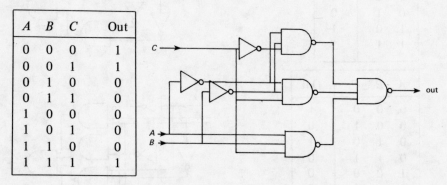

C2

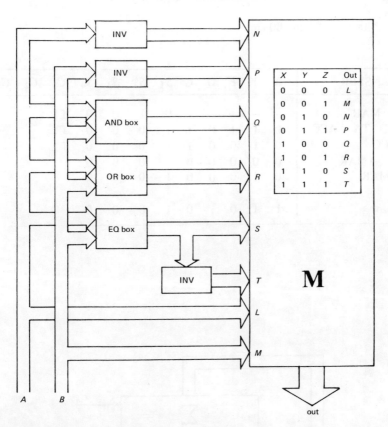

X	Y	Z	Out
0	0	0	L
0	0	1	M
0	1	0	N
0	1	1	P
1	0	0	Q
1	0	1	R
1	1	0	S
1	1	1	T

ASSIGNMENT 3

A1 true; **A2** false; **A3** all the flip-flops which need to change in any one machine cycle change at the same time; **A4** sequential; **A5** true; **A6** is a major factor in computer design; **A7** 1 word at a time; **A8** from one register to any number of others; **A9** can be either; **A10** the signal is indeterminate; **A11** 13; **A12** true; **A13** true; **A14** throw the chip away; **A15** true

B1

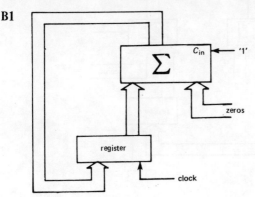

B2   2400 cm, 280 cm, 80 cm

B3

TRANSFER	X	Y	F	G	C	S_1	S_2	S_3	S_4	C_1	C_2	C_3	C_4
ACC => MAR	–	–	–	–	–	0	1	0	0	⊓			
ACC–DATA => ACC	0	1	1	0	1	1	0	0	0	⊓			
0 => ACC	0	1	0	0	1	1	0	0	0	⊓			
2*ACC => MAR	0	0	0	0	0	1	0	0	0				⊓
–1 => MAR	0	1	0	0	0	1	0	0	0				⊓
or	1	1	0	1	0	1	0	0	0				⊓

C2

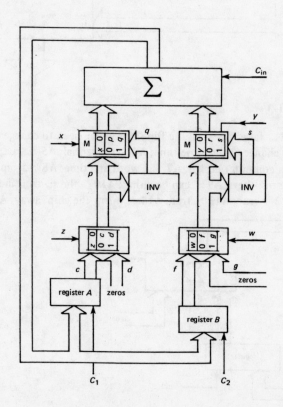

	x	y	z	w	C_{in}	C_1	C_2
$A = B$	0	0	1	0	0	⎍	
$B = A$	0	0	0	1	0		⎍
$A = (-B)$	0	1	1	0	1	⎍	
$B = (-A)$	1	0	0	1	1		⎍
$A = A + B$	0	0	0	0	0	⎍	
$B = A + B$	0	0	0	0	0		⎍
$A = A - B$	0	1	0	0	1	⎍	
$B = A - B$	0	1	0	0	1		⎍
$A = B - A$	1	0	0	0	1	⎍	
$B = B - A$	1	0	0	0	1		⎍
$A = A + 1$	0	0	0	1	1	⎍	
$B = B + 1$	0	0	1	0	1		⎍

ASSIGNMENT 4

A1 511; **A2** true; **A3** false; **A4** $B = 6$; **A5** no; **A6** $A = 39, B = 17$;
A7 something else; **A8** 34; **A9** 47; **A10** 51

B1

```
0  LDA  A  #361
1  SUB  A  #153
2  ADD  A  #7
3  END
```

B2

```
3  LDA  B  #1
4  ADD  B  #2
5  ADD  B  #3
6  ADD  B  #4
7  STA  B  2
8  END
```

B3

```
0  INA  A
1  STA  A  30
2  INA  A
3  ADD  A  30
4  OUT  A
5  END
```

B4

```
0  INA  A
1  STA  A  50
2  INA  A
3  INA  B
4  OUT  B
5  OUT  A
6  LDA  A  50
7  OUT  A
8  END
```

C AND does a logical 'and' independently in each pair of bits in the operands. ORA does a logical 'or' in the same way.

ASSIGNMENT 5

A1　yes; **A2**　−3; **A3**　nothing; **A4**　−4; **A5**　(a); **A6**　(c); **A7**　(a);
A8　when the action specified in *A* is complete, proceed to *B*; **A9**　6; **A10**　8

B1　62, 21, 29; **B2**　STA B 47, BNZ A 3; **B3**　The program displays the
number of leading zeros (on the left) of the binary representation of the
number used.

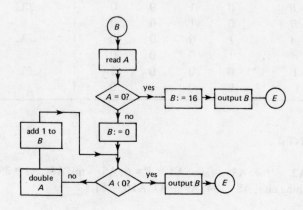

C1

```
0   INA   A
1   LDA   B   #0
2   STA   A   50
3   ADD   B   50
4   SUB   A   #1
5   BPL   A   2
6   OUT   B
7   END
```

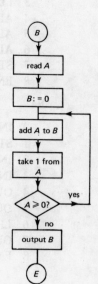

C2

```
0   INA    ,A
1   STA    A   50
2   LDA    B   #9
3   INA    A
4   SUB    A   50
5   BMI    A   8
6   ADD    A   50
7   STA    A   50
8   SUB    B   #1
9   BNZ    B   3
10  LDA    A   50
11  OUT    A
12  END
```

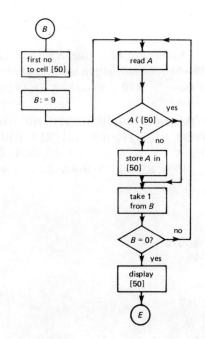

C3

```
0   INA    A
1   INA    B
2   STA    B   93
3   LDA    B   #0
4   SUB    A   93
5   ADD    B   #1
6   BPL    A   4
7   ADD    A   93
8   SUB    B   #1
9   OUT    B
10  OUT    A
11  END
```

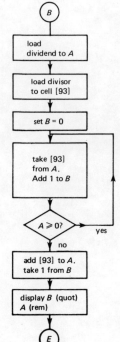

ASSIGNMENT 6

A1   there is no distinction; **A2**   true; **A3**   false; **A4**   true; **A5**   added to the address field when the instruction is executed; **A6**   false; **A7**   92; **A8**   11; **A9**   60 − 76; **A10**   something else (+2565)

B1   0000100000000000, 0011011000110010, 1001101000101000, 110000000000000, 0101111001001101; **B2**   BMI A 16, BZE B 511B, LDA A #0, SUB A 307, STA A 256A; **B3**   OUT B, ADD B 47A; **B4**   −28125, −4096; **B5**   LDA B 4A; **B6**   A #15, 59A, #, BNZ A 2;

B7

0	INA	A
1	LDA	A 3A
2	OUT	A
3	END	
4	+1	
5	+2	
6	+3	
7	+2	
8	+5	
9	+3	
10	+7	
11	+2	
12	+3	
13	+5	
14	+11	
15	+3	
16	+13	
17	+7	
18	+5	

B8

```
0   LDA  A  #31
1   LDA  B  #0
2   STA  B  19
3   LDA  B  19A
4   BZE  B  8
5   LDA  B  19
6   ADD  B  #1
7   STA  B  19
8   SUB  A  #1
9   BNZ  A  3
10  LDA  B  19
11  OUT  B
12  END
```

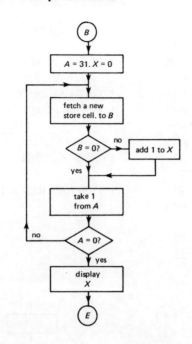

C1

```
0   LDA  B  #10      ↑ READ 10 NOS AND PLANT IN
1   INA  A           ↑ 70–79
2   STA  A  69B
3   SUB  B  #1
4   BNZ  B  1
5   LDA  A  #10      ↑ SET X (IN 69) = 10
6   STA  A  69
7   LDA  B  69       ↑ B := X
8   LDA  A  69B
9   STA  A  68       ↑ PUT XTH NO IN 68 (LARGEST SO FAR)
10  STA  B  67       ↑ PUT POSITION OF LARGEST IN 67
11  SUB  B  #1
12  LDA  A  69B      ↑ GET ANOTHER NO
13  SUB  A  68       ↑ COMPARE WITH LARGEST
14  BMI  A  18
15  LDA  A  69B      ↑ IF LARGER SET UP NEW VALUES
16  STA  A  68       ↑ IN 68, 67
17  STA  B  67
18  SUB  B  #1
19  BNZ  B  12       ↑ LOOP ROUND
20  LDA  B  69
```

```
21  LDA  A  69B      ↑ GET XTH NO
22  LDA  B  67
23  STA  A  69B      ↑ PUT IN PLACE OF LARGEST
24  LDA  B  69
25  LDA  A  68       ↑ GET LARGEST
26  STA  A  69B      ↑ PUT IN PLACE OF XTH
27  SUB  B  #1
28  STA  B  69
29  SUB  B  #2       ↑ LOOP ROUND
30  BPL  B  7
31  LDA  A  #10      ↑ DISPLAY RESULTS
32  LDA  B  69A
33  OUT  B
34  SUB  A  #1
35  BNZ  A  32
36  END
```

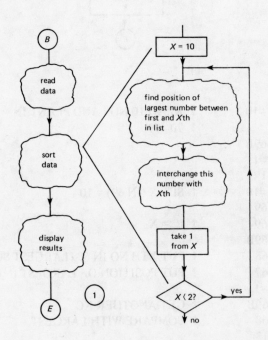

ASSIGNMENT 7

A1 a microinstruction; **A2** false; **A3** true; **A4** false; **A5** true;
A6 false; **A7** true; **A8** false; **A9** 8; **A10** 6

B1

11	31	63	64
A =) B	A =) B	A =) B	A*2 =) A
A*2 =) A	A*2 =) A	A*2 =) A	A*2 =) A
A*2 =) A	A*2 =) A	A*2 =) A	A*2 =) A
A+B =) A	A*2 =) A	A*2 =) A	A*2 =) A
A*2 =) A	A*2 =) A	A*2 =) A	A*2 =) A
A+B =) A	A*2 =) A	A*2 =) A	A*2 =) A
	A−B =) A	A*2 =) A	
		A−B =) A	

B2 $X + Y =) Z, X + (0) =) Y, Z - X =) X$

B3

Location	Transfer	Symbolic Sequence	Binary Address a	Address b	T_1	T_0	JKLMN	$S_1 S_2 C_1 C_2 C_3$
a (14)	0 =) Y	goto b (15)	001111	000000	0	0	11000	1 0 0 1 0
b (15)	NULL	if X = 0 then goto 37 else c	100101	010000	0	1	00000	0 0 0 0 0
c (16)	0 =) Z	if X < 0 then d else e	010010	010001	1	0	11000	1 0 0 0 1
d (17)	Y+Z+1 =) Y;	goto e	010010	000000	0	0	10011	1 0 0 1 0
e (19)	X+X =) X;	goto b	001111	000000	0	0	00000	1 0 1 0 0

C1   We note that $A \oplus B = (A$ OR $B) - (A$ AND $B)$. A suitable sequence for $A \oplus B =) A$ is

> A *and* B =) DR
> A *or* B =) A
> A − DR =) A

and similarly for $A \oplus B =) B$. We make the following changes

Location	New Contents
15	A *or* B =) A; goto 38
16	A *or* B =) B; goto 39
56	A *and* B =) DR; goto 15
57	A *and* B =) DR; goto 16

ASSIGNMENT 8

A1   a random access device; **A2**   a cyclic device; **A3**   the time needed to gain access; **A4**   by copying the information to another tape; **A5**   a system responsible for all three functions; **A6**   false; **A7**   getting the margins straight on both sides; **A8**   it simplifies alterations to programs; **A9**   a program; **A10**   to allow a large number of people to use the computer simultaneously and independently

B1   29 megabytes, 12 minutes; **B2**   72 megabytes, 6 minutes

ASSIGNMENT 9

A1 $X + Y - Z$; **A2** $(A + B)*(A + (A * B) + C)$; **A3**   false; **A4**   3; **A5** $ZC + I + W * E/I + C - AKUL + * + /$; **A6**   (2); **A7**   4; **A8**   *ade − c*x/−b+*; **A9**   true; **A10**   false

B1

OUT A   ⟨item⟩
            |
        ⟨addressless function⟩⟨acc⟩
            | |
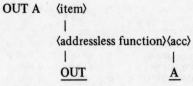
         OUT   A

BZE A 35   ⟨item⟩
              |
          ⟨addressed function⟩⟨acc⟩⟨address⟩
              | | |
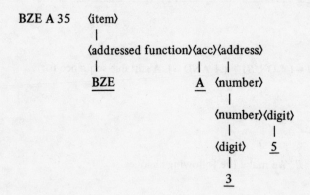
          BZE   A ⟨number⟩
                                  |
                              ⟨number⟩⟨digit⟩
                                  | |
                              ⟨digit⟩   5
                                  |
                                  3

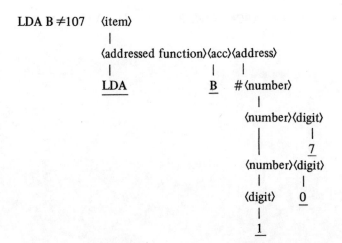

LDA B ≠107   ⟨item⟩

+346   ⟨item⟩

B2

	Cells visited	Correct?
345;	11, 21, 21, 25	Yes
+35.73;	13, 16, 21, 22, 26, 26, 30	Yes
−12.19.7;	13, 16, 21, 22, 26, 26, 32	No
44.;	11, 21, 22, 30	Yes
−1E7;	13, 16, 24, 31, 45	Yes
−3E+;	13, 16, 24, 33, 40	No

B3   AB +, XY3 − +, AB+CD−*, ABC*+ X2+/ABC/ −X2−/+, XY+5−sqrt

B4

```
LDA  B  #0
LDA  A  100      A
STA     A  90B
ADD  B  #1
LDA  A  101      B
STA  A  90B
ADD  B  #1
SUB  B  #1       −
LDA  A  89B
SUB  A  90B
STA  A  89B
LDA  A  102      C
STA  A  90B
ADD  B  #1
LDA  A  103      D
STA  A  90B
ADD  B  #1
SUB  B  #1       +
LDA  A  89B
ADD  A  90B
STA  A  89B
SUB  B  #1       /
LDA  A  89B
DIV  A  90B
STA  A  89B
```

(25 instructions)

B5

```
LDA  A  102
ADD  A  103
STA  A   90
LDA  A  100
SUB  A  101
DIV  A   90      (6 instructions)
```

C1

Symbol	State							
	1	2	3	4	5	6	7	8
⟨letter⟩	$\sqrt{2}$	$\sqrt{2}$					$\sqrt{8}$	$\sqrt{8}$
⟨digit⟩		$\sqrt{2}$	$\sqrt{4}$	$\sqrt{4}$	$\sqrt{6}$	$\sqrt{6}$		$\sqrt{8}$
:=		$\sqrt{3}$						
[	$\sqrt{5}$							
]						$\sqrt{7}$		
;		$\sqrt{0}$		$\sqrt{0}$				$\sqrt{0}$
⟨other⟩								

Note: Order of rows and columns is not significant!

Bibliography

Barron, D. W., *Assemblers and Loaders* (MacDonald/Elsevier, 1968)

Boulaye, G. G., *Microprogramming* (Macmillan, 1975)

Calderbank, V. J., *A Course of Programming in FORTRAN IV*, (Chapman & Hall, 1969)

Colin, A. J. T., *Programming and Problem Solving in Algol 68* (Macmillan, 1975)

Commodore Ltd, *PET User Manual* (October, 1978)

Findlay, W., and Watt, D. A., *Pascal – An Introduction to Methodical Programming* (Pitman, 1978)

Hartley, M. G., and Healey, M., *A First Course in Computer Technology* (McGraw-Hill, 1978)

Jackson, M., *Principles of Program Design* (Academic Press, 1975)

Jensen, K., and Wirth, N., *Pascal-User Manual and Report* (Springer-Verlag, 1975)

Kernighan B. W., and Plauger, P. J., *Software Tools* (Addison-Wesley, 1976)

Koestler, A., *Janus – A Summing Up* (Hutchinson, 1978)

Lavin, D., *Logical Design of Switching Circuits* (Nelson, 1974)

Lister, A. M., *Fundamentals of Operating Systems,* second edition (Macmillan, 1980)

Mowle, F. J., *A Systematic Approach to Digital Logic Design* (Addison-Wesley, 1976)

Scientific American, issue on Micro-electronics (September, 1977)

The TTL Data Book (Texas Instruments, 1980)

Weinberg, G. M., *The Psychology of Computer Programming* (Van Nostrand, 1971)

Weizenbaum, J., *Computer Power and Human Reason* (Freeman, 1976)

Index